Harvesting Experience: Reaping the Benefits of Knowledge

Jan Duffy

Production House: Justified Left
Compositor: Cover to Cover Publishing, Inc.
Cover Art: Jason Vannatta

ARMA International
4200 Somerset Dr., Ste. 215
Prairie Village, KS 66208

ISBN: 0-933887-80-9

Dedication

—To Rick—
my husband, my most enthusiastic
supporter, and my best friend

Contents

Foreword xi
Introduction..xiii

Chapter 1: Knowledge: What It Is, How to Get It
and Use It, and Why It Matters 1
    What Is Knowledge...3
        Data, Information, and Knowledge 4
        Why Knowledge Is Important......................................5
        Kinds of Knowledge...7
    Sources of Knowledge 10
        Best Practices..11
        Corporate Memory..12
        Communities of Interest 14
    Knowledge Economy and Knowledge Management.........15
        External Forces..17
        Internal Forces...23
    Conclusion 28
    Notes...29

Chapter 2: The Knowledge Connection: Learning,
Innovation, Productivity, and Performance 33
    Knowledge Work and Learning 35
        Sharing...36
        Collaboration 40
        Teamwork..41
    Knowledge Strategy Connections.......................................42

Innovation 44
Productivity 47
Performance 48
Learning as a Way of Life 50
Individual and Organizational Learning 51
Knowledge Management and Learning 53
Conclusion 55
Notes 56

Chapter 3: Preparation: Setting Direction,
Getting Commitment, Assessing Readiness 59
Setting Direction 63
Create the Vision 63
Develop a Knowledge Management Value
Proposition 67
Getting Commitment 71
Communicate Relentlessly 73
Assessing Readiness 73
Technology Environment 74
Business Environment 75
Organizational Environment 75
Conclusion 77
Notes 78

Chapter 4: Initiating the Knowledge Management
Project 79
Develop the Business Case 81
Costs 83
Benefits 84
Prioritizing Opportunities 87
Identify Project Team 90
Develop Project Plan 92
Prepare Project Planning Document 92
Identify Existing Knowledge Assets 96
Developing the Knowledge Map 96
Mapping Tools and Techniques—*How* to Get
What You Need 99

Review Business Processes—*What* You Need
to Get 102
Define Knowledge Management Processes 108
Acquiring and Capturing Knowledge........................109
Organizing and Storing Knowledge..........................112
Retrieving Knowledge..114
Distributing Knowledge 115
Maintaining the Knowledge Base 117
Conclusion 118
Notes..120

Chapter 5: Designing a Knowledge Management
Technology Infrastructure 123
A Technology Tour 126
Early Days and Limited Information..........................127
Dawn of Shared Ideas..127
Pull Technology and Unlimited Information............128
Push Technology 129
Intelligent Push Technology 130
Daily Work Supports 131
Decision Support Tools 132
Determine Functionality Requirements...........................134
Getting to Where You Need to Be..............................135
Finding What You Need 137
Storing What You've Found..139
Tracking Where You've Been 142
Support for Using Knowledge....................................143
Design Knowledge Management Technology
Architecture...145
User Interface 146
Knowledge Metamodel..148
Knowledge Map 150
Knowledge Repository or Source Repositories 151
Knowledge Access Tools 152
Select the Best Technologies (For You).............................152
Conclusion 159
Notes..160

Chapter 6: Implementing the Knowledge Strategy:
Making it Work 163
  Select a Team and Make a Plan 167
  Technical System Implementation 169
    Conduct Acceptance Tests 171
    Review and Approve Implementation Plans 172
    Conduct Training 172
    System Installation and Maintenance Strategy 173
  Cultural Transition 174
    Organizational Enablers 175
    Roles and Responsibilities 183
  Conclusion 196
  Notes 197

Chapter 7: The Next Few Years 201
  The Changes 203
    Organization 204
    Business Environment 207
    Technology 207
  The Challenges 209
    Moving from Concept to Reality 209
    Sustaining Knowledge Value 210
    Justifying the Expenditure 211
    Valuing the Resulting Asset 211
  Conclusion 213
  Notes 214

Appendix 215
Glossary 235
References 247
Index 255

List of Illustrations
  Figure 1-1 Turning Tacit Knowledge into
             Explicit Knowledge 8
  Figure 1-2 Knowledge Management Process 18
  Figure 1-3 Speed of Organizational Learning 27

Figure 2-1 Knowledge Strategy Connections....................43
Figure 3-1 Preparing for Knowledge Management 61
Figure 3-2 Situational Vision Statement 65
Figure 3-3 Strategic Vision Statement...............................66
Figure 3-4 Sample Knowledge Management
      Value Propositions 217
Figure 3-5 Knowledge Domains 70
Figure 3-6 Elements of a Communications Plan............218
Figure 3-7 Technology Readiness Assessment
      Checklist 220
Figure 3-8 Business Readiness Assessment Checklist 222
Figure 3-9 Organizational Readiness Assessment
      Checklist 224
Figure 4-1 One-time and Ongoing Costs.........................226
Figure 4-2 Prioritization Assessment Model.....................89
Figure 4-3 Developing the Knowledge Map 98
Figure 4-4 High-Level Classification Scheme 102
Figure 4-5 Sample Questionnaire 228
Figure 4-6 Interview or Workshop Guideline.................230
Figure 4-7 Sample Inventory Data Gathering Form 232
Figure 4-8 Knowledge Management Life Cycle 108
Figure 5-1 Knowledge Architecture..................................147
Figure 5-2 Incorporation of Existing Tools....................155
Figure 5-3 Framework for Collaborative
      Technologies...157
Figure 5-4 Potential Integrated Knowledge
      Management Environment 159
Figure 6-1 Implementation Guidelines and
      Challenges..166
Figure 6-2 Summary of Major Technical
      Implementation Activities 170
Figure 6-3 CKO Roles and Responsibilities 187

Foreword

During the past decade, we have witnessed a flood of materials focused on the knowledge society, the knowledge worker, intellectual capital, and knowledge management. Each function, including those represented by information management, is in the process of transforming, and its professionals are facilitating the transformation of their own organizations and industries as well as society as a whole.

Enabled by extraordinary advances in computer and communications technology, a movement is afoot—one that places knowledge at the core of business strategy. Not that reliance upon knowledge is anything new; it isn't. On the other hand, how well we carry our intellectual capability into the next generation is a function of effective management.

Changes we are experiencing are kaleidoscopic; their compounding effects defy interpretation. And yet, as effective managers in profit or not-for-profit enterprises, interpreting these compounding effects is precisely our mandate. With technological progress and the (re)focus upon knowledge (not only information) as the drivers of the economic engine come confusion, increased complexity, and inevitable connectivity.

The knowledge movement is one born out of practice—well ahead of many of the best management theories in the world. Because this focus on knowledge is intuitively obvious and pervasive, the movement enjoys significant momentum and is fueled by both individual and organizational innovation. Putting these new managerial concepts into practice represents the challenge of the millennium.

Jan Duffy, with *Harvesting Experience: Reaping the Benefits of Knowledge,* has made an extraordinary contribution to this emerging field of knowledge strategy. In a consistent, comprehensive and coherent format, she has structured the key trends, core concepts, available methodologies and suggested plans for action. Her reference list represents one of the finest in the literature.

Duffy has evolved the current thinking of information management into the realm of business strategy and has provided solid tools toward implementation. This book provides the foundation of leadership for the information professional by "turning vision into reality."

This rapidly evolving knowledge field has no cookbooks. All of our activities represent only "works-in-progress." We are learning from one another in real-time. However, *Harvesting Experience: Reaping the Benefits of Knowledge* certainly does represent an excellent recipe—at least the right ingredients—for moving forward effectively.

DEBRA M. AMIDON
FOUNDER AND CHIEF STRATEGIST
ENTOVATION INTERNATIONAL LTD.

Introduction

The benefits of preserving and organizing intellectual capital have not been quantified yet, but the sense is that millions of dollars can be saved and better work can be done as a result.
—THOMAS A. STEWART

Where We Are

Many of us are struggling to develop smarter, more competitive organizations. We know that knowledge is a most important asset, but we are having some difficulty understanding how it actually contributes to innovation and productivity. Business analysts tell us that, "By 2001, enterprises that lack ongoing enterprise transformation programs and an infrastructure that includes knowledge management will lag competitors by 30 to 40 percent in speed of deployment for new competitive capabilities."[1] We know that, in many cases, the collective experience and knowledge of our employees is better than that of our competitors, but we are having difficulty taking advantage of it. We are frustrated that it is so difficult to gain access to and profitably use the endless supply of "know-how" and experience that is available.

As a society, we are making a transition from a period when advantage could be gained from information to an era that depends on knowledge as an actionable asset for nonrepeatable competitive advantage. Learning faster than the competition is now fundamental to success.

The earlier era was characterized by relatively slow and predictable change that could be deciphered by most formal information systems. During this period, information systems based on programmable recipes for success were able to deliver their promises of efficiency based on optimization for given business contexts.[2]

Little that matters in these times of unsettling and dizzying change is "programmable" anymore. Fresh bursts of new knowledge have the effect of destroying the value of existing skills, goods, and services, and, indeed, some companies. These incursions can be so dramatic that they threaten the survival of an industry or an enterprise—incursions that Andrew Grove, Intel's co-founder and chairman, calls "strategic inflection points."[3] Ideally, an organization's leaders should want to identify a potential strategic inflection point long before it occurs in order to prevent financial instability. In an environment wherein knowledge and experience can be tapped and used to deflect or defuse the trauma, companies can survive and succeed in conditions of extreme stress.

Many professionals believe that a large volume of information is needed for them to do a satisfactory job. Others believe information overload to be the cause of lower job satisfaction and higher tension in the workplace. Whatever one's perspective, the torrent of information available to us will continue to grow, fed by the Internet and the greater range and connectivity of communication media. But, information by itself has limited value, and much time and effort is needed to digest it and determine its relevance in each specific situation. The process of moving information up the value chain to become *knowledge* will still require the accumulated experience (or know-how) of one or more individuals.

Unlike the industrial barons of an earlier time whose assets were physical things such as factories, the masters of the next century will be those who can make connections between pieces of information, thus generating knowledge and creative ideas more quickly than anyone else. Creating, harvesting, assimilating, and leveraging knowledge is now a core business process. The challenge is to be fast enough to capitalize on this wealth before anyone else and smart enough to learn how best to take advantage of it.

Moving Forward

In this intensely competitive and information-rich environment *everyone* in an organization needs to develop advanced research, analytical, and creative thinking skills. Everyone needs to be able to question assumptions, learn new techniques, thrive in the face of uncertainty, and be comfortable with ambiguity. Unlike technical skills, none of these skills ever becomes obsolete, so they are truly a sound investment—but they are never so valuable as when they are supported by a relevant and rich source of knowledge.

Understanding what knowledge is (and is not) and how to harvest it will help provide the basis for business advantage. Peter Drucker, one of this century's most influential management gurus reminds us, "We now know that the source of wealth is something specifically human: knowledge. If we apply knowledge to tasks that we already know how to do, we call it productivity. If we apply knowledge to tasks that are new and different, we call it innovation. Only knowledge allows us to achieve these two goals."[4]

In order to "harvest" knowledge, organizations need to have the ability and willingness to learn how to work with the people who have knowledge and who *know how to use it*. These people are employees, suppliers, customers, and other business partners. The knowledge market is like any other with supply, demand, and distribution considerations. It is also unlike any other because the asset of value is unlike other assets. Only recently has consideration been given to the notion that knowledge is a tangible asset—something to be considered as making a contribution to the financial value of an organization.

Knowledge is very different from and much more difficult to manage than other assets. First of all, it does not become less as it is used. On the contrary, new knowledge is developed as existing knowledge is used. Second, it is not easy to touch, see, and feel knowledge even though we know it is there. Collecting, hoarding, packaging, and protecting it cannot stimulate the value of knowledge. Knowledge is a dynamic, evolving product that depends on an organization and its network of relationships for its existence. Processes that encourage creativity and innovation—processes that are seeded by new knowledge as it is being created—enhance the value and growth of knowledge. Knowledge value comes from processes that allow continuous progress and that minimize regressive relearning and redeveloping activities. The value of knowledge increases dramatically when it is used and diminishes to the point of nonexistence when it is allowed to atrophy.

Capitalizing on knowledge and experience must begin in the same way as do other planning activities—with a clearly articulated strategy. A good understanding of what the organization as a whole is trying to accomplish is critical to defining what knowledge would be of most value. The starting point is to identify what knowledge is needed; what knowledge assets exist; where knowledge resides; how it can be deployed to improve products, services, and customer relationships; and last, but not least, what knowledge is missing. Once these questions are answered, the process of moving the organization from its current knowledge state to a more powerful one can begin.

What Is Knowledge Management?

Knowledge management is an emerging, but important, discipline that recognizes the value of knowledge and advocates a structured approach to using it wisely and well. It is ultimately a performance support strategy that aims to create an environment in which the organization and its people can be successful. It is neither possible nor desirable to "manage" what happens in people's brains. But managing the environment around those people can encourage the creation, growth, and use of knowledge. The environment includes systems, tools, and techniques that can be deployed to help people capture and share their ideas and experience. A successful knowledge management system provides all of these transparently, neither imposing new demands nor intruding on day-to-day work.

The American Productivity & Quality Center defines knowledge management as "the broad process of locating, organizing, transferring, and using the information and expertise within an organization."[5] The Gartner Group defines knowledge management this way:

> ...a discipline that promotes an integrated and collaborative approach to the process of information asset creation, capture, organization, access and use. Information assets include databases, documents, and, most importantly, the uncaptured, tacit expertise and experience resident in individual workers.[6]

"As a field of study," according to some academics, "knowledge management is concerned with the invention, improvement, integration, usage, administration, evaluation, and impacts of computer-based techniques for managing knowledge."[7] Knowledge management is treated in this book as a *process* that drives innovation by capitalizing on organizational intellect and experience. The process of knowledge management is the result of a carefully designed knowledge strategy.

To be successful, a knowledge management strategy must adhere to certain fundamental principles:

- Emphasize the creation of new knowledge by capitalizing on an organization's knowledge assets
- Promote an integrated approach to identifying, retrieving, sharing, and evaluating an organization's knowledge assets

- Stress *human interaction*, not technology, as the focal point for collection, distribution, and reuse of information
- Capitalize on "lessons learned" to help an organization gain insight and understanding from its own experience
- Enhance the ability of capable, accountable, empowered people to take appropriate action

As these principles indicate, knowledge management is a process for *facilitating*—not *controlling*—the creation, discovery, and distribution of knowledge. More than just extracting knowledge from existing databases and experienced workers, knowledge management as a process converts individual know-how, skills, and experience into organizational capital. An organization that is ready for the twists and turns of daily commerce, that knows how to find what it needs, how to focus its energies on what matters, and how to respond to its customers and market conditions can realistically expect the results that are most needed: innovative ideas, improved product and service development, and enhanced overall financial performance.

In efforts to implement a knowledge management strategy, as with other technology-enabled initiatives, there is a tendency to focus on the importance of the technology and pay less attention to the parallel cultural transformations needed for the initiative to succeed. When this happens, the results fall short of expectations. Knowledge management is as much about organizational development, human resources, communication systems, and management styles as it is about information systems. Finding a workable balance between fostering a supportive, collaborative culture, and providing effective technological supports and enablers is the biggest challenge for those who are implementing a knowledge strategy.

Of course, technology can have a positive or negative impact on the environment of people and processes into which you want to introduce knowledge management. Andrea Saveri, of the Institute for the Future explains:

> The expectations of what intranets can do are really high, and if you don't get the social part right—how the group governs

itself online, who makes the rules, how you get people to share, all those kinds of questions—the potential value won't be maximized.[8]

Without the right cultural climate, however, no amount of clever technology will have much effect on establishing a working knowledge management environment. Unless everyone is engaged to some extent in the knowledge development and sharing process, such an environment cannot be considered to be in place. Usually this means that most people will have to change—somehow, and to some extent—in the way they work, think, and behave. Thomas Davenport, respected knowledge management author and thought leader, observes that "knowledge management is a highly political undertaking. . . . If no politics appear around the knowledge management initiative, it is a good indication that the organization perceives that nothing valuable is taking place."[9]

Corporate culture consists of the "basic assumptions that drive an organization."[10] Michael Hammer, one of the world's foremost business thinkers, explains:

> The whole flourishing tangle serves to confirm old-timers, and to induct newcomers, in the corporation's distinctive identity and its particular norms of behavior. In myriad ways, formal and informal, it tells them what is okay and what is not.[11]

The successful introduction of a knowledge strategy requires the adoption of some new norms. Knowledge management is a natural extension of knowledge work, supporting the path to success in the twenty-first century.

About This Book

Harvesting Experience: Reaping the Benefits of Knowledge is designed to provide a territory map of knowledge management for those who are being introduced to its concepts for the first time or to those who are facing the challenge of implementing a knowledge management strategy. Readers who use the book for either purpose will find it easy to use because each chapter is a self-contained package of information. Essentially, the book covers four main topics: what knowledge management is (and is not) and why it is important; the infrastructure, culture and technologies needed for successful knowledge management; undertaking a knowledge management initiative; and the future of knowledge management.

This book is important because it fills a much-needed gap. Most published material about knowledge management is largely conceptual, providing little in the way of concrete guidance to those who are interested in working towards harvesting the knowledge in their organization. Whenever a new concept becomes popular, many people rush to rename existing processes or technologies to make them more marketable or acceptable—for example, many document management technology suppliers now promote their products as "knowledge management systems." Because of this tremendous hype, the useful meaning and application of knowledge management is threatened. This book provides a practical—not a theoretical—treatment of the subject and avoids jargon as much as possible. The primary purposes of *Harvesting Experience: Reaping the Benefits of Knowledge* are to:

- Make knowledge management understandable
- Restate knowledge management principles as management actions
- Provide a practical guide to implementing knowledge management strategies
- Offer a brief but comprehensive explanation of our own approach to knowledge management
- Provide the tools to support a quick start to knowledge management
- Outline the bottom-line benefits of knowledge management
- Make a case for knowledge management as a fundamental contributor to sustained competitive advantage

Harvesting Experience: Reaping the Benefits of Knowledge provides insights into the issues to be considered and choices to be made in addressing knowledge management in any organization. It is organized so that readers can apply the information in the most appropriate fashion. Chapter 1 provides the foundation by explaining what knowledge is and why it is important. How the individual and the organization acquire and use knowledge leads directly to the important issues of learning, innovation, productivity, and performance that are covered in Chapter 2.

Chapter 3 provides guidance in preparing for the knowledge management initiative. The design and implementation process will be much smoother if the commitment is real and if the team is prepared to deal with all obstacles. The business plan provides the information needed for budgeting and project planning. The processes needed to support the acquisition, organization, retrieval, distribution, and maintenance of knowledge are discussed in Chapter 4. They provide an ideal support mechanism for the design of the knowledge management technology infrastructure.

A brief tour of technologies that are applicable to the knowledge management infrastructure is included in Chapter 5 along with tools and techniques to help you to determine the functionality needed to support your organization. The knowledge management architecture provides the framework for technology selection and its five layers are described in detail in this chapter.

In Chapter 6, discussion of implementation begins, including the issues and challenges inherent in an initiative that is as far-reaching and important as knowledge management. This chapter continues the discussion of organizational issues begun earlier and outlines the roles and responsibilities needed to support the knowledge management initiative. Reference is made to many of today's information managers and the roles they might undertake.

Chapter 7 concludes the knowledge management odyssey and provides a sneak preview of what managers and other professionals can expect in the next few years. Knowledge management techniques and processes will be with us for a very long time, contributing to the growth and success of the business world as it moves into the twenty-first century.

The complexity of dealing with a topic such as knowledge management that, while grounded in reality, is rife with new concepts, new ideas, and new terminology, prompted the need for this book to address the issues with common sense and pragmatism. As the path to the future unwinds, the advantage of such a practical approach will become increasingly apparent because the material contained in the following chapters:

- Introduces knowledge management and related concepts, such as intellectual capital, learning organizations, and intangible assets

- Describes detailed processes for managing and capitalizing on knowledge

- Provides tools and implementation aids, such as checklists, questionnaires, interview guidelines, and frameworks

- Provides a blueprint for designing and implementing an enterprise knowledge architecture

- Features frequent headings and bullets to help in locating information quickly

Notes

1. V. Frick, "BPR TOPView," *Gartner Group Advisory Services* (24 September 1997), CD-ROM (Cambridge, MA: Gartner Group Inc., 1997).

2. Yogesh Malhotra, "Knowledge Management for the New World of Business," *Business Researcher's Interests* (1998), online, Available: http://www.brint.com/km/whatis.htm.

3. Andrew Grove, *Only the Paranoid Survive* (New York: Doubleday Currency, 1996).

4. Justin Hibbard, "Knowing What We Know," *Information Week* (20 October 1997), 46-64.

5. "Knowledge Management," American Productivity & Quality Center (1998), online, Available: http://www.apqc.org/prodserv/courses.htm.

6. J. Bair, "Knowledge Management Is About Cooperation and Context," *Gartner Group Advisory Services* (14 May 1998), CD-ROM (Cambridge, MA: Gartner Group Inc., 1998).

7. "Kentucky Initiative for Knowledge Management," *University of Kentucky* (1997), online, No Longer Available: http://uky.edu/man/dsis/KIKM.htm. 24 July 1997.

8. Recent Reports, "Institute for the Future," *The Institute for the Future*, online, No Longer Available: http://www.iftf.org/Whats_New.html.

9. Thomas H. Davenport, "Some Principles of Knowledge Management," *Knowledge Management Server* (1997), online, Available: http://www.bus.utexas.edu/kman/kmprin.htm.

10. Edgar Schein, *Organizational Culture and Leadership* (San Francisco: Jossey-Bass, 1990).

11. Michael Hammer, "The Soul of the New Organization," in *The Organization of the Future*, ed. Frances Hesselbein, Marshall Goldsmith and Richard Beckhard (San Francisco: Jossey-Bass, 1997), 25.

Acknowledgements

As a practitioner of knowledge management, I am a collector, sharer, and, most importantly, a collaborator. This book would never have been completed without the collaborative efforts and support of my friends and colleagues. I especially thank Margaret Tanaszi who patiently read and re-read the manuscript providing invaluable insights at every step. She prodded me to rethink statements that were without obvious foundation, she did not hesitate to question meaning where warranted, and she offered objective advice on content and readability. Her input added tremendously to the enjoyment factor of the book. My very good friend Amy Wohl has been discussing the concepts surrounding knowledge management with me for many years and perhaps one day the two of us will gather our thoughts and publish them for you to share.

Others also were very supportive of my efforts, and, again, I thank them. My friend and fellow innovator Debra Amidon was very supportive and enthusiastic in her review of the manuscript and I thank her for writing the Foreword. I also thank her for her suggestions and her introduction to David Skyrme, one of knowledge management's leading lights. Marilyn Carr was the recipient of my first brainstorms about the content of this book and helped to keep my ideas founded in reality. I would like to thank Amy Wohl, Ken Matheson, David Cattrall, Elizabeth Bluemke, Connie McCandless, Toni LoDico, Elizabeth Regan, David Skyrme, and, of course, the Publications Coordination

Committee of ARMA International for reviewing the manuscript and providing very valuable suggestions for improvement.

Working with Diane Carlisle of ARMA International and Sue Ellen Brown of Justified Left has been a tremendous pleasure. Their insights and constructive suggestions have helped to make writing this book a most enjoyable experience, and, I firmly believe, a more enjoyable and understandable book to read.

Last, but not least, I would like to thank the management and staff of my employer, LGS Group Inc., all of whom have been very helpful and understanding. Writing a book may be a labor of love, but it is almost all-consuming. I have benefited from my colleagues' support in many ways, but their recognition of the need to "get these thoughts on paper" was unfailing. I thank all of them for this encouragement.

—JAN DUFFY

1

Knowledge: What It Is, How to Get It and Use It, and Why It Matters

Do not wander without a purpose, but in all your impulses render what is just, and in all your imaginations preserve what you apprehend.
—MARCUS AURELIUS

Issues

- What does knowledge mean in a business context?

- What are the key sources of knowledge?

- What is the knowledge economy and why is it important?

- What is the link between knowledge strategy and knowledge management?

In today's highly sophisticated business environment, any company's products and services can quickly be duplicated, price reductions can be matched, and speed of distribution can be exceeded by others. Success is dependent upon actions that are triggered by anticipating a situation. Players rely on a mixture of insight, perception, experience, and foresight to give them an edge over the competition. These qualities are often called "know-how," the special blend of intellect and intuition that enables someone to "know how" to do something to determine the most appropriate action.

Managing this basis for action is the real meaning of knowledge management. **Managing** means capturing, using, generating, sharing, exploiting, storing, accessing, transferring, and gaining leverage from know-how. Know-how, or knowledge, takes time to develop and cannot be duplicated quickly; for knowledge to thrive, it must be nourished and harvested like any other resource. The payback is sustainable competitive advantage—something every organization covets.

Knowledge management is not a new concept, but it is still not commonly or effectively practiced. Many organizations realize too late that their efforts to capture knowledge provide nothing more than a casual accumulation of information, with little intrinsic benefit beyond its face value.

In order to "manage" knowledge, an organization needs to have an understanding of what it is, and what it is not. It is not data, nor is it information; it is more than both of these. Moreover, there are different kinds of knowledge, and many sources of it for an enterprising organization. Key sources are best practices, corporate memory, and communities of interest or of practice.

Knowledge is so important for business these days that it warrants being nurtured and managed in the workplace. The reasons become fairly apparent from even a cursory examination of the current knowledge economy. A combination of external forces in the global economy, and internal factors in today's businesses, has created an economic climate that puts special demands on businesses that, in turn, expect employees to do more with less, and to be better, faster, and smarter. Globalization has made everything bigger, and technology has made everything faster. Each enterprise needs to find its own way through this turbulence by managing knowledge in ways that work for the enterprise's own benefit.

What Is Knowledge?

Knowledge is generally recognized as a valuable asset, but to manage it requires a fuller understanding of what it is, what it means, how it is generated, and how it works. What it is *not* is data, nor is it information, although knowledge is based on both. Debated for many thousands of years, the precise nature of knowledge remains tenuous, with no agreement on a precise definition. According to *Webster's Ninth New Collegiate Dictionary*, knowledge is "the fact or condition of knowing something with familiarity gained through experience or association." Experience is defined as "the direct observation of or participation in events as a basis of knowledge." Since thoughts are conditioned and filtered by an individual's experience, knowledge can be considered a product of deduction and experience. Further detail is needed on the different features of data,

3

information, and knowledge in order to embark with some confidence on developing a **knowledge strategy**.

DATA, INFORMATION, AND KNOWLEDGE

Data are at the lowest level of known facts, with little value on their own. To be of value, data need to be organized, analyzed, and interpreted. When this is done, **information** is the result, an assembly of data into a message that is meaningful. Information is a commodity—plentiful, freely available. In today's world, "Information is pervasive and easy to transfer, it can be accessed through a variety of technologies (cable TV, computers, telephones), it can be combined in a variety of ways to create services, it can be filtered by various navigation tools to suit different situations, etc."[1]

Although it has meaning, information without **context** adds little value to the decision-making process. An assertion without rationale, for example, or opinion without validation, provides little insight and may render the information unusable. Information without analysis is a poor source of the interpretive intelligence (or context) needed to support action. Successful corporate decision making and planning require an appreciation of the relationships and interdependencies of information and its sources. A good understanding of the implications of these can mean the difference between appropriate and inappropriate use of information. This deep-seated understanding is the know-how that is knowledge.

A combination of knowledge and experience represents what we know, what we have learned, and what we can justify. A knowledgeable person can state, "I know because I've been there and can relate how I got there," or "I know because I've done it and have the proof." An informed person, however, can state only that he or she understands that it is so.

Knowledge is information that has been validated. It is information with context, which provides the understanding and rationale associated with knowledge. A living, evolving product, knowledge enriches the meaning of information, providing details of the relevant circumstances, insight into the source, and the derivation and previous experience associated with the information.

Knowledge is information that has been enriched by the user of information. It is influenced by the subjective context gained as a result of action taken by the user—action that was based on the available information. Knowledge is a collection of values and cognitive experiences; it is insight, judgment, and innovation. It is "the raw material, work-in-process, and finished good of decision-making."[2]

Although knowledge may sometimes appear to result from casual, serendipitous or random thoughts, it is really the product of discipline, of a methodical process. As individuals, we build knowledge in several stages: first, we speculate or believe that something is so; second, we justify our belief to ourselves and to others based on general principles; and third, we prove that our theories are valid through direct experience or deduction. The end result is **new knowledge**.

In the process of creating knowledge, we use experiences to define rules and to derive understanding. Because knowledge resides in people, it often becomes part of an organization's intellectual currency through stories the employees tell about their activities in order to help other people learn. Knowledge is generated by people during the process of social interaction, often through debate and discussion and even sometimes as a result of constructive conflict. Knowledge creation is a natural phenomenon. It is as simple as storytelling, as old as legends.

WHY KNOWLEDGE IS IMPORTANT

For centuries, craftspeople have been recognized for their know-how. The value of a highly skilled and experienced master craftsperson is appreciated, and the difference between such an individual's work and that of an apprentice is easily recognized. Apprentices learn their trade under the direction of a master of a craft. It is expected that the apprentice's work will increase in value as he or she gathers knowledge about a craft, develops a facility in doing it, and develops the ability to apply its nuances and peculiarities as experience is gained.

This system of knowledge transfer works well when the work is manual, comprises repetitive tasks, and is subject to continuous improvement. This is particularly true if the apprentice is allowed to experiment and test his or her own innovative ideas. Continued accumulation of knowledge and experience complements and enhances skills learned during the person's apprenticeship, resulting in a level of knowledge that is difficult to duplicate without the benefit of the same lengthy apprenticeship process.

In a **knowledge economy**, the number of manual craftspeople is small in comparison to the number of **knowledge workers** (a term first coined in 1959 by Peter Drucker) who are, in essence, intellectual craftspeople whose products are decisions, ideas and actions. Because so much of today's work involves decisions that are made on the spot, and decisions that are based on synthesis and idea construction, knowledge workers must have the ability to acquire and apply theoretical and analytical knowledge. Above all, because the environment in which they work is constantly changing, they require a habit of continuous learning.[3] In this world of **knowledge work**, the worker owns the key tools of competitive success—brains. Knowledge workers need to think and learn because innovation and idea generation depend not so much on the volume of information as on the connections that link it and give it greater meaning.

In the same way that a craftsperson develops knowledge, the knowledge worker adds to his or her value by building on and absorbing the lessons of experience through observation, imitation, and practice, but without benefit of a formal apprenticeship program. The development of knowledge is cumulative, adding value to prior experience. It keeps growing in scope and depth and richness. Unlike other assets, knowledge does not become depleted with use, but rather continues to grow and become more valuable as it is used and new knowledge is created.

"True knowledge is, in large part, found in the sophistication of the methods and attitudes by which that knowledge can be consistently renewed."[4]

Context and the continued capacity to renew itself, two key features of knowledge, are precisely why knowledge (and its effective management) is so important to business. For business, context consists of business strategy, organizational and cultural characteristics, and the knowledge needed to succeed. The advantage of context reduces the level of uncertainty in the decision-making process. Also, knowledge, and particular kinds of business knowledge, is important for business because it is dynamic, fluid, changing; it is a living, evolving entity. And in business today, the currency of both information and knowledge is critical. It is not enough to be satisfied with understanding yesterday's breakthrough ideas.

KINDS OF KNOWLEDGE

An organization's existing knowledge includes **explicit knowledge** (knowledge that is documented and public) and **tacit knowledge** (personal, undocumented knowledge).[5] Explicit knowledge is structured, fixed-content, externalized, and conscious. It is easy to codify, capture, and communicate and is the kind of knowledge most commonly captured and exchanged in organizations. It is found in filing cabinets, documents, on computer disk drives, and in other tangible media. It often exists in extremely high volumes and is embodied in one-way communication and exchanged at most meetings.

Tacit knowledge is context-sensitive, dynamically created and derived, internalized (often subconsciously), and experience-based.[6] It is gained through experience, and is often subjective and intuitive. It is difficult to capture, codify, and convey. This is because it consists of such things as know-how, judgment, perception, and intuition—all notoriously hard to express and explain. Tacit knowledge has a very high value because it is difficult for competitors to replicate.

7

As shown in Figure 1-1, these two very different kinds of knowledge are nevertheless complementary and interdependent. Tacit knowledge is made explicit in the form of metaphors, images, and anecdotes, and then combined with other explicit knowledge to create databases, documents, spreadsheets, and other material available to other people. These explicit forms of knowledge are interpreted by others to form new tacit knowledge. That tacit knowledge can then be made explicit again in conversation or reports, and the self-feeding cycle continues. Useful knowledge is passed on, and new knowledge is created. Explicit knowledge can be somewhat dated, however, since it is not as fresh as the knowledge in someone's mind. Therefore, it may be less valuable than tacit knowledge.

Development of a new concept, or new knowledge, is always founded on prior knowledge and experience. Ed Rogers, who is internationally recognized for his work in leveraging collective

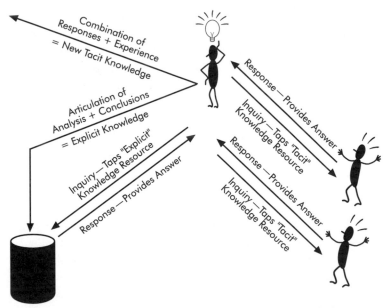

Figure 1-1—Turning Tacit Knowledge into Explicit Knowledge

assets, describes knowledge "construction" in the following way: "In order to put A and B together to get a new concept C, one must realize and know what A and B are and be able to formulate a question about how they relate. Furthermore, to get new concept X may require simultaneous and multiple modeling with concepts A through W."[7]

The key to developing new organizational knowledge is unleashing the tacit and often highly subjective insights, intuitions, and instincts of individual employees and making them available to others. Nothing replaces the value of the person who needs the knowledge being able to talk directly with the person who has the knowledge. But, making some aspects of relevant knowledge available other than by one-to-one communication does provide a measure of insight and availability to a wide audience that is otherwise absent. It is extremely difficult, however, to establish uniform methods for making the tacit knowledge of individuals available to other individuals. Knowledge is knowledge, after all, only because it is processed in someone's brain; capitalizing on it is dependent to some extent on that individual's cooperation.

Nurturing workplace knowledge—by a variety of means, for a variety of purposes—is one of the most important undertakings of smart businesses today. Gaining knowledge is a human process transferable only through learning (by another human being). As such, it needs a fertile environment in which to flourish. It is a by-product of communication and collaboration, which can be enabled and encouraged and supported in various ways. The flow of knowledge in the people associated with an organization—employees, associates, partners, and perhaps customers and suppliers—provides the raw material for fomenting more knowledge, in the never-ending cycle of knowing and learning. It is little wonder Dorothy Leonard-Barton, professor of business administration at Harvard Business School, refers to this dynamic as the "wellsprings of knowledge."[8]

One of the most enthusiastic supporters of workplace knowledge, nurtured for the benefit of the business and the people in it, is the president and CEO of Skandia Corporation, who says:

> There has never been a better time for a business revolution and quest for new heights than today. This is not a revolution of anarchists, however, but of activists and innovators: it's about daring to open the flow of ideas and propose that which has never been considered before; about tearing down walls between what were previously independent units; about fostering a climate of knowledge sharing within the group that is conducive to creativity and value creation. It's about having the courage to realize that the key word for the future is not only competition, but understanding that the future is more a matter of collaboration and context. About daring to understand that we do not need to do everything ourselves, but can collaborate with competence partners outside Skandia. It's about being innovative and accomplishing something neither we nor others in the industry have accomplished before.[9]

Opening the flow of ideas and capturing the value of knowledge are two valuable business strategies. They need commitment, creativity, energy and patience. The organization now has responsibility for nurturing knowledge, a role previously assumed by the craftmaster. Although much is to be gained from seeking knowledge from competitors and other organizations, the ideal place to look first is among the organization's own employees.

Sources of Knowledge

An enormous amount of valuable knowledge, both explicit and tacit, is available to enterprising individuals. Technology provides the means to tap vast reservoirs of potential knowledge. Employees can surf the Internet to seek out new ideas and recent developments. Also, one or more of the technologies described in Chapter 5 can be used to great advantage in the search for knowledge.

More now than ever before, businesses are working together, forming a network of interconnected nodes. Alliances, joint ventures, mergers, partnerships, and customers are all potentially valuable sources of knowledge. As well, links with universities and other research institutions, participation in conferences, visits to other companies, and business trips to other countries are all important threads in the creation of knowledge. They can present new insights and different views of a situation, broadening awareness and sometimes shattering previous truths.

Three of the most prominent areas of activity associated with the knowledge cycle are: best practices (applicable to nearly any activity, whether business, medicine, or industry); corporate memory (archival material revived for current purposes, wisdom of predecessors, and corporate ethics, as well as databases); and communities of interest (the natural home of specialists, generalists with a particular passion, or the curious). All of these offer an ideal starting point for the organization interested in capitalizing on what it knows.

BEST PRACTICES

Best practices are business processes, or major subsets of business processes, that represent the most effective way of achieving specific objectives. Best practices databases capture both these proven, successful practices, and the context and performance data connected with them. Capitalizing on internal best practices is done by systematically replicating practices that have already proven to be successful within the company—that is, repeating successes and not mistakes. By doing this, many companies have been able to turn the knowledge incorporated in best practices into measurable performance improvements.

Best practices are not merely directives; they are intended to stimulate thinking and action. After all, there is no single best practice for any business or function, since a process that works well in a certain situation may not be suitable under a different set of circumstances. Users can modify or augment best practices in the database for specific situations, thereby creating new knowledge in the process. Elements of several similar scenarios can be combined to work well in the situation in question.

Capturing and capitalizing on best practices effectively supports knowledge management because it externalizes tacit knowledge, shares organizational expertise, and reuses knowledge. It saves time and money, and thus maximizes the value of a company's knowledge resources, making effective implementations easier. It works for managers, too, because it is easy to understand, it is a low-cost, relatively low-tech solution, it is fast, and it delivers substantial results.

A knowledge management perspective on best practices would include not only specific examples, but also information about technology, people, and tools appropriate in various circumstances. In this sense, the term best practices "refers not just to a set of information, but also to all of the processes and tools necessary to identify and apply that information to business process design."[10] Because an effective best practices database contains the context or history and rationale surrounding success or failure, assessing applicability of each best practice to a new situation is made easier.

CORPORATE MEMORY

Corporate memory constitutes a historical record of an organization's significant events and decisions. It is the organization's corporate records *and* the accumulated knowledge, experience, expertise, history, stories, strategies, successes, and mythology of an organization as these exist in its employees. Much of this is likely to be maintained in the records or archives that form a history of an organization.

If the records management program provides good access to legacy records, it can provide a valuable and relevant reference for today's problem solvers. Lawyers, for example, base much of their work on precedent, often using closed court cases and legislative bill-drafting files. But, how many of the rest of us have said, in the throes of a burning issue, "I wish we had something about how this has been handled in the past," or even, "I didn't know we had *that* on file!"

The advances in technological hardware and software, each issue of which can do more astonishing feats than the last, and which become nearly outdated in a matter of months, have stretched the traditional notion of what constitutes a "record." In addition to paper documents, a record can now be digital in many forms: documents, images, graphics, videotapes, audio tapes, streaming video, news clips, pointers to database entries, e-mail records, listserve "push" items, and the list goes on. This turns the traditional notion of corporate memory upside-down.

These items can all be considered part of a record, a history, a base of reference. They can all be considered part of an evolving base of corporate knowledge—if the organization can establish the taxonomy that can incorporate these resources into a corporate reservoir that can be easily tapped for current purposes. On the other hand, it may also be that the evolving content of a knowledge management initiative can then be incorporated, as time goes on, into the reservoir of corporate memory, now with more new attributes of context. This may mean that the notion of corporate memory may change from that of corporate archive to corporate experience.

Knowledge management is not just the creation of a corporate memory. **Knowledge management** pertains to a whole process that uses particular means to codify, capture, and make generally available the collective experiences of the organization. The content evolving from knowledge management practices can itself eventually be considered part of an organization's corporate memory in a broad sense.

The most fundamental part of knowledge management is about capturing and recording pertinent business knowledge, be it the facts associated with events, or the iterative development of a strategy, or the wisdom of a respected and experienced employee. Otherwise, the knowledge will be difficult for others to access. It seems, therefore, that the management of knowledge and the management of records of knowledge will be merging more cohesively than we can even imagine at this stage of development.

COMMUNITIES OF INTEREST

Communities of interest exist in every organization, on either a formal or informal basis. They are people who have joined together to use and develop their skills and resources, and to work together on issues of common interest. They share ideas and experiences to identify new opportunities in their field or to solve problems confronting them as a community. In so-called **communities of practice**, members belong to a specialty within a particular field of work and are held together by a common goal and purpose that is supported by a desire to share knowledge.

Membership in such a community is open to all who are interested in the goals of the group, and the members are leaders and advocates for the ideals and principles in which they believe. Their activities often focus on developing solutions to well-defined problems, or to "wicked problems," whose definition, specifications, or requirements cannot be fully determined or understood until the solution is produced. In both cases, the process of problem identification and resolution generates new knowledge and innovative ideas that are worthy of capturing and sharing. Debra Amidon, founder of ENTOVATION International, suggests that, "If the future belongs to those who are able to transform boundaries, then participants in these communities of practice may represent the leadership of tomorrow. . . . (T)hese communities do have a distinct purpose in this evolving knowledge economy . . . they provide the counterbalancing force to offset the inevitable negative aspects of quality, re-engineering and downsizing."[11]

In organizations where universal access to technology and discovery is encouraged, employees will join technology-based communities of interest—on the Internet, their own intranet or through groupware. Like other communities, they form around common interests, flourish through communication and inter-action, and develop their own norms on the basis of shared values and meanings.

Members of these communities assume the responsibility for assessing facts and clarifying values about their field of interest or practice. Over time, they come to trust one another, to develop processes for sharing information and values, and to engage in symbiotic learning and teaching. The interaction contributes to developing new relationships, while supporting a continuous learning process.

What is really significant for knowledge management purposes is that the knowledge developed by these groups is of the highest quality: subject to peer review, and based on genuine open dialogue and multiple viewpoints. Much new knowledge is created through the energy generated in these groups, because interactive dialogue, collaborative creation, debate, and discovery all act as powerful filters on raw information, fusing and focusing good ideas.

Precisely because of these qualities, communities of interest are natural places to begin probing the kinds of knowledge the organization might possess, and to begin formulating a knowledge strategy for the whole organization. This is because any enterprise contains a wide variety of diverse competencies, all of which are in the service of the company's goals. To be successful, any company needs to capitalize on these distinctive competencies. Particularly in times of resource constraints, distrust from downsizing, and a general sense of jeopardy from economic uncertainties, many employees may be reluctant to share ideas or time or effort. For communities of interest or practice, collaboration makes sense. Chapter 2 will discuss this notion further.

Knowledge Economy and Knowledge Management

In *The Organization of the Future*, Michael Hammer described the twenty-first century organization as "characterized by re-

15

sponsibility, autonomy, risk, and uncertainty."[12] Whether this is entirely true or not, it will certainly look and act differently from the organization of this century. Radically new types of organizations are starting to appear—bookstores without books, car dealers without cars. Physical space is no longer needed to initiate or complete a business deal. De-materialization of the trading economy is occurring, as evidenced by the trading in intangibles, and "disintermediation," or removal of the "middleman," is now a feature of many businesses. All of this is fueled by widespread access to the fundamental electronic communications infrastructure—the Internet. These developments bring new power to organizations, large or small, that are willing to innovate. Valuing an organization according to a labor + capital + land formula appears hopelessly quaint in view of some of today's corporate giants. They trade by allowing invisible bits to move along equally invisible atmospheric trade routes in wireless bandwidths, providing services that are in great demand, often generating fabulous profits and share prices that bear little relationship to traditional asset measures. Intellect has become the kind of capital most in demand.

In this new environment, customers have the same information available to them as suppliers; small organizations can make themselves look like large organizations; workers are no longer a cost but, rather, assets valued for their intellectual contribution. Rosabeth Moss Kanter, whose optimistic book on business possibilities is titled *When Giants Learn to Dance*, is equally buoyant in commenting, "The years ahead should be a good time for dreamers and visionaries of the business world, for the barriers to innovation, the roadblocks to inspiration and imagination, are being knocked down one by one."[13]

As we move towards a new century, the transition from an industrial economy to a knowledge economy is well under way, but the ripple effect of the impacts has only just begun. First, more than 75 percent of the population is employed in service and knowledge-intensive activities in the knowledge economy. Second, the employee base is vastly changed. Pedro Saenz, an economist who focuses on the linkages between technology and human capital, explains it this way:

> [the] knowledge economy . . . makes substantial use (greater than most economies) of well educated workers rather than unskilled ones since the structure of production uses technologies that demand many skills . . . which, furthermore, requires know how, know what, know who (and frequently know why) of a 'sophisticated' nature. Basic to these workers is their capacity to learn and adapt continually since technologies being developed or imported are changing continuously . . . in a knowledge economy the exchange between producers and customers, producers and producers (suppliers) is increasingly based on information technologies (computer, INTERNET, INTRANETS, etc.).[14]

The effects of the knowledge economy will also affect the impetus for knowledge management and the direction of its development. There are many environmental forces, internal and external, wide-ranging, unpredictable, and uncontrollable, that can have significant impacts on the organization and its future. Corporate strategies will have to respond to market demands and then change again in response to new demands. The same forces that drive the corporate strategy also move the knowledge management strategy forward. If the corporation needs to have quicker response times to customer needs, it may decide to establish a best practices program. The next year, it might need to have better business intelligence, so an intranet is installed along with client-management software. The results of the process then become driving forces unto themselves, influencing and propelling the future direction of the organization and its business. This dynamic is illustrated in Figure 1-2. Forces buffeting businesses, both external and internal, are discussed in the following paragraphs.

EXTERNAL FORCES

The major economic shift that is under way as we come to the end of the twentieth century is both unrelenting and complex.

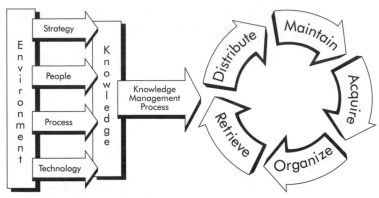

Figure 1-2—Knowledge Management Process

It involves a multiplicity of driving forces: globalization, need for constant renewal, accelerated speed of change, intense competition, and customer relationship building, to name a few. Moreover, the complexity increases as the energy created by one driver causes another one to emerge and further complicate the mix. Most people instinctively recognize that new processes are needed to "ride the wave," but unless they understand the forces that are driving these changes, it is difficult for anyone to take appropriate action in response to them. Some of the major forces of change that are buffeting all businesses these days are described below.

Globalization. The ability and need to trade on a worldwide basis is at the root of much of today's economic and business upheaval. Money markets are now worldwide in scope; no longer is a country totally in control of its own economic future. The highs and lows of currency values in a country on the other side of the world may have a more profound impact on a trading partner's competitive effectiveness than a local event. Increasingly, companies, even quite small ones, have to be run as transnational businesses. Their markets may still be local or regional, but their competition is global.[15]

The global trading environment has created a need for an international integration of cultures, economies, and markets. The increase in markets has resulted in more competition and

18

fostered a need to capitalize on widely dispersed talent. Companies now find it advantageous to reach out across national boundaries in their search for employees, business partners, and allies.

Globalization affects all levels of the organization, not just the senior management level. The global team is the engine that pulls an organization forward, enabling it to compete in the new global marketplace. Success depends on the ability of multicultural teams of workers to overcome the barriers of conducting global work. It is the organization's responsibility to support the global team's efforts to compete in an international trading environment. This requires relentless and systematic pursuit of knowledge, regardless of its source or location; the best brains available to assist in these global efforts may be in other parts of the world.

An organization that pays little heed to the forces of globalization risks its future. As computing costs continue to decline and worldwide connectivity increases, remaining ahead of the crowd will become increasingly difficult. Trade and financial barriers will become less apparent, and multinational companies will have a global pool of resources from which to draw and to whom to sell. Access to knowledge in this environment is critical to any company's future.

Need for Constant Renewal. Organizations achieve market success because they design, make, reproduce, and deliver the best products and services. Along with the trading environment, these products and services are themselves becoming more complex. In an environment where consumer goods are essentially obsolete as soon as they are introduced, renewal and innovation at every level and in every location are fundamental to survival. An innovative company will expect the majority of its sales or products to be made up of those that have been recently introduced, and less and less on products that are more than five years old.

Neither individuals nor organizations can achieve or sustain excellence without constant renewal—renewal of strategies, offerings, and expertise. Constant renewal can be achieved only by building on experience in "a culture where learning is constant; where coaching and feedback are pervasive, given and received from countless sources on an ongoing basis; and where expanded consciousness is the order of the day, simultaneously supporting growth, performance and self esteem."[16] Often, an organization is unable to repeat a success because everyone who contributed to the original achievement has left the organization, leaving behind no meaningful history or knowledge to be applied for a second time.

As the demand for innovation continues to increase, knowledge must be developed and assimilated at an ever-increasing rate. Employees have less and less time to capitalize on what they and others have learned. The results are poor customer service, poorly configured products and services, sales people who know little about what they sell, continuous rework, and continual employee retraining.

An organization that does not learn how to develop and capitalize on its own knowledge runs the risk of running out of good ideas—having no new products or developing products that do not satisfy customer requirements. There is also a high risk of letting employees' creativity and innovation atrophy and stagnate. When this happens, it becomes even more difficult for the organization to compete, even survive. On the other hand, when knowledge is nurtured, shared, and created, it is an unlimited resource, its value increasing the more it is shared. The organization gets better at getting better.

Speed and Complexity of Change. Debra Amidon suggests that we view today's changing environment as we would a kaleidoscope: "No longer can changes be viewed independently. It is the compounding effect that must be taken into consideration as an organization charts its new direction."[17] Coupled with this complexity is the unrelenting pace at which change is occurring. Markets are shifting, products are obsolete before they hit the shelf, competition is coming from unfamiliar sources, technology mutates itself regularly, and the world economy continues to take wild swings. Somehow, businesses must keep up with each of these individual changes, but more importantly they must recognize, interpret, and take action to capitalize on the compounding effect referred to by Amidon.

Along with having to handle a greater scope of markets and complexity of products and services, every organization needs to adapt to the changing needs of its stakeholders. New products constantly eclipse those of yesterday and a market position based on a single product or market image can be tenuous. Every organization must be willing and able to reinvent itself and move on faster and better than its global competitors. Gary Hamel and C.K. Prahalad, leading thinkers in the field of global competition, refer to this as "global pre-emption."[18]

Successful transformation depends on speed and agility, which themselves can be accomplished on the basis of excellent decisions, made with excellent insight, intuition, experience, and knowledge. Informed, timely decision making is a prerequisite to intelligent action. If an organization has no systematic and enterprise-wide process for managing its knowledge, it will be unable to satisfy this demand for rapid development and deployment of high-quality ideas.

Intense Competition. Competition is intense, and it is coming from all directions, within industries and from firms that were previously not competitors. Product life cycles continue to decrease, and competitors introduce new products on a daily basis. Former customers become competitors, and technology continues to change the competitive landscape.

Competition from other organizations in the same industry demands that attention be paid to efficiency and productivity because the cumulative effect of even minor improvements in process and outcomes can become critical for revenues and margins. Introduction of streamlined processes is a partial solution, but its effect is magnified if processes that encourage the capture and reuse of knowledge support the efficiency improvements.

Products and services based on new technologies and delivery mechanisms generate some of the fiercest competition in the market. Often, the products and services come from new

21

sources—software companies that become music and video distributors, office furniture companies that become consulting firms, banks and car dealerships with no physical buildings. In this kind of environment, firms that succeed will be able to develop systems that support rapid conversion of intriguing ideas into commercial ventures. Every organization needs to encourage continual innovation, enhance its offerings, and build, maintain, and grow its market share. The most successful will be those that have knowledge assets that are organized and ready to be applied.

Added value and product or service differentiation are the core of an organization's business success. Knowledge workers are the keys to that success because they are the carriers of the tacit knowledge that generates innovation. A knowledge-friendly environment, where exchange of ideas is encouraged, innovation is rewarded, and change is welcome promotes the successful transformation of products and services. Research and development need not be restricted to a formal program. Every employee has ideas, and smart firms take advantage of them.

Developing competitive advantage means reducing time to market and improving quality and value. This, too, can be achieved through implementing strategies for innovation and intellectual capital development. However, it needs as well a full understanding of the external business environment and the forces that are driving it. In some cases, the organization's only knowledge of that environment resides in its employees' individual and cumulative experience. Accordingly, it is beneficial for the organization to capture the business intelligence in the minds of its own human resources.

Customer Relationship Building. In this environment of intense competition, customers' needs and expectations are more complex and demanding. All competitors need to develop a deep and lasting relationship with customers, but loyalty is short-lived if the products and services do not satisfy customers' needs. That is why "listening to current clients represents perhaps the best source for developing and testing new products and services."[19] To satisfy customers, firms must have knowledge about customers. An organization needs to monitor the market (existing and potential) and tap every available source of knowledge in order to know and anticipate its customers' needs. Also, its employees need that knowledge in order to effect any noticeable customer service improvements.

If relationship building is a company's objective, as it should be, then it is just as important to know the customer as it is to know about the customer. Knowing the customer can lead to many kinds of valuable insights and benefits. Market leaders often demonstrate strong commitments to all stakeholders, including customers, partners, suppliers, and employees. Removing barriers and increasing communication between suppliers and customers can pave the way for cost savings, increased revenue, and increased customer satisfaction. The knowledge management environment needs to accommodate this source of valuable insights.

In this day of call centers, help desks, and e-mail customer support, there are many opportunities to gather customer information. Every interaction with customers is an opportunity to get to know them better, to gather intelligence about their likes, dislikes, perceptions, intuitions, and other subjective insights. Building this base of knowledge is a key competitive weapon.

INTERNAL FORCES

It is obvious that the external forces described above will have a significant impact on the inner workings of the organization, but there are other forces internal to any organization that, in themselves, will drive major changes. Every organization, whether large or small, has felt the impact of technology and the increase in information available and demanded. There is a universal shortage of resources, coupled with increased demands on existing employees—again, impacting most organizations.

As companies come out of restructuring, downsizing, and business process re-engineering, many are realizing that they

23

have sacrificed vital knowledge that was built up over many years. In many cases, downsized or retired employees have been asked to return because the knowledge they took with them was considered irreplaceable. Organizations now agree that it is good practice to capture knowledge on an ongoing basis. Videotaping certain processes and using voice narrative to describe why certain actions are being taken, supported by descriptive contextual information, are two of the ways knowledge is being captured.

Technology. In every organization, technology continues to change traditional business practices, resulting in ongoing internal transformation. Gartner Group analyst Richard Hunter suggests that:

> As enterprises are continually challenged to go higher, faster and further than their competitors with whatever products or services they provide, rapid technological innovation is narrowing the differentiation gap between competitors. As a result, enterprises are viewing the collective knowledge of their employees as a key competitive tool from which innovation can emerge, and are encouraging, supporting and rewarding the collaboration between people.[20]

Business processes are constantly being updated to reflect technological change because many functions that previously involved extensive human intervention are now performed by technology. Human intervention, however, is needed at key decision points and requires the knowledge worker to have access to experiences, lessons learned, and other forms of knowledge support.

The relatively low cost of technology has made it available to all organizations, regardless of the size of the organization. Similarly, access to the Internet and other advanced information sources has made information available to all organizations. While on the surface this may appear to be an advantage, too much information can cause inefficiencies and interfere with an individual's own effectiveness. The knowledge worker needs to be able to locate and apply information that is specifically related to the task at hand.

24

Because technology enables an organization to represent itself electronically, especially using the Internet and intranets, small organizations with vision can now trade on a global basis, making size irrelevant in the knowledge economy. The important factor is the breadth of experience that can be brought to bear in critical situations.

It is possible to gather information about almost anything—customers, competition, markets, performance. It is also possible to collaborate and cooperate across timelines and geographic boundaries. Technology provides the means for an organization to be flexible, but robust; creative, but well managed; innovative, but prudent. What matters is to exploit the technology, to use it to maximum benefit. This means taking its traditional role as a labor-saving device to the higher realm of cognitive support. As a support to knowledge management, technology is invaluable. It allows maximum advantage to be taken of existing knowledge and provides a powerful means of searching for new insights.

Increased Complexity. As the working environment increases in complexity, so do individual jobs. More and more positions are imprecise; people are performing multiple roles and assuming positions that are very broadly defined. Roles and responsibilities change almost daily to reflect the demands of external forces, and in such fluid conditions, employees are required to make instant decisions about actions to be taken in connection with a particular event or circumstance. In many cases, the decision needs to be made in circumstances not previously encountered, but which share similarities with previous situations. If the lessons learned from those other similar situations have been captured, the employee already has some advantage in knowing something about what to do, and the organization benefits.

Layered on top of this complexity is the constant pressure to do more with less, as performance demands on workers continue to increase. At the same time, the cost of mistakes continues to increase. No longer just the cost of paper and pencil, a mistake in today's highly competitive market could result in the loss of a customer, revenue, and market share. The ability to capitalize on lessons learned—avoiding the same mistakes and repeating successes—is highly valued in this increasingly complex world. Making relevant knowledge and experience available to those on the front line gives the lessons learned some continuity and value in the organization, and gives the organization some easy points in the market stakes.

Shortage of Resources. Knowledge tends to be scattered throughout an organization's systems, structures, processes, procedures, culture, and, most importantly, its people. Competitive pressures continue to reduce the size of the workforce. Unfortunately, relentless downsizing has left many organizations stripped of valuable experience. The people who have the knowledge are leaving to join other organizations, to start their own businesses, or to retire, and experts are, therefore, in short supply.

In this environment, the responsibility for knowledge development and transfer is left to the few who remain, and these people often lack the scope and depth of understanding needed to pass on important knowledge effectively. The generation, capture, and use of knowledge ought to be ingrained in the very fabric of the organization, or else its value for future use is at risk.

Anthony Smith, director of Keilty, Goldsmith & Company, and Tim Kelly, president of National Geographic Television, illustrate the difference between speed of learning in traditional and future organizations in the diagram shown in Figure 1-3.[21] Long learning curves are a luxury that no organization can afford today. To ensure that core knowledge is preserved, organizations would be prudent to ask today's knowledge workers some key questions: "What is important about your job?" and "What does someone need to know in order to fully understand what you do?" The recorded answers to these can provide valuable guidelines to future workers.

Rapid growth is difficult to sustain without leveraging employees' knowledge. New hires need access to the knowledge and networks if they are to become valuable contributors in a

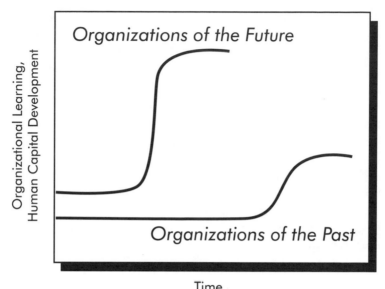

Figure 1-3—Speed of Organizational Learning

short time. The most cost-effective way to provide the necessary background, insights, and guidelines is through the implementation of a knowledge strategy.

Increase in Information. The Internet now provides access to the same information to everyone at the same time, regardless of geographic location. Reproduction of this information is easy and relatively inexpensive. Consequently, there is almost no advantage to be gained from having access to the information. *The real advantage is gained by probing and analyzing the information and then acting on the results more quickly and more intelligently than anyone else.* This requires three key things: a systematic way to collect information; a well-organized and carefully considered store of knowledge and experience to use as the starting point for analysis; and knowledgeable and experienced employees to take advantage of these rich resources. The deliberate use of knowledge and experience provides a unique advantage for organizations that want to be leaders. Those are the organizations that enthusiastically embrace knowledge management to get an edge.

Geographic Dispersion. When all the staff are in a single location, the corporate grapevine provides organizational memory and is the source of much folklore and many anecdotes. When staff are geographically dispersed, such informal mechanisms for sharing knowledge fail and need to be replaced by something more formal. It is now possible, through the Internet, intranets, and features of groupware such as discussion databases and collaborative networks, to develop and support global teams of knowledge workers that operate as a single entity. Knowledge management takes advantage of these technologies to provide an infrastructure that supports the work of such enterprises, so they can systematically capture and use critical knowledge.

Conclusion

It is important to "know what you know"—to know what corporate knowledge assets the organization has. Few organizations have considered what they need to know, what they already know, and where this knowledge is located. There is a growing realization that employees—not computer databases—represent an organization's best knowledge. Consequently, a corporate environment that values knowledge, that encourages workers to share their ideas, generate new knowledge, and capture it for reuse by others is the foundation for any effective knowledge management system.

Knowing what you know is necessary but not sufficient. It is equally important to "use what you know." It is the use of the knowledge, not the knowledge inventory, that provides competitive advantage. Dynamic and creative use of knowledge is enabled by a culture of sharing, motivated by positive business energies, and supported and streamlined by clever new technologies. That's the "pull." The "push" for knowledge management is a combination of business drivers that are remaking the marketplace, that demand greater responsiveness and quicker time to market, and that are blurring the lines of products, suppliers, services, and technologies. Knowledge management is already becoming a way to stay afloat; it will soon become a way of doing business.

Notes

1.   Charles R. McClure, "Network Literacy in an Electronic Society: An Educational Disconnect?" *The Aspen Institute* (1993), online, Available: http://www.aspeninst.org/dir/polpro/CSP/IIS/93-94/McClure.html.

2.   "Kentucky Initiative for Knowledge Management," *University of Kentucky* (1997), online, No Longer Available: http://uky.edu/man/dsis/KIKM.htm. 24 July 1997.

3.   Peter F. Drucker, *Managing in a Time of Great Change* (New York: Truman Talley Books/Dutton, 1995).

4.   Thomas M. Koulopoulos, "Leverage Knowledge Management to Create Corporate Instinct," *The Delphi Group* (1998), online, Available: http://www.delphigroup.com/km/KMandInstinct.html.

5.   J. Bair, J. Fenn, R. Hunter, and D. Bosik, "Foundations for Enterprise Knowledge Management," *Gartner Group Advisory Services* (7 April 1997), CD-ROM (Cambridge, MA: Gartner Group Inc., 1998).

6.   R. Hunter, "Knowledge Capital: Essential Active Management," in *The IT Revolution Continues: Managing Diversity in the 21st Century: Proceedings of Gartner Group Symposium/ITxpo96*, Lake Buena Vista, Florida, 7-11 October 1996 (Stamford, CT: Gartner Group, 1996).

7.   Edward W. Rogers, "Knowledge Construction," *Mayjjer Corporation* (1995), online, Available: http://www.mayjjer.com/knowledge.html.

8.   Dorothy Leonard-Barton, *Wellsprings of Knowledge: Building and Sustaining the Sources of Innovation* (Boston: Harvard Business School Press, 1995).

9.   Björn Wolrath, "Power of Innovation," *Supplement to Intellectual Capital* (Copenhagen: Skandia Corporation, 1996).

10.   V. Frick, "Best Practices and Knowledge Management," *Gartner Group Advisory Services* (22 January 1998), CD-ROM (Cambridge, MA: Gartner Group Inc., 1998).

11.   Debra Amidon, "Evolving Communities of Knowledge Practice," *International Journal of Technology Management* 16, nos. 1/2/3 (1998): 45-64.

12.   Michael Hammer, "The Soul of the New Organization," in *The Organization of the Future*, ed. Frances Hesselbein, Marshall Goldsmith and Richard Beckhard (San Francisco: Jossey-Bass, 1997), 31.

13.   Rosabeth Moss Kanter, *When Giants Learn to Dance* (New York: Touchstone, 1989), 17.

14.   Pedro Saenz, "The Knowledge Economy," *Vita* (n.d.), online, Available: www.vita.org/technet/kaarch/0013.html.

15.   Peter F. Drucker, "Introduction: Toward the New Organization," in *The Organization of the Future*, ed. Frances Hesselbein, Marshall Goldsmith and Richard Beckhard (San Francisco: Jossey-Bass, 1997).

16.   Deepak Sethi, "The Seven R's of Self-Esteem," in *The Organization of the Future*, ed. Frances Hesselbein, Marshall Goldsmith and Richard Beckhard (San Francisco: Jossey Bass, 1997), 236.

17.   Debra Amidon, *Collaborative Innovation and the Knowledge Economy* (Hamilton, Ontario: The Society of Management Accountants of Canada, 1998), 24-5.

18.   Gary Hamel and C.K. Prahalad, *Competing for the Future* (Boston: Harvard Business School Press, 1994), 23.

19.   Ric Duques and Paul Gaske, "The 'Big' Organization of the Future" in *The Organization of the Future*, ed. Frances Hesselbein,

Marshall Goldsmith and Richard Beckhard (San Francisco: Jossey-Bass, 1997), 36.

20. R. Hunter, "The Whys and Hows of Knowledge Management," *Gartner Group Advisory Services* (4 February 1998), CD-ROM (Cambridge, MA: Gartner Group Inc., 1998).

21. Anthony F. Smith and Tim Kelly, "Human Capital in the Digital Economy," in *The Organization of the Future*, ed. Frances Hesselbein, Marshall Goldsmith and Richard Beckhard (San Francisco: Jossey-Bass, 1997), 204.

2

The Knowledge Connection: Learning, Innovation, Productivity, and Performance

A learning business today is one that leverages the economic value of knowledge. It is always figuring out how to define, acquire, develop, apply, measure, grow, use, multiply, protect, transfer, sell, profit by, and celebrate the company's know-how.
—STAN DAVIS AND JIM BOTKIN
The Monster Under the Bed

Issues

- What are the critical linkages between knowledge, learning, and performance at individual, team, and enterprise levels?

- How do learning and knowledge contribute to innovation and improved economic success?

- Are organizational and individual learning the same and what role does collaboration play in the learning process?

Knowledge has strong linkages to learning, and both are fundamental to innovation, productivity, and performance. The critical success factor common to all is the requirement for new ideas, new thoughts, and creative concepts—every one of them dependent on accessibility to a pool of knowledge. Successful organizations are committed to the creation of a learning culture, and development of an innate ability to capitalize on and learn from what they know. In these organizations, the knowledge worker is empowered to make critical decisions and provided with the knowledge needed to assume responsibility in such situations. The twenty-first century organization, of necessity, will adopt learning as a way of life and will recognize that the development of learning skills is a worthwhile investment. It will deliberately seek out and apply the best available knowledge.

There are two new demands in the current business environment: to anticipate and simulate the future, and to identify and assemble sometimes-elusive kinds of knowledge. "The new world of knowledge-based industries is distinguished by its emphasis on precognition and adaptation in contrast to the traditional emphasis on optimization based on prediction."[1] Interpreting messages using lessons learned in the context of anticipating the future is very different from formulating projec-

34

tions based on history. It requires an open and inquiring stance in the face of volatile changes in the marketplace.

Peter Senge gave the term "learning organization" its popular currency in his book *The Fifth Discipline*. He describes such an organization as one "where people continually expand their capacity to create the results they truly desire, where new and expansive patterns of thinking are nurtured, where collective aspiration is set free, and where people are continually learning how to learn together."[2]

A **knowledge-intensive organization** is one that capitalizes on creating, harvesting, assimilating, and applying knowledge to gain economic leverage, producing a smarter and more competitive organization. In *Competing for the Future*, Hamel and Prahalad remind us:

> A firm is a reservoir of experiences. Every day employees come in contact with new customers, learn about competitors, think up new ways to solve problems, and so on. What differentiates firms may be less the relative quality or depth of their experience stockpiles than their relative capacity to mine learning from out of these stockpiles.[3]

The ability to learn from every experience and innovate quickly is one of the key skills of the new order, allowing smart companies to achieve competitive levels of performance and productivity. A knowledge-friendly organization exhibits a spirit of collegiality and a social climate of interaction.

Knowledge Work and Learning

As discussed in Chapter 1, knowledge workers are the new and much-valued assets of the knowledge economy. But what exactly do knowledge workers do, and why is knowledge work important? Since he coined the term, it is reasonable to rely on Drucker for further definition of knowledge work:

> "(I)n knowledge work, as we have seen, the organization is increasingly composed of specialists, each of whom knows more about his or her own specialty than anybody else in the

> organization. . . . The knowledge-based organization. . . has to assume that superiors do not know the job of their subordinates."[4]

Consequently, in a knowledge-intensive organization, everyone shares the responsibility for the organization's performance; it is not limited to a specific group or category of employee. Every worker makes critical decisions, so that everyone becomes a contributor and has the power to make a difference. It is the organization's responsibility to help all workers identify their strengths and weaknesses and then to match opportunity with the right mix of strengths and competencies. When employees, suitably equipped and empowered, are held responsible for their behaviors and actions, they typically act responsibly.

How are employees suitably equipped and empowered? The organization has the responsibility for the renewal of the "wellsprings of knowledge" from which all its vitality comes, and this will be addressed in subsequent sections. How can knowledge workers evolve into such talented assets? And how can they keep up with the pace and complexity of change? It takes intellectual skills and knowledge of various kinds, of course. A true learning environment needs to promote the circulation of those intellectual skills and knowledge through sharing, collaboration, and teamwork. For this discussion, these activities are understood to be on a continuum of professional interaction from the least to the most formal.

SHARING

Over the years, individuals have learned how to acquire and use knowledge, but **knowledge sharing** is a more complex phenomenon. Children are encouraged to share and to learn from each other, but at some point, sharing loses its favor; independent accomplishment becomes the way to get ahead, get attention, and get approval. Sharing is often contrary to the organization's culture. In many businesses today, those who *have* knowledge are rewarded, rather than those who *share* knowledge. So, the climate itself is not conducive to the sharing that takes advantage of an organization's intellectual resources. Richard Hunter explains:

> Organizations resemble formal political entities in their internal structures. Politics is about power and information is power. Therefore, information distribution and sharing are strongly affected by the political structure of the organization. A balkanized organization in which political power is distributed among numerous warring "fiefdoms" is unlikely to share information of any importance across political boundaries. In a "monarchy" information sharing is directed from the top of the organization and is essentially limited to officially sanctioned topics. The monarch may be benign, but may also be capable of sudden retribution against those seen as usurping the monarch's rightful authority.[5]

Sharing information and knowledge is rarely built into the normal day-to-day processes of an organization. It occurs, of course, but often guardedly, since it is dependent on established relationships and trust. Both of these are in short supply in a business climate characterized by downsizing, restructuring, merging, global work teams, reassignments, and real-time everything.

C. Jackson Grayson, Jr., founder and chair of the American Productivity & Quality Center, suggests that most people are not accustomed to sharing knowledge. They may not realize that what they have learned is valuable to others in the organization. They may not know how to share knowledge or with whom to share it. They may be busy, and sharing takes time. The result is that valuable knowledge generated every day remains locked up in the minds of individuals all over the organization.[6] Many people, in fact, see sharing as providing more chances for them to be proven wrong.

But why is sharing so important for the organization that wants to succeed? It needs knowledge to be transferred, moved around, cross-fertilized, and used by those who see these activities as fundamental to becoming successful individuals, as well as to the success of the overall organization. Robert Buckman, head of Buckman Laboratories International Inc., of Memphis, Tennessee, is both a good spokesperson and an exponent of organizational sharing. His organization estimated the average of the amount of time that its associates were in one of its offices and found that 86 percent of them were outside the office and in any one of 90 different countries. Obviously, the office was not the place where the business of the company was being done. Since cash flow was generated outside the office, and barriers to company-wide results were structural barriers of hierarchical organizations, the company sought a solution. Buckman explains:

> We believe that it is essential to have clear communication . . . so that the individual in need of information will be able to provide a rapid response to the customer. You do this by radically changing the span of communication of the individual from his immediate work group to the entire company and beyond to anybody on any network that they need to go to for information. If the greatest data base in the company is housed in the individual minds of the associates of the organization, then this is where the power of the organization resides. . . . We have to connect these individual knowledge bases together so that they can do whatever they do best in the shortest possible time.[7]

Sharing knowledge requires individuals to share intuitions, feelings, assumptions, and ways of working. In a knowledge environment, this means exposing previously hidden competencies and making other people aware of what is important to you and to the work you do. Both individuals and the organization as a whole become more powerful from effective sharing. Buckman's own words are again worth quoting:

> The greater the span of communication that you give to individuals, the greater the span of influence they will have. The greater the span of influence, the more powerful the individuals will be. . . . As you expand the ability of individual members of the organization, you expand the ability of the organization. As you change the span of the influence of the individual you change the power of the individual and you change the power of the organization.[8]

An environment conducive to sharing will evolve when the organizational culture, as in the case of Buckman Laboratories, demonstrates to workers that sharing is valued by the organization; and that developing new ideas, sharing ideas, and accepting the ideas of others will be the norm and not the exception. It needs open dialogue in order to develop new knowledge and to reuse what it knows in creative ways to meet real-time demands. It needs the participation of experts and knowledge holders in the collaborative activities of the knowledge marketplace.

When Monsanto was building its knowledge-management architecture in the mid-1990s, the project director, Bipin Junnarkar, now director of knowledge management, noted that the emphasis moved from "How do I get information?" to "How do I exploit it?" He summed up the knowledge-learning challenge: "Typically, people make buckets of information—finance, operations, competitive intelligence—with no flow between them, the question is how to link them to create a learning and sharing organization. Then the fun starts."[9]

A Word about Perspective. Knowledge sharing, to be useful, demands that people listen to one another with open minds and engage in lively discussions and debate in the course of creating and using knowledge to their advantage. In the course of listening, even openly, people do apply their own natural "filters" to the information or knowledge they receive. Perspective provides the "lens" through which a person views a situation. Some filtering is good; too much is limiting.

Perspective is necessary for applying knowledge appropriately. It gives an individual some context from which to derive meaning from experiences, events, information, and knowledge. A broad perspective is beneficial because it provides the most opportunity for comparison, for reasoning, and for determining the benefit of knowledge. As Leonard-Barton observes, deep knowledge in one particular area of expertise, coupled with sufficient breadth to be able to relate that experience to many other areas of corporate activity, is a valuable capability and one that

39

should be much sought after, both in individuals and as an organization.[10]

Subject-area perspective is very useful for the way business works. T. Austin states:

> People interpret, understand and use shared information in situation-specific and task-specific contexts, relating objects to one another in multiple ways. A customer's financials are used differently by a credit manager, the assigned salesperson and a senior executive with a scheduled customer visit. Perspective is important. Each user has a different perspective on the same object and each organizes his or her papers in ways that have personal and context-specific meaning.[11]

Perspective can also be limiting if the lens of perspective is actively constrained by different backgrounds, training, professional expertise, and nationalities. Since most organizations are made up of people with a range of perspectives like these, the likelihood of divergent views is very high. When people take great pride in emphasizing their differences, applying their own interpretation of reality, and seeking recognition for their own group, difficulties can arise from a reluctance to consider other perspectives.

COLLABORATION

It is the collective ability of employees to apply knowledge in innovative ways that provides continuous strategic renewal to an organization. For this to occur, the organization needs to provide a cooperative, collaborative environment, in which everyone will learn from each other, as well as from mistakes and successes, and new ideas will emerge from the interaction. It needs to provide ways to renew the wellsprings of knowledge.

The creation, sharing, and combining of knowledge within and among different knowledge communities needs as a key dynamic the exchange of tacit and explicit knowledge. It also needs to be coordinated and managed. New flexible technologies are needed to support networks of workers in a workable and robust collaborative environment. One of the biggest challenges for such an environment is to support the making of tacit knowledge sufficiently explicit to be recorded and documented, and efficiently shared and reapplied, for the benefit of both the enterprise and individual development. The other great challenge for the utility of a collaborative environment is to strike a workable balance between two important aspects of a knowledge environment: enough *structure* and formality to be able to capture and redistribute knowledge on a recurring basis, but enough *flexibility* to allow random connections and interactions that lead to new insights, new knowledge, and innovative strategies.

One of the reasons collaboration works and can yield such rich results in short times is that the participants share an **interpretive context.** They are part of the same corporate culture or subculture; they understand the same concepts, meanings, experiences, and implications; they subscribe to the same norms of structure and behavior; they "speak the same language." When this is the case, collaborative technologies (like groupware, and others discussed in Chapter 5) can play a central role in the acquisition, combination, and dissemination of knowledge. When knowledge is primarily tacit, communication is best accomplished using interactive technologies like e-mail and video-conferencing. Another way is to identify certain people as sources of specific content and expertise, in a map of corporate knowledge resources, so the rest of the organization can benefit from their knowledge.

Encouraging and maintaining collaboration in an extended business environment, such as home office, virtual teams, and telecommuting, is one of the special challenges of making knowledge management work. Experience, like Buckman's and others', has shown that people will share what they know and reuse the know-how of others if it is easy for them and if it is worth their while.

TEAMWORK

Knowledge work starts with individuals and then gravitates to smart work teams. Because a smart team is one that continues

41

to learn from its own and others' experiences, its work is likely to be highly interactive, spanning the entire tacit/explicit knowledge cycle. To encourage learning and the generation of new knowledge, the smart team allows debate, challenge, and creative tension to occur. Sometimes a facilitator or coach can be useful in these circumstances, but difficulties can nevertheless occur. According to Professor Linda Hill of the Harvard Business School, once the team has been established, the manager needs to keep a vigilant eye on the competitive environment and at the same time maintain the team's relationship with key internal and external stakeholders.[12]

As they form and build, teams cycle through several stages on the way to becoming efficient and effective. It is estimated that it takes some three to five years for team members to learn how to work together through a continuous process of educating each other. This includes learning what everyone's responsibilities are; what is important to them; and what they have done to make themselves successful. Also, time is needed just to ascertain what the team needs from technological and other support mechanisms since this is often influenced by geography, work styles, and of course, the task at hand.

In order to be efficient, teams must move beyond conflict, while maintaining the climate of debate. In order to be effective, teams need to share a set of common values. One of the most important is that although knowledge has intrinsic value, its value is enlarged by being shared; this greater value accrues to both the individual and the organization. If individual team members hoard knowledge, the group cannot be considered a team. Real teams have respect for the members, the ability to interpret and use shared knowledge appropriately, and they avoid getting stuck in frustrating, wasted effort.

Knowledge Strategy Connections

Knowledge work is learning work. Intellectual growth must be ongoing so the worker can maintain an ability to respond appropriately to the changing demands of the business environment. The organization needs to support the worker in this endeavor if it expects to have top-quality employees who are committed to advancing the organization's vision and goals.

An organization that wants to succeed in today's tough business climate strives for innovation to stay competitive, productivity to stay profitable, and top-quality performance to distinguish itself in the market, support its bottom line, and energize and retain its best staff. All are linked to learning; they are enabled by learning; and the activities of each contribute to learning.

The relationships connecting knowledge and learning, innovation, productivity, and performance are like those between tacit and explicit knowledge. Each can be considered independently, but they are self-referential, each informing the other.

The environmental forces discussed in Chapter 1 demand that businesses pay attention to learning, innovation, productivity, and performance. These can be considered the key drivers of business success. All are needed to successfully manage the environmental forces affecting today's enterprises. Each of them needs the support of strategy, people, processes, and technology.

Figure 2-1 provides a simple framework that portrays the synergistic connections among these drivers. The model also shows critical success factors for each driver. Credit for this representation is due to Lotus and IBM, which use a similar model to portray their interpretation of knowledge management.[13] What is significant about this model is the interrelationship and interdependence among and between each of the drivers. For example, **smart reuse** needs learning, sharing, adaptability, and responsiveness. None of the synergy can happen without a good strategy for facilitating the flow of knowledge.

Managing these interrelationships, and putting into place the conditions that support each of the drivers and that enable communication and cross-fertilization among them, is the heart of a knowledge strategy. Knowledge management is a way to orchestrate and benefit from learning *in* the organization and enhancements to the performance *of* the organization. A

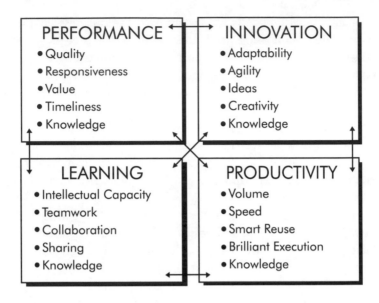

Figure 2-1—Knowledge Strategy Connections

knowledgeable workforce enhances everything in a business. Learning stimulates innovation, which improves performance and energizes the whole enterprise.

INNOVATION

Since the forces of change are expected to accelerate, the complexities of doing business in the twenty-first century will multiply. Innovation will be the key to success. The need to generate and capitalize on new ideas is more important now than ever before; in fact, innovation has become a preoccupation of business, and in some cases it is considered to be a core competency—something that is critical to survival.

Debra Amidon defines innovation—for business—as "the creation, evolution, exchange, and application of new ideas into marketable goods and services for the excellence of an enterprise, the vitality of a nation's economy and the advancement of society as-a-whole."[14] Margaret J. Wheatley, renowned business-thought leader, academic, and author, describes innovation as a dynamic phenomenon:

> The literature on organizational innovation is rich in lessons ... [and] describes processes that are also prevalent in the natural universe. Innovation is fostered by information gathered from new connections; from insights gained by journeys into other disciplines or places; from active, collegial networks and fluid, open boundaries. Innovation arises from ongoing circles of exchange, where information is not just accumulated or stored, but created. Knowledge is generated anew from connections that weren't there before.[15]

For the reasons cited by Wheatley, innovation relies on learning and knowledge. As discussed in Chapter 1 (Figure 1-1) this interdependency is fundamental to the knowledge life cycle; learning takes place as tacit knowledge becomes explicit, and innovation occurs as the result is applied. According to a leading authority on Japanese business, Nonaka Ikujiro, it is this ability to translate subjective understanding into objective information (and then apply it) that makes Japanese organizations learning-rich innovators.[16]

Many business leaders engaged in building new types of organizations are committed to fostering innovation, but few have been successful in developing breakthrough products and services, despite achieving market dominance.[17] Neither is there a very good track record for capitalizing on acquisitions that were meant to contribute innovative capabilities. Why is this? Ric Duques, chairman and CEO of First Data Corporation, and Paul Gaske, managing director of Keilty, Goldsmith & Company, suggest that this is partially because of a lack of attention to generating innovation in a systematic way. They also suggest that the fact that many acquisitions were only speculative and not seriously integrated into business operations reduces the likelihood of increased innovation following an acquisition.[18] It is likely that the outcome might be different if a well-designed knowledge strategy and/or culture that encourages continuous learning and sharing supported these efforts.

Innovative business applications and breakthroughs are not accidental, and only rarely serendipitous. Often, the conditions that foster new, out-of-the-box thinking are carefully planned and put in place. Great new corporate ideas are the result of combining many small, individual ideas into a larger, often elegant solution or opportunity. But combining and synthesizing those small ideas does not always occur with ease.

People are often reluctant to share unfinished thoughts or bits and pieces of information—perhaps because raw information is not valued. Corporate thinkers often feel comfortable sharing only thoughts that have been honed and refined. Except for the most aggressive firms, organizational culture, with its hierarchical and competitive characteristics, often discourages many people from contributing their early insights. As a result, many potentially rich new combinations and insights are missed and withheld from the energies of dialogue, so potentially fruitful avenues are not explored, and opportunities are missed.

Employees may be uncomfortable sharing ideas for one (or more) of many reasons. Examples of potential barriers are: individual competition is encouraged and individual success rewarded; some reward systems do not recognize raw information, but only polished thoughts; professional egos may get in the way of teamwork and collaboration; and dysfunctional organizational behavior resulting from past experiences may flare up.

The quality of innovation, in any business, has the potential to change the traditional ways of working, and change them in previously unconsidered ways. If an organization wants to reap the rewards of innovative and creative thinking, it needs to create opportunities for debate and change, allowing employees to challenge ideas without fear of recrimination. Team brainstorming sessions with no risk of censure are essential for encouraging learning. All this should ideally occur in an

Real-Life File: Monsanto Scores Innovation Points through Collaboration

For Monsanto Life Sciences, a division of Monsanto Company, business success is driven by innovative, value-added products that can be patented. The patent establishes a barrier to entry so the company can generate substantial profit margins on its products—such as Nutrasweet—for a protected period of time. For companies such as Monsanto that focus on innovation, substantial R&D investments are critical to success, even though many initial product development efforts will fail. The typical person hired by the Life Sciences division is highly educated, often a Ph.D., with an established network of scientists and researchers around the world.

Monsanto focuses its knowledge management efforts on innovation by leveraging the talents of these highly skilled professionals. Using electronic discussion forums to help bring its people together to share ideas and brainstorm, Monsanto created fertile ground for innovation. [It] has had better success with collaborative discussion forums than most other companies.[19]

environment in which workers understand the importance of innovation to the organization's goals.

PRODUCTIVITY

During the last 25 years, many attempts have been made to resolve the **productivity paradox**, wherein the investment in technology over the last decade or so has not produced identifiable commensurate returns in **productivity**. Many productivity improvement efforts focused on employee empowerment (giving workers more control over their work), delayering (reducing the number of management layers), and process re-engineering (re-

47

thinking the process of doing work). All of these were supported by the latest technology. But it is safe to say that of the many improvements made, not all of them were noticeable, and many fell short of expectations. Technology alone, we are realizing, cannot do the work of brainpower.

Knowledge can certainly contribute to improving productivity, but only if it is applied in a systematic fashion throughout the organization. In other words, it must be managed in order to provide a meaningful contribution to the synergies that result in productivity improvements. Capturing and sharing best practices, lessons learned, and other reusable assets can shorten cycle times (for development or delivery). However, people need to: (1) be aware that there are repositories of knowledge for them to use, and (2) be provided with a simple way to tap into the repositories. Also, they need to know that reuse is both acceptable and desirable in the organization. The awareness, the database, the user-friendliness of the technology, and the message of approval from management—all these are part of a knowledge strategy for capitalizing on knowledge.

PERFORMANCE

An organization committed to high-quality performance is one for which success, that is, long-term sustained growth, is achieved through its ability to create ideas and move them into the marketplace profitably and expeditiously. This depends on the organization's ability to anticipate the marketplace and to recognize and capitalize on intuition and other organizational perceptions and insights.

Innovation and productivity pave the way for the cost-effective production of dynamic new products and services. Companies that enjoy sustained success rely on outstanding product quality, service delivery, and service reliability. An organization needs to perform well across all three elements to satisfy its stakeholders—customers, suppliers, shareholders, and employees. Some suggestions follow:

- **Product quality.** Although it is no longer a means of competitive differentiation, quality is still extremely important to overall economic success. Quality output means there is little rework necessary—a positive influence on the cost of "before sale" production. Quality products result in satisfied customers and reductions in warranty work, resulting in reduced "after sale" costs. In some cases, early products do not entirely satisfy customer requirements, since it is almost impossible to predict exactly how a product or service will be received. This is true whether the product is a car, a computer, a food, or a software program. Market testing and knowledge gathering are extremely important to this learning process of market exploration. But, any knowledge gathered should be retained for future use. Even though future products and services will differ from existing ones, lessons can be learned from features the customer liked as well as from features the customer did not like or did not identify as needed.

- **Service delivery.** Time-to-market is important in gaining or maintaining market share. Product life cycles are getting shorter, development times are getting tighter, and speed is of the essence in today's business world. Reducing the number of iterations involved in production—from development to launch—is critical to cost effectiveness and to capturing a market space. Knowledge and learning are important ingredients in this process; each iteration provides an opportunity to apply what has been learned either to the same or to other products and services. In many cases, the process (or part of the process) can be reused or duplicated in other processes.

- **Service reliability.** Customers expect almost instantaneous service, and knowledgeable, responsive service representatives. In these circumstances, shared knowledge and experience are essential for those providing service to customers. The customer is a source of valuable material for the organization's knowledge base and to the overall learning process. No one else can provide better information about existing products. Similarly, no one else can provide more insights into what products might be ideally suited to a future market than can the potential buyer. One of the oldest applications of lessons learned is in the customer service area. Help desks take advantage of large "frequently asked questions" databases to respond to customer inquiries. Supported by case-based reasoning software, these systems reuse and manipulate similar situations, often combining elements of multiple scenarios to construct a situation similar to the current one and then providing an appropriate answer.

One of the risks, of course, in basing decisions entirely on accumulated knowledge and past experience is that of being over-conditioned by an existing direction. Anthony Patrick Carnevale explains:

> Learning processes begin with incremental choices, but the subsequent accumulation of experience eventually magnifies and reinforces these small events in the development of industries, technologies or products and services, especially when they occur early in the learning process. Alternatives that are marginally superior now may lock us into developmental paths that prove inferior later.[20]

Dorothy Leonard-Barton cautions that there is a risk of an organization's core capabilities becoming its core rigidities.[21] The learning process must include an exploration of alternatives and an active search for input from other organizations and external experts to complement internal knowledge.

Learning as a Way of Life

The organization of the future, for the sake of its own future, is wise to encourage learning as an ongoing activity and make it effective enough to develop "experts" relatively quickly. Where there is a comfortable environment of sustained coaching and feedback, learning becomes a real-time activity, a way of life rather than a task done only occasionally as it is needed. This is becoming less a luxury and more an imperative in today's business world. As Professor for Leadership, Ethics and Corporate Responsibility at Harvard University Graduate School of Business, Shoshana Zuboff, summarizes it, "Learning is not something that requires time out from being engaged in productive activity; learning is the heart of productive activity. To put it simply, learning is the new form of labor."[22]

Smith and Kelly assert that "organizations that can develop methods for increasing the need for and impact of learning will clearly have a competitive advantage, not just in terms of advanced human capital, but also in their ability to attract the best and the brightest."[23]

The recent emphasis on learning has sparked major investments in training and education, much of it administered en masse in classroom-style settings. The amount of money invested in training or the number of people put through a training process are not, in themselves, indications of progress. If there is no evidence of performance improvement or other meaningful metric, then the training itself is of questionable value. Moreover, in any training initiative, it is important to understand and take into account the individual needs and learning styles of the participants. This is extremely difficult when the class consists of 10, 20, or sometimes 30 people. Consequently, the training itself is not always beneficial.

The real value of training sessions often lies in the opportunities they provide for participants to establish networks and learn from one another. This suggests that the money invested in training might be better spent in supporting communities of interest and the technology that serves them. Kanter suggests that training centers and educational events are excellent ways to increase communication. She cites the example of General Electric's facility in Crotonville, New York, as much more than a corporate college, calling it "in effect a synergy center that helps people identify shared interests across businesses and tackle common problems together."[24]

INDIVIDUAL AND ORGANIZATIONAL LEARNING

It cannot be assumed that an increase in individual learning automatically leads to an increase in organizational learning. For knowledge to be effectively transferred across the organization, attention should be given to how work groups might learn from one another and how this will facilitate continuous improvement.

In a demanding business environment, most business leaders recognize the value to be gained by the corporation from developing a "learning organization." In a resource-constrained market, moreover, part of the competitive challenge is to make the organization itself an attractive place to work for high-value employees. Employees respond to stimulation and challenge and are unlikely to stay in a poor-quality work environment that does not offer them this. Indications of dissatisfaction include higher than usual absenteeism and turnover, reluctant participation in new programs, and lack of interest in developing new skills. It is important to recognize the needs of individuals and to support their personal development. An organization that can emphasize and encourage learning among its employees and recognize their acquisition of new skills is likely to produce a highly motivated workforce.

The collective knowledge, skills, and experience of workers can be harnessed by informal networks of people who do similar work, regardless of whether they are in the same geographic location or in the same business unit. These informal networks are typically known as communities of practice (or interest) and they are held together by a sense of mutual interest, or by a common desire to solve a problem that is shared by the members. As mentioned in Chapter 1, these communities represent a major source of knowledge for an organization.

Communities of practice are ideal environments for developing, sharing, and disseminating best practices as well as for developing a sense of trust and of community. The kind of open, sharing culture found in such communities is generally receptive to the introduction of technology, particularly as part of a knowledge development cycle. The automated capture of knowledge in a groupware-supported environment immediately transitions an individual's tacit knowledge to explicit knowledge that is available for use by a group of people. Stated differently, the passive sharing of knowledge turns into collective ownership of the knowledge, thereby making the knowledge actively shared. It is this sharing and noncompetitive exchange of ideas, concepts, and experiences that contribute to organizational learning.

Cooperation means sharing the pie; collaboration means creating multiple new pies. Since knowledge is the product of human interaction, and a key objective of knowledge strategy is innovation, new ideas, and new pies, the organization should support and encourage collaboration. When there is a serious commitment to capitalizing on knowledge assets, collaboration becomes a core competence.

Understanding the connection between knowledge and learning, innovation, productivity, and performance allows an organization to better capitalize on its knowledge resources in a systematic way through a knowledge strategy. Figure 2-1 provides a framework for this. The factors operating in this dynamic mix of intelligence, energy, and activity are all mutually enhancing; each helps to advance the others. All can be harnessed in the service of a knowledge strategy and all contribute to corporate success.

KNOWLEDGE MANAGEMENT AND LEARNING

A knowledge-intensive organization promotes and supports excellence, autonomy, and responsibility. The knowledge worker in this environment is someone who is capable of acting independently, is often the first point of contact in a variety of circumstances, and is empowered to make decisions. These knowledge workers are constantly learning and, in the process, are capitalizing on lessons already learned (by themselves or others) and experience gained (again by themselves or others). All the while, they are generating new knowledge, since knowledge is the product of learning. This new knowledge, if captured and structured, will contribute to the learning of other individuals. These workers are expected to contribute knowledge as well as to take advantage of it, and act as role models for the entire organization.

In an environment where work methods are standardized, best practices are relatively easy to capture, and these can then be used to spread ideas for improvement throughout an organization. For such processes to be effective, the workers should be involved in a process of identifying problems, defining improvements and opportunities, and implementing the new standards. This is an opportunity for the organization to support the learning process because it provides an environment for exposing workers to responsibilities and activities that are not normally in their own domain.

All knowledge workers require skills similar to those defined by Distinguished Professor Charles McClure, of the School of Information Studies, Syracuse University, in connection with network literacy in 1993, that are clearly relevant today. These skills include the ability to define a task, determine the best way to access information, identify ways to use and synthesize information, and evaluate the quality of the information and the methods used to gather it.[25] In a business environment, workers use these same skills, with available tools and sources of information, to solve a problem from start to finish.

In this intensely competitive and information-rich environment, everyone in the organization needs to develop advanced research, analytical, and creative-thinking skills. Everyone needs to be able to question assumptions, learn new techniques, thrive in the face of uncertainty, and be comfortable with ambiguity. All of these skills are essential to tackling the "wicked problems" associated with the knowledge economy. Unlike technical skills, none of these skills ever becomes obsolete, so they are truly a sound investment, but they are never so valuable as when they are supported by a relevant and rich source of knowledge.

Another way that learning and knowledge management can be linked for enterprise benefit is by capturing lessons learned. In order to be useful to people who consult it in the future, the lesson has to include both facts and context. This requires identification and capture of the theories, authorities, justifications, precedents, beliefs, and other features that were used to develop an approach to solving a problem. In the simplest terms, this is anything that was important to the problem and to its resolution. This could be captured graphically, as a flow chart, or it may be a simple goal, objective, or resolution statement. The effort of recording the lesson, and the reasons it can be understood as a lesson, is a cultural activity and needs official reinforcement in the organization. Gathering this kind of information is valuable in itself because it demands that people think through a process, thereby determining the critical success (or obstructive) factors.

Conclusion

It is in the organization's best interest to remove the boundaries to communication and learning, and to openly acknowledge the connection between individual growth and corporate achievement. By now, most organizations are aware of the importance of innovation to getting and keeping a competitive edge in business. They also know that innovation is dependent on knowledge and learning and stimulation of creativity.

A work culture that fosters teams and collaborative teamwork fosters innovation. All this can happen only in a culture that recognizes that knowledge is its most valuable corporate asset. Knowledge workers are most valuable when they are able to make knowledgeable decisions. An individual without knowledge cannot take responsibility and cannot make informed decisions. An organization that leverages the economic value of knowledge provides its workers with the motivation and the ways to acquire, develop, apply, grow, use, transfer, and celebrate the company's know-how.

The most important thing is to recognize the enormous benefit to the organization of the knowledge assets of its own employees. The next step is to determine what kinds of knowledge are important to the enterprise. Then, a knowledge management strategy can begin to evolve. That strategy needs to target the culture of the organization. If employees truly understand the importance of knowledge management for the organization, their own place in it, and the benefits they as individuals can derive from it, the organization can move into a new dimension of fruitful effort and business health.

Notes

1. Yogesh Malhotra, "Knowledge Management for the New World of Business," *Business Researcher's Interests* (1998), online, Available: http://www.brint.com/km/whatis.htm.

2. Peter M. Senge, *The Fifth Discipline: The Art and Practice of the Learning Organization* (New York: Doubleday, 1990), 3.

3. Gary Hamel and C.K. Prahalad, *Competing for the Future* (Boston: Harvard Business School Press, 1994), 165.

4. Peter F. Drucker, *Post-Capitalist Society* (New York: HarperCollins Publishers, 1993), 106-7.

5. Richard Hunter, "Knowledge Capital: Essential Active Management," in *The IT Revolution Continues: Managing Diversity in the 21st Century: Proceedings of Gartner Group Symposium/ITxpo96*, Lake Buena Vista, Florida, 7-11 October 1996, (Stamford, CT: Gartner Group, 1996), 10.

6. C. Jackson Grayson, "Taking Inventory of Your Knowledge Management Skills," *Continuous Journey* (Winter), American Productivity & Quality Center, online, Available: http://www.apqc. org/b2/b2stories/story1.htm.

7. Robert H. Buckman, "Collaborative Knowledge: The Worldwide Implications," (Austin, TX: International Knowledge Management Summit, 11 March 1997, transcription).

8. Robert H. Buckman, "Collaborative Knowledge: The Worldwide Implications," (Austin, TX: International Knowledge Management Summit, 11 March 1997, transcription).

9. Thomas A. Stewart, "Getting Real About Brainpower," *Fortune*, 27 November 1995, 201.

10. Dorothy Leonard-Barton, *Wellsprings of Knowledge: Building and Sustaining the Sources of Innovation* (Boston: Harvard Business School Press, 1995), 156.

11. T. Austin, "Information Sharing Chaos: Much Change," *Gartner Group Advisory Services* (3 July 1997), CD-ROM (Cambridge, MA: Gartner Group Inc., 1997).

12. Linda Hill, "Faultlines a Manager Must Walk on the Way to the 21st Century," Harvard Management Update (June 1996). Harvard Business School Publishing. http://www.hbsp.harvard.edu/groups/newsletters/update.html.

13. Lotus Institute, "The Lotus/IBM Knowledge Management Framework: Structuring the Problem," *Lotus*, Hp, 1998, online, Available: http://www.lotus.com/news/topstories.nsf.

14. Debra Amidon, *Collaborative Innovation and the Knowledge Economy* (Hamilton, Ontario: The Society of Management Accountants of Canada, 1998), 6.

15. Margaret J. Wheatley, *Leadership and the New Science: Learning about Organizations from an Orderly Universe* (San Francisco: Berrett-Koehler, 1992), 113.

16. Nonaka Ikujiro and Hirotaka Takeuchi, *The Knowledge Creating Company* (New York: Oxford University Press, 1995).

17. Peter M Senge, *The Fifth Discipline: The Art and Practice of the Learning Organization* (New York: Doubleday, 1990), 15.

18. Ric Duques and Paul Gaske, "The 'Big' Organization of the Future," in *The Organization of the Future*, ed. Frances Hesselbein, Marshall Goldsmith and Richard Beckhard (San Francisco: Jossey-Bass, 1997), 33-43.

19. Lotus Institute, "Lotus, IBM and Knowledge Management Index," White Paper, 1997, Lotus, Hp, 1998, online, Available: http://www/lotus.com/news/topstories.nsf.

20. Anthony Patrick Carnevale, "Learning: The Critical Technology," *Training and Development* 46, no. 2 (February 1992), S1-16.

21. Dorothy Leonard-Barton, *Wellsprings of Knowledge: Building and Sustaining the Sources of Innovation* (Boston: Harvard Business School Press, 1995), 30.

22. Shoshana Zuboff, *In the Age of the Smart Machine: The Future of Work and Power,* in Britton Manasco, "Enterprise-Wide Learning: Corporate Knowledge Networks and the New Learning Imperative," Knowledge Inc., 1995, online, Available: http://webcom. com/quantera/enterprise.html.

23. Anthony F. Smith and Tim Kelly, "Human Capital in the Digital Economy," in *The Organization of the Future*, ed. Frances Hesselbein, Marshall Goldsmith and Richard Beckhard (San Francisco: Jossey-Bass, 1997), 203.

24. Rosabeth Moss Kanter, *When Giants Learn to Dance* (New York: Touchstone, 1989), 113.

25. Charles R. McClure, "Network Literacy in an Electronic Society: An Educational Disconnect?" *The Aspen Institute*, 1993, on-line, Available: http://www.aspeninst.org/dir/polpro/CSP/IIS/9394/ McClure.html.

3

Preparation:
Setting Direction,
Getting Commitment,
Assessing Readiness

Vision is the art of seeing things invisible.
—JONATHAN SWIFT

Issues

- What strategies and tactics will lead to the effective adoption of knowledge management?

- What is the knowledge management value proposition? How does it link to tangible business value?

- What steps need to be taken prior to embarking on the implementation of a knowledge management environment?

To introduce and implement knowledge strategy in any organization is a major undertaking, and it will require a major change in the culture and processes of the organization. It needs strong support from senior management, and leadership, commitment, enthusiasm, and courage from sponsors and advocates. A number of activities are involved in preparing for a knowledge management initiative, which will begin as a project, but continue as a "way of life." As shown in Figure 3-1, the preparation activities are not necessarily sequential, but all of them precede the design and implementation stages of the project. It is recommended that no more than a few months be spent on the preparatory work, so that the knowledge management project can get off the ground quickly and carry much-needed momentum with it.

Three of the most important preparatory activities are these: setting the direction for the effort; getting commitment for the process; and determining the organization's readiness for the various dimensions of knowledge management that need to be in place and working.

Setting the direction of the initiative involves articulating that direction at various levels of specificity. First, the business drivers that provide the impetus for a knowledge strategy need to be: (1) identified, (2) articulated in a **knowledge management**

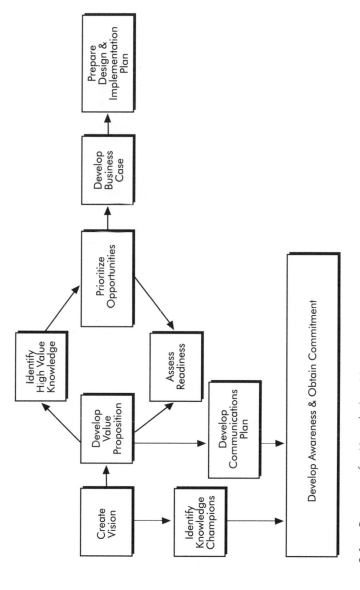

Figure 3-1— Preparing for Knowledge Management

61

vision statement that propels all aspects of a knowledge strategy, and (3) shared throughout the organization. As discussed in Chapter 1, these strategic drivers could be of various kinds: economic, innovation, quality, competition, or customer-relations related.

Next, a knowledge management value proposition needs to be articulated. Any business needs to know the benefits that can be derived from any initiative it considers undertaking. Knowledge management is particularly tricky to justify. It is not only difficult to measure the value of knowledge assets, it is even more of a problem to determine the return on investing in them. But it can be done and needs to be done, on the basis of the vision that will propel the organization forward in the knowledge economy. Then, a strategic high value definition of knowledge management can help to bring the articulations developed so far to a more practical, tactical level. This is when the organization brings out the magnifying glass of analysis and applies it to the company's own resources—processes, people, patents, expertise, know-how, experience, methodologies, innovations, reusable components, and revenue-generating or industry-leading capabilities. At this point, the planners find out what the organization knows, and how it can use that knowledge to get better and to get to where it wants to go.

Getting commitment is critical to the success of a knowledge management initiative. Too often, there is a temptation to leap immediately into designing the knowledge management environment before there is real commitment to and recognition of its value across the organization. There are many reported failures resulting from efforts undertaken without an explanation as to why and how the organization would benefit from knowledge management. Commitment has to be present at the executive as well as the operational level. If management is not serious about an initiative, few employees will be fooled for long. It has been proven many times—in countless business initiatives that demand change in attitudes or behaviors—that if workers, the end users, don't understand and accept the change, they will ignore or sabotage the new system/procedure.

Assessing readiness is part of laying the groundwork for a knowledge management initiative. Knowledge management needs **enabling conditions** in three key dimensions: technological infrastructure, business strategy/operations, and management/organizational environment. All of these must be able to support what knowledge management needs in order to flourish. At the very least, planners need to be able to identify the barriers to implementing a knowledge strategy in any of these dimensions. Also, it is important to recognize that conditions in *all three* dimensions must be amenable to supporting knowledge management processes because one kind of enabler without the others will be ineffective. Planners need to know what they are up against, as well as what can work for their purposes.

Setting Direction

CREATE THE VISION

Knowledge management is a journey through unfamiliar territory. As with any untravelled path, someone needs to be able to visualize where the path leads and to go forward in that direction with passion about what is possible. As Rosabeth Moss Kanter, professor of business administration at Harvard Business School, reminds us, "No lasting achievement is possible without a vision, and no dream can become real without action and responsibility."[1] There is likely to be a knowledge management innovator who will be ahead of all others in taking the leap of faith needed to move the vision forward, and to introduce knowledge management and its benefits to the organization. This person can be found in any part of the organization, and is usually someone who can foresee benefits to his or her area of function or influence.

This person takes on the responsibility of articulating a **knowledge management vision** that supports corporate goals and objectives. The advocate of knowledge management, as with any other innovative and leading-edge concept, is likely to be a visionary who has imagined what the future of the organization might be like with knowledge management—one in which knowledge will flourish.

Such visionaries continue to believe in their ideas even when no one else does and, according to organizational development specialist Richard E. Byrd, are usually admired and probably feared, viewed as radicals, and rarely at the head of the most-liked list.[2] Innovators can sense the promise of breakthrough ideas, and they are often the architects of corporate futures. These are people who dream of things not yet created, and who are capable of turning dreams into reality. Sowing the seeds, nurturing support, and generally developing and sustaining a high level of interest are some of their strengths.

Articulating a vision for knowledge management is the first step in selling the concept to people who are not yet committed to it. To make the case for managing knowledge to those on the front line, says Richard Baumbusch of U.S. West Communications (a baby Bell), "the pivotal insight was finding a language that engages operations managers."[3] These people need to understand how they can take a leap of faith and share the same convictions as the primary knowledge management advocate.

The vision, whatever its scope, provides clear direction and a declaration of what and how knowledge management will contribute to achieving the stated objective. Often, it will reflect the organization's areas of difficulty and point out how knowledge management can contribute to ease them. *Computerworld* columnist Rick Saia has identified some of the ways knowledge management could help reduce an organization's struggles. These include things such as faster, more informed response to customers; improved efficiency of knowledge workers; increased innovation in designing new products and services; better decision making; enhanced flexibility; and the ability to change and adapt to change more rapidly.[4]

The knowledge management vision is a positioning statement and, at the same time, it is a marketing tool. It must be bold and passionate and create a sense of excitement, energy, and, most important, confidence that it can be achieved. The vision should be unambiguous, coherent, and clear, but not so much that it becomes prescriptive and is seen as an order or instruction. It should be innovative, expressing what is possible and, at the same time, be realistic and achievable. From the vision will come the short- and long-term knowledge management goals and objectives and the action items that will turn the vision into reality.

The scope of the vision will depend upon how broadly the application of knowledge management is viewed. In some instances, it is reasonable to develop a vision that is situational in nature, i.e., that pertains to a specific activity or area of business, as shown in Figure 3-2. The following examples describe situational objectives, all of them narrowly focused and tactical:

- The knowledge base will contain all information needed to approve a new loan, including business rules, corporate policies, and competitive programs. The knowledge base will be updated as "new" knowledge is created.

- Whenever a manufacturing problem occurs, the technicians will be able to search a knowledge base to find out whether it has

---

Knowledge is power.
Aggressive attention to its capture,
distribution, and maintenance will allow us
to resolve our manufacturing problems
more quickly than any of our competitors.
We will take advantage of our worldwide associates,
using their experiences to help solve our problems.
Never again will we "reinvent the wheel."

Figure 3-2—Situational Vision Statement

happened before and how it was solved, at any location across the world.

- New and temporary workers are fully productive after only a few hours of orientation. Policies, procedures, and frequently asked questions are all available instantly in the context of the particular activity being performed.

In other instances, the knowledge management objectives are broad and strategic. For example, it may be that the stated objective for knowledge management is to "support the organization in its effort to grow." This objective would clearly have much broader implications for the knowledge management process than would the situational objectives described above. What matters is to identify what the organization wants to achieve through the knowledge management initiative and how its success will be determined. The sample strategic vision statement in Figure 3-3 reflects ABC Company's stated strategic objective of becoming number one in its marketplace and suggests how knowledge management will contribute to its achievement.

A knowledge management vision embraces the principles, direction, and goals for knowledge management and supports

---

Knowledge is power.

Aggressive attention to its creation,
distribution, and maintenance will allow
ABC Company to see things that others don't see,
understand things that others don't understand,
and be creative where others are repetitive.
It is this ability to innovate that
will ensure ABC Company's
sustainable elevation to market leader.

Figure 3-3—Strategic Vision Statement

the vision of the organization. Some advice in writing a strategic vision:

Ground it in reality and make it specific enough so that anyone who reads or hears it will understand it.

DEVELOP A KNOWLEDGE MANAGEMENT VALUE PROPOSITION

As the knowledge management vision is needed to set the scene, a **knowledge management value proposition** is needed to articulate the real value of knowledge management to everyone in the organization. The value proposition identifies the key benefits of knowledge management to the organization, and states which critical business issues it will solve. A simple return-on-investment formula is not necessarily appropriate in the case of knowledge management; in many cases, the pay-offs are things like better information, better knowledge connections, better insights, and better and wider perspective. Carla O'Dell, of the American Productivity & Quality Center, suggests that organizations ask:

- What knowledge do we have that is valuable?

- If we were to use it in a different way, how would it add value to the organization?

- Can I articulate the value proposition?

She suggests six main ways that knowledge can add value to business enterprise:

- Knowledge management as a business strategy—in products and processes

- Innovation and knowledge creation—new products, rapid commercialization, and renewal

- Transfer of knowledge and best practices—improved customer service and reduced order cycle or repair times

- Customer-focused knowledge—building customer relationships, loyalty, and joint efforts

- Intellectual asset management—realizing value from assets such as patents

- Personal responsibility for knowledge—encouraging individual learning and development[5]

Accordingly, preparing a meaningful value proposition depends on understanding a number of key issues: (1) the organization's current state and what is driving the knowledge management initiative, (2) the organization's capabilities, constraints, strengths, and weaknesses, and (3) comparable situations in other organizations and the value gained from knowledge management.

Because different layers of the organization are motivated in different ways, there is a potential need for at least two and sometimes three slightly different value propositions. One each is needed for:

- Senior management team members most interested in strategic results

- Middle management team members most interested in satisfying operational demands

- Nonmanagement employees most interested in making a contribution that is valuable to the organization and satisfying to themselves

As Figure 3-4 (on page 217 of the appendix) demonstrates, the differences in these statements may be subtle, but they are nevertheless important for making the target audience receptive to the message and more likely to understand and support it.

High Value Knowledge Definition. The **high value knowledge definition** is a subset of the value proposition. It confirms at a more tangible and quantifiable level what the organization expects to accomplish through its implementation of a knowledge management process.

The high value knowledge definition must reflect a senior management perspective rather than focus on user needs, but it must nevertheless demonstrate how sharing knowledge will pay off for everyone in the organization. Above all, it must be in line with the issues that are considered most important for the business. Accordingly, it identifies what knowledge the organization needs in order to succeed; what knowledge is of most value to the organization; and what specific contribution the capturing, managing, and exploiting of that knowledge will make to the business health of the company.

As the first indication of the value of knowledge for the organization, this information will be important to the next preparation step: the development of a sound business case. As well, this specific articulation paves the way for: (1) discovering the organization's knowledge needs and holdings, (2) identifying benefits from filling knowledge gaps, and (3) providing the basis for planning and prioritizing the implementation of knowledge management.

The task for advocates, then, is to prepare a high value definition statement based on answers to these questions: How can we add value? What do we already have that is valuable? In what groups and areas will further knowledge increase value? These questions, in more detail, are:

- What are the key business drivers for knowledge management for this organization?

- What knowledge is needed to meet strategic goals and in which domains does this knowledge reside?

- What is the value of knowledge for this organization? What could it contribute to innovation, competitive strength, job enrichment and expansion, retention, and leveraging of expertise?

- What are the organization's core capabilities (not competencies); that is, what does the organization do that is not easily imitated, and what are the core elements of these core capabilities (for example, physical systems, skills, managerial systems, values, etc.)?[6]

- What are the key groups (for example, business units or functions) that have the potential to increase revenue?

- What are the proven practices in the organization that can be turned into measurable results and thus become reusable best practices?

69

- What are the key topics or knowledge domains that contribute value to the organization? Some key knowledge domains are suggested in Figure 3-5, based on a model presented at Lotusphere98 by Christopher Andrus, senior manager, Arthur Andersen's Business Consulting Practice.[7]

When drafters of the high value definition statement identify the key knowledge domains (the categories representing major stakeholders, business drivers, and other major influences), they can determine the topics and "knowledge objects" that belong in each domain. Only then can the interrelationships amongst them be identified and the scope of knowledge requirements fully understood.

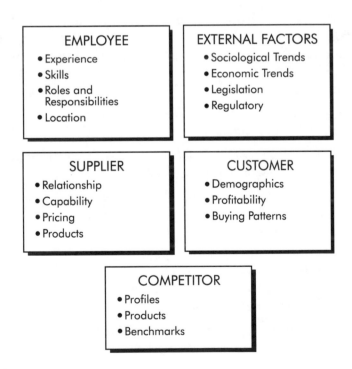

Figure 3-5—Knowledge Domains

Another perspective for the planners to keep in mind is the company's competition and its own competitive strategy, with respect to the following questions:

- How does the organization compete—what is its competitive advantage? What are the strategic initiatives that will keep it competitive five years from now? What are the organization's areas of competitive weakness, and what core capabilities are lacking?

- What are competitors doing about knowledge management?

Getting Commitment

Knowledge management can never be separated from the organization's main work; it needs to be built into the core processes of the organization, rather than as a layer on top of other activities. Because it needs to be pervasive in order to be effective, knowledge management needs to be understood and accepted by everyone in the organization. It also needs a high degree of participation and support, which will not be forthcoming without widespread appreciation for knowledge management and why it is important. Employees are unlikely to actively support something they neither comprehend nor value.

The initiative may begin at any level of the organization, but until leadership is committed, the chances for long-term success are limited.[8] The organization's senior management team, therefore, has to embrace the idea of a corporate knowledge strategy and support it actively. Otherwise, it will likely fade.

When senior management is "on board," it is time to "spread the word," to get people's attention, and to engage all employees in the energy of the initiative. If the knowledge management vision is to become reality, it needs the enthusiasm and commitment of a large proportion of the people in the organization— it needs critical mass. It needs commitment from all levels of the organization, from decision makers near the top, and from people who need the tools and leverage of knowledge management to make them successful. Commitment from decision makers can help propel the initiative forward by setting an example for others in the organization. Commitment from people in various functions and specialties can create grassroots support for a knowledge management initiative if they see realistic benefits for their own work.

To help get the initiative moving during this "getting commitment" phase, it is a good idea to identify and recruit energetic supporters of knowledge management from all parts of the organization to form a cross-functional, multidisciplinary task force. These individuals will need to work and communicate with both senior managers and front-line employees. They must have organizational savvy and be able to move throughout the organization without regard to level or function. Ideally, this same task force will continue to be involved in the knowledge management initiative until it is fully implemented.

Knowledge management champions must quickly grasp and internalize the value of knowledge development and sharing, and be active promoters of its adoption. The champions will typically be natural leaders—those to whom others look for cues about how to react to new situations and change. They will probably be adventurous and willing to try new concepts without a guarantee of 100 percent success. The champions must be adaptable, flexible, and resilient in order to handle shifting expectations. If they have a bias towards continuous improvement, that is a bonus.

Because knowledge management is a relatively abstract concept, it is difficult to articulate its value and the contribution that it makes. Employees are more likely to commit support to the initiative if they are given an opportunity to discuss and debate the concept. This requires open communications that present knowledge management in a practical and easy-to-understand way. The messages for this purpose must be reinforced consistently and continuously.

COMMUNICATE RELENTLESSLY

A message or announcement to everyone in the organization is often the first tangible indication that some kind of change is imminent. Some will welcome it; some will resist. Because knowledge management is a wide-ranging concept that serves corporate strategic objectives, and thus affects many functions or business units, random communications are unacceptable. It is important to treat communications as a project unto itself, with its own project plan.

Any time a major change is the topic, the communications objective is to provide information, encourage dialogue, and manage expectations. Each individual will want to understand how he or she will be affected, and how knowledge management principles will be incorporated into day-to-day activities. If any information is available about new reward and recognition programs designed to support the success of the knowledge management initiative, it should be clearly and widely communicated.

The **communications plan** sets out the methods and mechanisms to be used for making knowledge management principles and objectives well understood by the organization. It describes how and when the importance of knowledge management will be communicated; identifies and communicates potential cultural issues and how they will be mitigated; and states what the processes for creating and sharing knowledge might be. Figure 3-6 (on pages 218–219 of the appendix) provides guidelines for the development of a communications plan.

Assessing Readiness

Adopting a knowledge strategy means sanctioning significant changes. Success in any new endeavor comes when its participants are ready, willing, and able to change. It is of little use to attempt to introduce a sharing, nurturing knowledge environment into an organization with a feudal information culture without first trying to lessen some of the technological, business, and organizational pitfalls.

Organizations that are considering a knowledge management initiative would be wise to assess their readiness for it in three important areas: technology environment, business environment and organizational environment. Sample **readiness assessments** are provided for guidance (see Figures 3-7, 3-8, and 3-9 in the appendix), but each can be customized for any particular organization. The assessments are designed to provide insights into potential problem areas so the project team can mitigate any identified risks.

The scores are unlikely to be the same across all areas of an organization. For example, some departments or locations could be quite advanced technologically and others not; some could already be working in a highly collaborative, team-oriented style; and others working in a hierarchical structure that rewards individual accomplishment. The important thing is to take stock of the situation and be prepared to deal with the findings.

TECHNOLOGY ENVIRONMENT

How much technological wizardry does an organization need to have in order to embark on knowledge management and have some hope of sailing to business advantage in favorable winds? Since knowledge management is inherently collaborative, and collaboration is no longer constrained by time and geography, organizations that are widely networked will find the technical implementation of knowledge management less onerous than will those organizations with less networked infrastructure. Also, organizations with installed and working elements of a technology infrastructure that could serve knowledge management may have a shorter learning curve and certainly a less complex and expensive technology requirement than others. The role of technologies is discussed in Chapter 5.

The higher the score in this section (see Figure 3-7 on pages 220–221 of the appendix), the greater the technological readiness of an organization for a successful knowledge management initiative. However, if the installed technologies are used only to inform and not to support collaboration, the organization may still face some serious cultural impediments. A score of 50 is likely to be the norm, indicating enough existing technologies that knowledge management could be implemented without enormous capital expense. A low score indicates a need for a major investment in technology before knowledge management should be considered.

BUSINESS ENVIRONMENT

This section of the Readiness Assessment (Figure 3-8 on pages 222–223 of the appendix) seeks to determine whether or not the organization is suffering from known problems that could, in many cases, be resolved through the introduction of knowledge management. If the organization shows a willingness to capitalize on lessons learned for continuous improvement, then it is amenable to thinking about knowledge management as a way to achieve this. However, if the lesson learned was a painful one, like a product failure or loss of a customer, the organization may shirk from exploring that failure too closely or learning from it.[9]

A high score here ("strongly agree") indicates that the organization does *not* routinely learn from its past mistakes. Consequently, employees are spending time "reinventing the wheel" and customers are subjected to the same problems on a recurring basis. Even a median score suggests that a knowledge strategy is warranted. If good ideas are not shared, there will be little innovation; without innovation, the only potential competitive edge is price. Also, mistakes and duplication are costly, which minimizes the chance to compete on price. To be successful in today's highly competitive marketplace, it is recommended that companies be able to respond with "strongly disagree" to every point in this section.

ORGANIZATIONAL ENVIRONMENT

This last section of the Readiness Assessment (Figure 3-9 on pages 224–225 of the appendix) focuses on the internal cultural

75

environment of the organization that could affect the success of a knowledge management initiative. The more "agree" responses an organization gives here, the fewer problems it will face in establishing a workplace cultural environment that is conducive to a flourishing and fruitful knowledge management undertaking. *Success or failure in this endeavor will depend on the cultural environment more than on any other factor.*

What an organization learns from its responses to the Organizational Readiness Assessment will provide the basis for further investigations that can uncover important obstacles to implementing a knowledge management initiative. Here are some potential negative scenarios:

- **Are existing processes under stress?** Is the organization in growth mode? Are new employees being hired more rapidly than they can be trained? Is existing staff expected to transfer knowledge "on the fly"? Is the work becoming increasingly complex? Are people being asked to undertake multiple roles and broadly defined jobs?

- **Is the current employment environment negative?** Has the organization recently undergone a downsizing process? Are the remaining employees empowered to make decisions? Are the employees required to make decisions in areas where they are not knowledgeable, resulting in errors, costly rework, and mounting frustration?

- **What is the existing climate of information sharing?** Do underlying cultural norms support or discourage information exchange between individuals or departments? Does the company consistently miss opportunities to take advantage of the information it owns?

- **What is the existing climate of knowledge sharing?** Most people are hired and promoted on the basis of their real or perceived level of knowledge and job competence. Do people resist sharing their knowledge for fear they will create more competition for the limited number of roles in the organization? Are there structural, geographic, technological, or cultural barriers to knowledge sharing? Does the reward structure actively promote knowledge sharing?

Each of these situations could introduce another element of complexity into the already-complex milieu of managing change. The knowledge management team needs to fully understand these, and ensure that they are reflected in any plan to initiate a knowledge management project.

Conclusion

Any major undertaking that involves and affects a variety of players, special interests, motivations and constraints needs to be grounded in sound planning, or it will founder on the many obstacles that can arise from its complexity. In undertaking a knowledge management initiative, much of the initial planning pertains to preparing the ground: making a case for the project; getting people's support for it, notably management support; communicating its value for the organization; and generally estimating its proportions.

Developing and communicating the vision and fostering a good understanding of how and why knowledge management is important to the success of the organization are ways to establish the foundation on which the knowledge management environment will be built. A sound business case for knowledge management is necessary to launch the initiative and to communicate the value proposition associated with knowledge management to everyone in the organization. Although it has longer term dimensions, the development and implementation of a knowledge strategy is initially undertaken as a project. As such, it will benefit a great deal from adhering to good project management principles and practices. Before its launch, the knowledge management project needs a sponsor in management, a champion in the ranks, and critical mass throughout the organization.

Notes

1.   Rosabeth Moss Kanter, *When Giants Learn to Dance* (New York: Touchstone, 1989).

2.   Richard E. Byrd, *The Creatrix Inventory* (San Diego: Pfeiffer & Company, 1986).

3.   Thomas A. Stewart, "Getting Real About Brainpower," *Fortune*, 27 November 1995, 201.

4.   Rick Saia, "Thirsting for Knowledge," *Computerworld*, 10 May 1997, 70.

5.   David Skyrme, *Measuring the Value of Knowledge* (London: Business Intelligence Limited, 1998), 114.

6.   Dorothy Leonard-Barton, *Wellsprings of Knowledge: Building and Sustaining the Sources of Innovation* (Boston: Harvard Business School Press, 1995), 3-28.

7.   Christopher Andrus, "Knowledge Management: Components and Methodology," Lotusphere98, Walt Disney World, Florida, February, 1998.

8.   Richard Hunter, "Knowledge Capital: Essential Active Management," in *The IT Revolution Continues: Managing Diversity in the 21st Century, Proceedings of Gartner Group Symposium/ITxpo96*, Lake Buena Vista, Florida, 7–11 October 1996 (Stamford, CT: Gartner Group, 1996).

9.   Art Kleiner and George Roth, "How to Make Experience Your Company's Best Teacher," *Harvard Business Review*, September-October 1997, 172-177.

4

Initiating the Knowledge Management Project

A philosopher of imposing stature doesn't think in a vacuum.
Even his most abstract ideas are, to some extent, conditioned
by what is or is not known in the time when he lives.
—ALFRED NORTH WHITEHEAD

Issues

- What are the critical success factors and best practices for designing a successful knowledge management environment?

- What systems best create, capture, and disseminate valuable knowledge across the enterprise?

- How do we ensure that technology does not have a negative impact on the process?

Successful initiation of the knowledge management project involves further definition of its benefits and articulation of the project completion process, followed by analysis of existing knowledge and then determination of how the knowledge management life-cycle processes might be implemented. This presupposes satisfying three key conditions:

- Committing project resources and preparing a plan for making it happen

- Discovering what information and knowledge you have and would like to have

- Tracking and mapping the processes you use to create, move, use, and store knowledge

An initiative as complex as a knowledge management undertaking needs to be solidly justified and supported by a sound **business case.** The business case builds on the value proposition and high value definition that have already been developed, and it grounds these principles in practical business realities. The exercise is necessary for management approval, but it is also useful for encouraging planners to think through their reasons for wanting to introduce knowledge management practices into the organization.

Like any project, this initiative needs a plan that sets out its scope, objectives, and the roles of its participants. Without people assigned to it, the project will founder. It is important to have a plan that lays out what needs to be done, how it will be done, and who will do it. Everyone knows how easily projects can be driven off track, torn apart by dissent, or slowed by distractions or inertia. A plan helps stay the course.

The next part of the project is to find out where the organization's information and knowledge resources reside, and how they are created, transferred, used, and stored. The investigative work in this exercise involves consulting a wide range of employees by a variety of means. Out of this comes the development of a knowledge map or K-map. This is what will form the basis of the organization's knowledge base and provide the guidance for accessing the firm's knowledge resources.

Finally, the planning team needs to identify and record the processes by which the organization's information and knowledge are circulated. The phases of the knowledge management life cycle—acquire, organize, retrieve, distribute, and maintain—are used as a guideline.

Develop the Business Case

Knowledge management can be an expensive endeavor, not only to set up, but also to maintain, especially for enterprises in which knowledge is the key commodity. For example, 6 percent of Ernst & Young's consulting revenue is spent on internal knowledge management programs, and 10 percent of the consulting revenue of McKinsey & Co. is spent on managing intellectual capital.[1] Robert Buckman of Buckman Laboratories estimates that his firm spends 7 percent of its revenues on knowledge management.[2] The high cost of knowledge management can be attributed to the investment in human resources: the people who create, use, and maintain information.

Any undertaking of this magnitude needs to be carefully and solidly justified. By itself, of course, knowledge is difficult to value. The objective of a knowledge strategy and its implementation is to produce a more tangible asset—one that can be reflected on the "bottom line." The business case provides the justification for moving forward. It documents the estimated costs and the potential benefits of identified knowledge management opportunities. The valuation of assets comprising knowledge capture and reuse, plus innovation, should form the basis of the business case. Because the environments of business and knowledge management change continually, the business case should address the year immediately following implementation of a working knowledge management environment.

The focus of the business case will depend on the organizational culture. Gartner Group identifies three kinds of organization according to the organization's responses to change and technology:[3]

- **Type A enterprises.** Type A enterprises are aggressive, high-risk pioneers whose senior management plays the role of an agent of change. Type A has sophisticated IT and plenty of funding.

- **Type B enterprises.** Type B enterprises are balanced, low-risk, moderate organizations whose senior management is focused on increasing productivity. They have moderate to high IT sophistication and a variable supply of funding.

- **Type C enterprises.** Type C enterprises are cautious, risk-averse followers whose senior management is fixed on cost efficiency. They are low to moderate in IT sophistication and have constrained funding.

Accordingly, as Gartner subsequently pointed out, each type of enterprise would likely put forward a different kind of business case for knowledge management:[4]

- Type A enterprises accept value based on less tangible benefits.

- Type B must look for cost savings.

- Type C enterprises will wait until knowledge management can be implemented on the existing enterprise computing infrastructure.

Real-Life File: Chrysler Capitalizes on Engineering Know-how

Chrysler identified its problem as an inability to transfer knowledge within the enterprise, among distinct divisions that nevertheless had common engineering challenges. Chrysler's objectives were to share engineering knowledge across divisions, avoid duplicating work, and ensure reuse. Knowledge was understood to include leading practices and lessons learned. The company hoped to increase engineers' efficiency and maintain a competitive advantage by building on the best knowledge regardless of which organization it came from.

The solution was an *Engineering Book of Knowledge*, provided online, using Lotus Notes. For a year, cross-functional and cross-divisional teams undertook intensive discussions. Then, a five-phase "knowledge process map" was developed. The phases were: determine book content; define suppliers and their inputs; establish knowledge ownership and review responsibilities; define outputs and customers; apply knowledge.

According to the Gartner Group, bottom line benefits are these: "KM has high perceived payoff at Chrysler because of its focus on an appropriate core business process and people, engineering design and engineers. It is enabling critical components to be designed once and used many times through a transfer of the design knowledge, not of the physical parts."[5]

Costs

Costs include all anticipated monetary outlays, risks (both technical and nontechnical), organizational and cultural implications, and potential impacts on other key initiatives that are planned or are already under way. Many potential costs are dependent on the existing organization and infrastructure, as well as on the scope and complexity of the knowledge management initiative, so cost estimates are not provided here. There is a relatively standard set of one-time and ongoing costs, though, that will occur in every organization contemplating a knowledge management initiative. Figure 4-1 (on pages 226–227 of the appendix) describes how and when these costs might arise.

BENEFITS

The most successful knowledge management initiatives are those that demonstrate measurable results. Benefits must therefore be clearly linked to corporate goals and objectives. Much of this linking was accomplished with the preparation of the vision, value proposition, and high value definition. The question to be answered now is how the benefits will affect the bottom line. However, because its primary focus is on stimulating growth and increasing revenue, rather than on streamlining operations, the benefits of introducing knowledge management to an organization will fall mostly into the "strategic" category and may thus be difficult to quantify.

Benefits are either tangible or intangible and should be identified as such, although all benefits are quantifiable. Their value should be estimated, and the time frame over which they are expected to accrue should be identified. Whoever will be responsible for actually delivering the benefit must validate the benefit. When identifying benefits:

- Be **specific**.
- Be **clear**—benefits should be understandable to everyone.
- Be **conservative**—limit statements to valid benefits.
- Be **sure** there's a relationship between the knowledge management process and the benefit.

Each organization will have a unique set of strategic business drivers and therefore can expect to achieve different benefits from knowledge management. Some generic benefits, all of them potential spurs to competitiveness and growth, can be found in any organization. For example:

- **Improved communications (internal and external).** Introduction of up-to-date networked technology and collaborative processes provides immediate access to information for everyone regardless of time or location. The information being shared is common, current, and relevant.

- **Employee skill-set development.** Organizations can improve communication and knowledge sharing through organization-wide, online, just-in-time discussion, electronically shared best practices, and widespread electronic access to training programs. The benefits are significantly reduced training costs; opportunity for employees to learn what they need, when they need it; and improved productivity and effectiveness from access to expertise and lessons learned. Accordingly, the organization's skill base is updated and enlarged to target the best-qualified people within the organization for any new project.

- **Increased responsiveness to customers.** Although customer service is among the top three focus areas for most companies, customer service excellence remains a distant goal for many service providers and customers alike. Good customer service means having instant access to the knowledge and information needed to respond to inquiries, such as product information and usage tips, information about a sales transaction, or policies and procedures or government regulations. Most customers consider a service interaction completed in one call or visit to be a success. Reducing callbacks and follow-ups saves company time and improves the customer's perception of the service.

- **Improved efficiency.** White-collar workers spend up to 40 percent of their workday looking for information, consolidating it, and trying to find answers to various questions. Although some of this is necessary thinking time, much is nonproductive because workers have no single place to go to look for information and advice. Paper is an inefficient method for storing and retrieving information compared to electronically indexed material. A well-designed knowledge management system provides universal access and sophisticated electronic search and navigation tools for locating information quickly. Eliminating both the expensive duplication of thousands of quickly outdated manuals and other paper documents and the loss of time needed for distribution are definite benefits of knowledge management.

- **Improved quality.** Knowledge management can support improved quality by ensuring that all of the rules, methods, and procedures required to produce the business outputs are readily accessible. A knowledge management repository can also store lessons learned and the resolutions of previous quality issues, so that the same mistakes are not repeated. High-quality products and services minimize the time and effort required to support them.

- **Faster problem solving.** In large organizations, it is very easy to be solving the same problems over and over again because workers do not know that someone else has faced the same situation. This is particularly troublesome when there are time gaps or geographically dispersed locations, so that delays in resolving issues result in downtime and divert effort from core activities. Faster, better problem solving results from easy access to relevant information, lessons learned, and subject experts.

- **Better decision making.** The best decisions are made on the basis of near perfect information that is applied intelligently. Of course, it is possible only to minimize the risk of a bad decision and maximize the likelihood that the right choice is made. A knowledge base or repository can contain the knowledge to support good decision making. Knowledge management tools can also assist in analyzing and consolidating information to streamline the decision-making process.

- **Better ability to change and adapt to change.** A knowledge management program encourages people to share knowledge and information and to collaborate on problem solving and work ideas. This in itself promotes an environment that can adapt better to change. The contents of the knowledge base can be used to support advancement and to forge new directions as required. The corporate history of an organization can help to position it in the face of new challenges and provide the knowledge needed to avoid repeating mistakes.

- **Reduced duplication.** A substantial number of business documents are re-created simply because no one knew they already existed. Searching a knowledge base can produce a list of existing relevant information on a certain topic, so that the starting point for adding more information is clear. As a central access point, it stores information only once and ensures that the most current sources are provided for information seekers.

- **Innovation in product/service design.** Innovation requires the creative application of knowledge. Often, new products and services are developed from threads of ideas that have been around the organization for some time. Knowledge management provides a framework for collaboration and encourages sharing of experiences. Collaboration maximizes productive time by minimizing the effort of searching for and consolidating existing resources. New concepts based on a combination of old and new experiences provide a continuous source of product or service-related ideas.

PRIORITIZING OPPORTUNITIES

Some of the benefits of knowledge management will need a while to percolate through the organization's day-to-day business activities and to show real value. It is important to recognize this and to understand that some benefits will be strategic, some tactical, some long term, and some short term. Understanding how benefits will be realized can then be taken into consideration when prioritizing opportunities.

Development of the vision, value proposition, and strategic high value definition reveal a range of advantages to be gained from knowledge management. Some of these, for example, could include patent and intellectual capital development; sales and reseller communication; customer service improvement; investor communication; product life-cycle management; and

Real-Life File: Dow Converts Knowledge Properties to Cash

"Dow Chemical took the plunge into knowledge management . . . when the company decided to get more out of its patents by taking stock of its intellectual assets. Today Dow uses SmartPatent Workbench, a decision-support tool . . . to analyze a database of its 30,000 patents, as well as those of competitors. By identifying valuable patents, Dow expects to boost licensing royalties from $20 million . . . to $125 million by 2000; it also plans to cut $40 million in tax maintenance over 10 years by identifying unused patents that it can let expire.

"These projected revenues and savings have convinced top managers at Dow to make knowledge management a companywide initiative. . . . [Gordon Petrash, Dow's director of intellectual asset management] is evaluating ways to capture business processes and workers' expertise and share them internationally. Petrash says the ability to share knowledge with companies in developing nations could lead Dow to some lucrative partnerships. For example, he says the company could offer pure know-how to another company that could provide manufacturing facilities and supplies in return. That, in turn, has convinced top executives at Dow of the need for knowledge management."[6]

employee and organizational development. What needs to be done at this stage, in the course of developing a business case, is to put these benefits in order of priority and significance. Like any careful shopper, the organization needs to evaluate where it can get the most value for its money.

A simple way to do this is to measure benefits against the Prioritization Assessment Model shown in Figure 4-2. It provides a simple way to determine priorities based on the potential benefit to the organization versus anticipated risks,

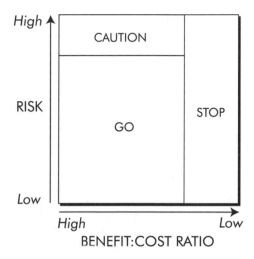

Figure 4-2—Prioritization Assessment Model

including costs. When risks and benefits have been carefully analyzed, the model can reveal the following categories of knowledge management opportunities:

- High or medium benefit opportunities with low or medium risk are a definite "go."

- Caution is recommended for high or medium benefit opportunities with high risk.

- Low benefit opportunities, regardless of whether the risk is low, medium, or high are inadvisable, as the effort will far exceed the results.

When assessing benefit versus risk, it is useful to recognize that, in the early stages, the knowledge base will be populated with information (since it is unlikely that context has been captured), and that the information will be predominantly explicit (knowledge that is documented and public). Applications that will benefit from this type of content are logical choices for demonstrating early results. For example, primary contenders for short-term knowledge management results are activities that are information intensive. These are activities in which a person relies on a variety of sources of explicit information in order to complete tasks or activities that involve a long learning curve before the person is fully competent.

In businesses that have large seasonal fluctuations, such as retail or financial services, it is often necessary to hire temporary staff to meet the demand. Knowledge management can help meet the challenge of getting these workers up to speed quickly on required processes, policies, and procedures. This is also true for new employees entering any highly regulated or process-intensive business.

A word of caution is warranted here. When considering the balance between risk and benefits, there is a tendency to try to minimize the cost. In the case of knowledge management, however, this could be very shortsighted. According to Richard Hunter, in an address to Gartner Group's ITxpo96, investing in the human and automated mechanisms associated with knowledge management is subject to a "threshold" effect. When the overall level of investment is below the threshold, there is little likelihood of developing noticeable knowledge assets. Additional investments without exceeding the threshold are unlikely to yield benefits that are commensurate with the investment. Only when the threshold is exceeded does the organization's culture suddenly and dramatically "flip," leading to benefits that are noticeable and worthwhile. A reversal may occur as a result of seemingly small investment reductions that result in a cumulative drop below the threshold.[7]

Identify Project Team

Designing and implementing a knowledge management initiative requires a broad range of skills and experience and a well-placed team of supporters and workers across the organization. The champion of the knowledge management strategy, identified earlier, should continue to participate in all phases of the project, as well as should other individuals who were involved in developing the knowledge strategy. Many skills will be needed to fully round out the team's competencies. In addition to senior management support, the knowledge management project will require the following:

- **A strong team leader** with good project management skills, excellent people skills, and a broad knowledge of the organization. Since the knowledge initiative will introduce change, this individual should be experienced in using change-management techniques to ease the transition process.

- **Business analysts** to help knowledge workers identify what knowledge they need to solve their business problems, what knowledge they have, what is missing, and how the knowledge will be used.

- **Subject matter experts** to assist in determining what does and does not add value. These individuals need to be familiar with the objectives of the project and the overall knowledge strategy—in particular with how the objectives and strategy relate to business processes.

- **Information systems specialists** who understand existing systems and how they might be customized to accommodate identified knowledge management requirements.

- **Librarians and records managers** who are familiar with organizing and categorizing information and who understand the retrieval patterns associated with supporting the business processes. These individuals can assist with designing filters to minimize the risk of information overload.

Disruptions to the composition of the project team can seriously affect the team's cohesion and the project's schedule, and generally have a negative impact on the outcome of the project. To the extent possible, the team members should remain together for the duration of the project, since they will be learning together and benefiting from this process.

Develop Project Plan

A vision that is grounded in a carefully considered value proposition and strategic high value definition provides the momentum needed to get the knowledge management initiative going. A business case provides a professional rationale for proceeding with the initiative. Next, a more detailed definition of the scope and objectives of the initiative is needed. The successful implementation of knowledge management, like the introduction of any change, requires careful planning. After all, the knowledge management initiative is a project like any other until such time as the process is woven into the fabric of the organization.

The purpose of planning is to determine a specific course of action to achieve stated objectives. Plans set direction and help the project team to achieve its objectives, but the plans should be sufficiently flexible to allow for modification if required. Throughout the project's life, the plan is monitored and may require adjustments based on changes to project scope, staffing availability, or shifts in the environment. Plans should respond to changes in the environment in which they are being used.

PREPARE PROJECT PLANNING DOCUMENT

Planning tasks usually begin immediately after a project has been approved. They begin with defining the project's scope and setting objectives, and ultimately result in terms of reference for the project. It is important to document the dimensions of the project so that everyone—project team, stakeholders, and sponsors—knows what to expect. The **project planning document** makes these dimensions explicit in a summary of all activities required for the design and implementation phase. Here are some general guidelines for preparing this document:

1. **Define the objectives of the project.** The knowledge management project (as opposed to the knowledge management strat-

egy and environment, which are the result of the project), like any other project, has a finite and well-defined life span. It is not an activity that is expected to be an ongoing part of an organization's existence. At the outset, therefore, it is very important to determine what will indicate that the project is complete. The project objectives are the specific and measurable results that will be achieved. For example:

a. Implementation of an environment that will electronically capture and catalog all of the information created by and required by the marketing department so that the information can be easily accessed and preserved.

b. Implementation of a system to capture the lessons learned and knowledge created by the product team so that they can be easily shared both within the team and with other plant locations.

c. Implementation of processes to ensure that all product problems and their resolutions are captured and stored as they occur.

2. **Define the scope of the project.** Ensure that there is a common understanding of the initiative. The scope defines the boundary of what is and is not included. For example, the initiative might focus only on revenue-generating business activities, rather than support or administrative tasks, or it might be restricted to specific geographic areas.

3. **Define the context of the project.** This may include the state of the technological infrastructure, the extent of process bottlenecks, attitudinal obstacles, or the level of management support for the project. Urgency may also be part of the context, as knowledge management may be considered critical to the firm's survival. Some aspects of the context can be identified as constraints, others as supports. What is important is that the project team is aware of them.

4. **Define the roles and responsibilities of project participants—who will be responsible for what.** There should be a description of the responsibilities of key roles, so that people in those roles understand their jobs, and project team members know whom

to consult for directions, decisions, and support. A chart to depict project structure can help clarify how things will get done.

5. **Identify critical success factors.** Doing so will establish how the success of the project will be demonstrated. The critical success factors are the conditions that are necessary to achieve the predicted benefits and the measures against which the success of the project will be evaluated. These may include staff buy-in and commitment; a stable and appropriate knowledge database; updates of knowledge and information added every day; or active usage by 80 percent of the target audience. The critical success factors will be used during a postimplementation review as one measure of success, along with the measurement of tangible benefits achieved to date.

6. **Identify project deliverables.** It is useful to identify "products" for each stage of the project to provide milestones of progress and demonstrations of success in order to build greater support for the project at both the management and grassroots levels. A **project deliverable** is any predetermined entity to be delivered as a result of the project. Deliverables may be tangible, such as reports, inventories, and architectures, or less tangible, such as improved processes or trained staff.

7. **Articulate project strategies.** It is often important for the smooth functioning of the project to document significant strategies in order to reduce the possibility of confusion or unintentional conflict. Strategies can be developed about topics such as training, techniques, or testing, or they can pertain to behavior or protocols, such as the following:

   a. Build a relationship with staff based on respect so that their understanding of the project gives them the comfort to be interviewed.

   b. Build and use a consistent query tool for questioning staff so that they all have the same understanding of what the project team is trying to achieve.

   c. Secure management approval for internal staff time for various project activities needing staff cooperation and collaboration.

8. **Prepare schedule and work plan.** A global project plan, comprising discrete tasks, with associated time and staff resources, is essential for an orderly progression of project work. Minor schedule adjustments may need to be made in response to changing or unforeseen circumstances, but the schedule will serve to move the initiative forward steadily because each stage and each task component will have been thought through for reasonableness and completeness. Some tasks that are relevant to each other can be undertaken in an overlapping time frame so that the findings of each can give insight to those of the other.

   There are many ways to develop and represent schedules and work plans. The use of a simple computer-based tool that produces Gantt charts and other graphic representations of the project and its progress are recommended. Estimating the work effort and identifying the types of resources needed for the project are included in this step.

9. **Prepare communications plan.** It is important to continue the emphasis on communications, particularly since the outcome of the knowledge management project will, in the longer term, affect almost everyone in the organization. Some considerations:

   a. Conduct a project team orientation. The project planning document can serve as a basis for this orientation. It is important that all project team members have the same understanding of the project's purpose and activities as well as the same level of commitment to its successful execution.

   b. Consider a similar but more general orientation for all staff. This will help to promote widespread understanding of the intent and potential benefits of the project, and secure cooperation and support.

   c. Develop a project toolkit. Consider developing a technology-supported environment with groupware features (a database on the company network or intranet) that would allow project team members to record their findings, collaborate on developing issues or conducting research, and co-create reports and other products. The sharing would be a microexample of knowledge management principles and would keep project activities consistent and current.

10. **Communicate relentlessly.** Experience has shown that even brilliant business transformation projects have foundered on the shoals of poor communication. Everyone needs to know what's happening, why, when, and who's doing what. As a small knowledge management initiative, project planning activities would do well to be exemplary information-sharing and knowledge-sharing processes.

Identify Existing Knowledge Assets

In order to properly determine how the high value knowledge identified earlier in the knowledge management initiative can be provided in the most accessible form without duplicating existing valuable assets, it is important to understand what currently exists, where it is, and in what form it is stored. The most practical way to do this is by developing a knowledge map (often called K-map). A **knowledge map**, or **K-map**, is a visual representation of the overall knowledge management environment, and it points to knowledge sources and locations.

DEVELOPING THE KNOWLEDGE MAP

Few organizations are aware of the knowledge they have in their own files or computer systems and in the minds of their employees. This knowledge is neither inventoried nor cataloged and therefore is not generally available to the organization. Even if some people know the knowledge is somewhere, they do not know who has it, where these knowledgeable people are, or how to reach them. Effective knowledge management must provide a simple means for people to find the knowledge they need.

The knowledge map displays the whereabouts and structure of knowledge holdings that allow users to navigate the organization's resources and expertise. "Simple K-maps are like a presentation graphic with hyperlinks from boxes on the screen to the Web resources . . . [allowing users] to navigate to an enterprise's digital information resources and people (e.g., experts)."[8] It is a multidimensional matrix in graphical form.

K-maps can be many levels deep and can combine hierarchical and thesaurus-like structures. The complexity increases as the connections, categories, and associated layers of detail increase. Moreover, the K-map can provide not only hyperlinks to digital information but also location pointers to nondigital information, such as the location of paper holdings. In the early stages of implementation, it may be that the K-map provides live links to primary knowledge repositories and location pointers to others.

The knowledge-mapping phase of a knowledge management project has many steps, as shown in Figure 4-3. Some steps will take place concurrently, and the entire process will be iterative. It is recommended that a K-map:

- Be representative of the business model
- Reflect knowledge domains identified earlier
- Be understood and used throughout the organization
- Support multiple "information object" types, such as documents and Web pages
- Keep pace with changing needs through continuous reassessment of content and structure

It is a good idea to identify key individuals from various parts of the organization who can be part of the "mapping team." This ensures that important functional areas are represented and takes advantage of the energy and commitment of early supporters. Although the K-map is more complex than the traditional classification scheme, the foundation skills needed to create them are very similar. Therefore an organization's records management specialist or librarian is an ideal member of the mapping team, providing special insights into the organization of knowledge, augmenting other expertise provided by **subject**

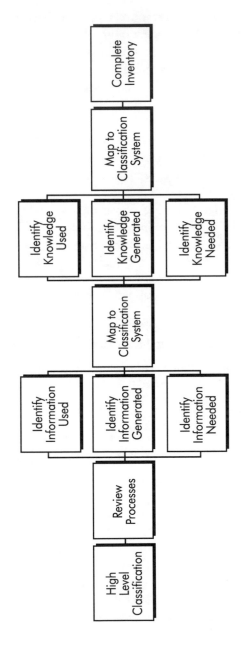

Figure 4-3—Developing the Knowledge Map

matter experts. A number of organizations are developing specialized positions, called **cybrarians**, to support the development and ongoing maintenance of K-maps.[9]

The K-map should be organized to provide maximum flexibility for users conducting searches, but at the same time, it should promote efficient searching. As representatives of users of the knowledge base, subject matter experts will have the responsibility of providing input into what links are most appropriate, which sources are most valuable, and, ultimately, what should be included in the knowledge base. As noted, the K-map itself can provide either a link to the knowledge source, similar to the hyperlinked indices used on the World Wide Web, or simply an indicator or pointer to the location of the knowledge.

MAPPING TOOLS AND TECHNIQUES— *HOW* TO GET WHAT YOU NEED

The preparation of a K-map is a classic process of gathering information, analyzing findings, and documenting results. Information that has already been gathered—for example, questions that were answered during the preparation of the vision, high value definition, and value proposition—should not be asked again. However, it may be necessary to validate that information with more detail. Various tools and techniques can be used for information gathering, including the questionnaire, interview, and workshop. Each of them has merits and is suited to specific circumstances; some of the tools and techniques are described in the following paragraphs.

Questionnaire. Questionnaires provide an easy way to gather information from a broad base of participants and can be used to reach many more people than can interviews. The structured format allows many questions to be asked, but for the same reason, there is always the risk of superficiality.

A questionnaire is best suited to nonsubjective, easy-to-answer questions (who, what, where, when) that are designed to provide quantifiable results. The questionnaire should be relatively short (no more than 20 to 25 questions) and the distribution memo should provide an insight into why the questions are being asked as well as how long the respondent needs to complete a response. In all instances, a deadline for responding is recommended, as well as follow-up telephone calls for nonresponses. The promise of a reward might do wonders for encouraging prompt responses.

Successful questionnaires incorporate the following features:[10]

- Questions that can be rated on a five- or seven-point scale, avoiding simple "yes" or "no" questions

- Simple, short, terse wording to avoid confusion

- Sectioned questionnaires to distinguish different subjects and to maintain respondent interest

- Pretested questions

The questionnaire is ideal for gathering information about internal, explicit knowledge assets—things that an organization owns that enable it to generate business and profits—and external explicit sources of knowledge. The result will be a volume of information, not knowledge, which can then be used to populate the knowledge inventory.

Interview. A series of interviews will be needed to validate and enrich the data gathered through the questionnaire. Interviews provide a richness of facts, perceptions, feelings, and opinions that cannot be obtained through any other method.[11] This feedback, however, represents the view of a single individual and needs to be validated in other less subjective ways. For example, bias can be controlled through group interviews or workshops, but participants are often reluctant to speak frankly in a group setting. Consequently, a combination of both one-on-one and group interviews is recommended.

A representative group of individuals, from all levels of the organization, should be selected for interviews. The group could consist of a team that currently works together; a group of people who need to collaborate; or multiple people sharing similar jobs or involved in the same process. Interviewing is an exercise in active listening and ideally suited to obtaining answers to the "who" and "why" questions. The interviewer's comments should be brief, but should encourage the interviewee to respond openly.

Two types of input will likely be obtained from an interview: fact and personal opinion. Direct questions encourage factual responses; for example, starting the question with "How many" or "What is" will discourage personal opinion. If the objective is to obtain opinion, then the questions need to be worded differently. Asking questions such as, "What do you think is working well?" will elicit very broad answers that need to be followed up with qualifiers such as, "Why do you think that way?" or "What makes you say that?"

Mapping Tools. The actual preparation of a map might involve several types of tools, some involving database development, some that are graphical, some using specialized software. A simple graphic drawing tool is adequate in a "situational" knowledge management initiative that involves minimal links and layers. A more complex or enterprise-wide undertaking would be better documented using a tool that is specifically designed to show threaded indices and hyperlinks.

It is a good idea to develop a high-level classification scheme early in the process, so that a general layout of the kinds of knowledge resources available can be used to guide further refinements and to identify knowledge gaps. This should be based on the domains identified earlier, using knowledge categories and subcategories that reflect the knowledge management vision, the value proposition, the high value knowledge proposition, the priorities, and the overall business. Figure 4-4 provides a visual representation of a high-level classification scheme containing conceptual, functional, and physical models for knowledge classification. This model was prepared using Dataware Technologies' Knowledge Suite II.

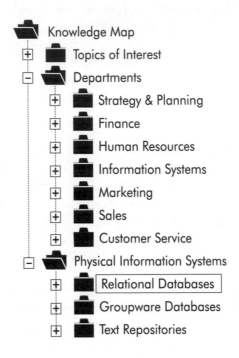

Figure 4-4—High-Level Classification Scheme

REVIEW BUSINESS PROCESSES— *WHAT* YOU NEED TO GET

To properly identify what knowledge is most important, the project team needs to fully understand what the organization does and how; they need to understand workflow and decision-making processes. Only in this way can they assess the relevance and importance of the information and knowledge pertaining to the organization.

An excellent starting point is a review of key business processes, since these incorporate business practices and management systems, job definitions, organizational systems, and beliefs and behaviors that underpin any business operation. The knowledge-mapping process should concentrate on those business processes identified as priorities in earlier stages according to knowledge management objectives and benefits. Priority processes probably contain knowledge that is critical to the business.

This phase of the project seeks to determine what people rely on most in order to do their jobs—their own experience and available knowledge, information and documents, or consultation with others. The key activities and roles in priority business processes need to be examined in relation to:

- What information and knowledge are *used* and *generated*, and how this is done

- What information and knowledge are *needed* and why

- The *sources* of what is used, generated, and needed

Focusing on priority business processes allows knowledge management to be more easily integrated into the core work processes, which is essential for the success of the knowledge management process.

The next sections provide some practical guidance in discovering and documenting the organization's information and knowledge resources. A reminder about the difference between explicit information and tacit knowledge:

- Explicit information is documented, public, structured, and has fixed content and known facts.

- Tacit knowledge is personal, undocumented, context sensitive, experience based, and often subconscious.

Another reminder: Because there is a significant risk of gathering an unmanageable volume of information or knowledge in this exercise, it is important to put everything in the context of supporting the priorities identified in earlier stages of the project. For example, if the priority for knowledge management is customer service improvement, then information (or knowledge) used, created, and needed in connection with that particular process will be the focus of the exercise.

Information Used, Generated, and Needed. This stage of information gathering is designed to answer the following questions for each key business process, focusing on priority processes:

- What information is *used* and where is it obtained?
- What information is *generated* and where is it then stored?
- Who *needs* what information and when it is needed?
- Who knows what, and where are these individuals located?
- Is all of this information essential or is some of it just nice to have?

A questionnaire can provide a relatively easy way to gather responses to questions about information resources. Figure 4-5 (on pages 228–229 of the appendix) shows a sample questionnaire. It should be noted that during interviews designed to gather insights into information use, for example, it is not unusual for the discussion to venture into knowledge use. This is acceptable and quite natural, as long as the discussions stay on topic, and the digressions contribute to the whole process.

The quantifiable responses to the questionnaire are organized in terms of the high-level classification scheme and mapped to identified knowledge domains. Analysis of the results will reveal context, and when this is included with the hard facts, the early form of a **knowledge base** begins to take shape. Answers to the supplemental questions at the end of the questionnaire are intended to provide further insight into the way people currently work. The answers to these last seven questions will be extremely useful in future steps of the design and implementation process.

Knowledge Used, Generated, and Needed. After questionnaire responses are analyzed, a series of follow-up interviews or workshops will be needed for an understanding of the subjective aspects of how knowledge is used and generated. For example, tacit knowledge may have a limited life span because certain methods, assumptions, and ways of working become outmoded and are supplanted by better ones. For this reason, it is important to understand how people who use it confirm its validity, particularly when the knowledge is being used to make important decisions. The responses gathered in this step will provide insights needed to address the human issues associated with designing a knowledge management environment—relevant to both the technological infrastructure and cultural behaviors.

The next step, then, is to interview or conduct workshops with people whose main responsibility is the business process identified as the first priority. For example, if the primary objective of the knowledge management environment is to support customer service, then the first people to invite to participate in a workshop would be the customer-service representatives—the people on the front line. If the customer-service process has been documented, this could be used as a starting point for the interview or workshop discussion.

At the outset of the workshop, it is useful to reiterate the difference between information and knowledge and to share with the participants the beginnings of the knowledge map developed earlier. It is also very useful for the participants to share in understanding the vision, the value proposition, the high value knowledge proposition, the priorities, and the business case.

Figure 4-6 (on pages 230–231 of the appendix) provides a guideline for obtaining further input about what knowledge is used, what is created and how, what is needed, and what would be nice to have. To make the interview or workshop more productive and meaningful, it is helpful to use pertinent questionnaire responses and **business process diagrams** in conjunction with the interview or workshop. Also, a set of clearly identified knowledge domains available to respondents might help them to structure their responses to be more relevant to the knowledge management initiative. It is good practice to discuss the purpose of the inventory and various information-gathering methods with interviewees and workshop participants so that any questions about them can be resolved immediately.

Compile Information/Knowledge Inventory. The results gathered from questionnaires, interviews, and workshops provide the first picture of the **information and knowledge holdings** of the organization. Such a picture reveals:

- Who knows what about what

- How information/knowledge is retained, by whom, and in what form

- Availability of context associated with information

- Oversupply or lack of information/knowledge

- Level of awareness of information/knowledge elsewhere in the organization

To make the inventory meaningful and accessible, information is needed about the attributes of the content, such as location or source, subject matter, owner, format, age, and use of internal and external information. A sample form for gathering such information is shown in Figure 4-7 (on pages 232–233 of the appendix). When completed, the inventory can be used to further develop the K-map, and it can provide guidance for further developing the knowledge base itself.

The inventory comprises information and knowledge that is available and used in the organization. The responses to the knowledge-mapping activities also reveal what should be available and used in order to serve important business functions. Accordingly, the gaps between what is available and what is desired need to be identified. The potential for these gaps to weaken an organization's ability to compete effectively is the basis for evaluating their criticality or significance. The knowledge gaps can then be ranked in order of the importance of filling them.

From this base line, the project team can determine what is important enough to include in the initial or foundation inventory, regardless of whether these are currently available or not, as well as what the team should plan to include in the future. Using all of the information gathered as a result of the knowledge management project—vision, value proposition, high value knowledge proposition, priorities, business case, questionnaires, interviews—the project team needs to assess what it has and what it wants. Both of these will comprise the organization's knowledge base.

Although it is important to know what the organization knows, who knows it, how it can be accessed, and how it is maintained, there is a risk of trying to document everything known or knowable. Dilution of the knowledge holdings must be discouraged to keep them workable and meaningful. Enhancement, however, should be encouraged. As mentioned earlier, the organization's knowledge base is likely to contain more information (without context) at first than knowledge (with context). As the organization pays increasing attention to recording associations and experience, the content of the knowledge base will be enriched with high-value, business-critical knowledge that is made more valuable by relationships of meaning. This will make the knowledge more useful to users.

Peter Vogel, application systems supervisor for Champion Road Machinery, advises, "Your whole implementation must ensure that the answers to your users' questions are in the repository and easy to find. Once you accomplish those two things, you'll have reached critical mass: enough people will find the knowledgebase useful often enough to make it self-perpetuating. . . . You've achieved success when people put enough faith in the knowledgebase to be let down by it."[12] So, some tips to achieve that critical mass include:

- Focus the material. People use a knowledge base because there is some hope that what they are looking for is in it.

- Ensure that it will grow. If contributions are optional, they won't happen. If there is no real-life content, it will be ignored.

- Make access easy. The knowledge base must be the closest source of information available. Provide as many ways to get to it as users need. Then, provide great links to internal knowledge and to sources outside the organization.

- Maintain content constantly. If content stops being relevant, the system will stop being used.

Define Knowledge Management Processes

Knowledge management processes refer to the ways that an organization handles knowledge at various stages of its life in an organization. The organization needs to acquire and capture knowledge; organize and store it; retrieve it as needed; distribute it as needed; and maintain its currency, relevance, and value. These five stages in the life cycle of knowledge are illustrated in Figure 4-8. Keep in mind that these five life-cycle phases do not work in a neat or predictable pattern. According to renowned training authority Anthony Carnevale:

> "The proper analogy is not the relay race, in which each runner hands off to the next in a prescribed sequence, but the basketball team, in which each player interacts with the others in a complex set of patterns while moving toward a common goal."[13]

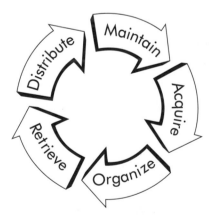

Figure 4-8—Knowledge Management Life Cycle

In order to ensure the absorption of knowledge management into day-to-day processes for each of the five phases of the knowledge management life cycle shown in Figure 4-8, the organization needs to document and communicate what is done, who does it, and when. It needs to identify continuing processes and the roles and responsibilities associated with them. Unless accountability for these processes is assigned, there is little chance of anyone taking ownership; thus, the likelihood of success will diminish.

Identifying knowledge management processes, as defined here, is a valuable undertaking for the organization. In explaining how you reach a conclusion, for example, you need to look at what factors you consider, what assumptions or preexisting knowledge you use as a foundation, what information you disregard and why, and what judgments you are required to make. All this can lead to reassessing the process used, and thus further validating the conclusion.

In this exercise, the question to be answered by those engaged in establishing a knowledge management environment is: "How can we put knowledge management processes in place in order to establish a workable knowledge management life cycle that is advantageous to the business functions and objectives of the organization?" Each of these processes will be discussed in turn.

ACQUIRING AND CAPTURING KNOWLEDGE

Knowledge is acquired in several ways: it is created by employees in their day-to-day activities; it may be purchased from external knowledge sources such as specialized online feeds; or it can be rented on an as-needed basis from consulting companies or other external experts. An organization can use all of these sources and more, depending on the type and complexity of its business functions.

In activities where workers rely mostly on their own knowledge, the challenge is to elicit that knowledge from them and make it transferable. Remember that much of the most valuable knowledge is unstructured and buried in day-to-day processes; it is often only available as tacit knowledge in the minds of skilled practitioners. Thus, capable people are the most important aspect of capturing and transferring knowledge.

If knowledge of varying complexity from all these sources is not captured systematically, it will be knowledge "on the fly," unavailable to the organization as a whole, and lost to future workers needing facts, advice, and assistance. First, the organization needs to decide what kinds of knowledge to acquire and capture. C. Jackson Grayson suggests the following questions as a starting point:[14]

- Do you know what knowledge you have now?

- Are you systematically transferring knowledge inside your own organization?

- Are you creating new knowledge? Is it being captured?

- Are you leveraging knowledge?

- Are you measuring your knowledge assets?

- Are you using technology to acquire, disseminate, and transfer knowledge?

Then, it needs to identify which people will ensure that particular kinds of knowledge are captured, how often, and from where. Dataware Technologies advises, "The capture and management of tacit knowledge requires more than a searchable repository. A knowledge management system . . . should enable the capture and later location of not just documents, but related information such as lessons learned, previous experiences, and relevant people."[15]

In the course of making these decisions, the planners will need to consider the following topics and questions:

- **Knowledge Sources.** Is the organization taking advantage of the many available knowledge sources? Can it get leverage from information in back-office applications, customer service systems, human resources data, documents, and news services? Is it aware of the knowledge generated from meetings, focus groups, observations, and the company grapevine? What will be the organization's primary sources of knowledge?

- **Authority to Acquire.** What role will the subject matter expert play, and what role will other knowledge workers play? Who is authorized to acquire (buy or rent) external knowledge? Is one particular mode of acquisition favored, or can knowledge be acquired from any source?

- **Systematic Acquisition.** How frequently will new knowledge be acquired? How can the organization use information searches, reverse engineering, competitive intelligence, and sales force feedback to acquire outside knowledge? Is it taking advantage of industry benchmarking, or of finding, learning, and adapting best practices from others?

- **Systematic Creation.** Is new knowledge being captured and shared? Is the organization routinely capturing lessons learned? One technique that can readily be transferred is the U.S. Army's "After Action Review." It analyzes previous operations, regardless of whether the outcome was negative or positive, to answer the questions: What did we do? Why did we do it that way? What happened? Why did it happen? How can we do it better in the future?

- **Turning Tacit into Explicit Knowledge.** Have ways been found to convert the intangible to the tangible, the inaccessible to the accessible? Is the organization capturing expertise, insights, previous experiences, and the knowledge of relevant people?

- **Converting Individual Know-How and Experience into an Organizational Resource.** Does the organization recognize (on a formal basis) the value of individual knowledge? Does it routinely seek the advice of its specialists; its astute middle managers; its business-savvy, front-line sales team?

Capturing organizational knowledge is no longer a luxury, nor something that should be done if only there were time to do it. A review of Price Waterhouse's employees determined that "more than 40 percent of the staff was either in their first year with the firm (and in need of institutional knowledge) or in their last year with the firm (and about to leave with substantial knowledge)."[16] Leif Edvinsson, vice president and corporate director of intellectual capital for Stockholm-based Skandia, describes one company that laid off "as many as 2,000 employees in a day, each of whom had more than 20 years experience. Imagine the organizational memory lost when 40,000 years of experience walk out the door in one day."[17]

ORGANIZING AND STORING KNOWLEDGE

Capturing knowledge is of little use if it is not organized in such a way that it can be understood, indexed, accessed easily, cross-referenced, searched, linked, and generally manipulated for maximum benefit for everyone in the organization. The K-map provides a framework for identifying the location or source of high value knowledge, and for defining common terminology to enable constructive analysis and meaningful collaboration.

The objectives of the knowledge management initiative and the capabilities of supporting technologies will certainly influence how knowledge is organized in any particular enterprise. Perhaps the least effective way to organize knowledge resources is according to the physical systems that house the knowledge, which requires users to know the location of the knowledge they seek. Neither is it particularly beneficial to organize around functions or departments, since this encourages the continuation of information islands.

The most effective approach to knowledge organization is to start with the knowledge domains identified earlier, building on these layer by layer, topic by topic, and concept by concept. In this way, for example, all information about a particular customer or product will come together, regardless of its location or department of origin. Thus, users do not need to know the physical location of the knowledge, nor take the time to check the knowledge repositories of every function or department.

The use of filters can assist in navigation to ensure that the most relevant knowledge is presented in the first layer of access.

Each contribution to the knowledge base should be accompanied by its own metaknowledge, which provides some detail and attribute data about the knowledge asset—why it was created, what the results were, what to watch out for when it is used. Also useful is the inclusion of expert commentary and annotation. "End users are typically the most knowledgeable resource for capturing metaknowledge and categorizing their own contributions. . . . [K]nowledge editors may perform or provide additional categorization information since they are able to see across departments or functions and recognize other uses for the information."[18] Each contribution should also be associated with one or more of the knowledge domains included in the K-map, for ease and speed of navigation.

Any time a document is created electronically, certain information about the document is captured—for example, author, sender, date of creation, subject, document name. The system can be set up in such a way that all of this information is automatically entered into the knowledge management system to form metaknowledge. Sophisticated knowledge management technology can automatically produce a synopsis of a document as it is processed for inclusion in the knowledge base.

Storing the knowledge is another issue to be addressed by planners. Solutions that facilitate access to original source data, information, or knowledge are often the most cost effective. This would make use of pointers to knowledge located in various repositories or at other Web resources accessible to users. However, better performance and security can be gained from designing the knowledge base around a staging platform similar to a data warehouse.[19] Properly classified and "cleansed," the contents can be searched, targeted, synthesized, and manipulated like a Rubik's cube of valuable gems, refracting different kinds of insight as its properties are variously aligned.

Responsibility for the initial organization of the knowledge base is shared between the knowledge team and subject matter experts. On a continuing basis, however, dedicated knowledge stewards may be needed to take care of maintaining integrity in the content and structure of the knowledge base.

Real-Life File: Teltech in the Business of Knowledge Management

Teltech, a small company in Minneapolis, has built a successful business by helping other companies get access to external technical expertise and information. Teltech offers four kinds of services: (1) it maintains a network of thousands of technical experts who can be called by clients, (2) it offers assisted database searches with access to over 1,600 online databases, (3) it provides a vendor service, and (4) it provided a technical alert service for topics deemed critical by clients. For such a range of services, Teltech needs complex knowledge maps of its resources, plus a useful, accessible structure for them.

Teltech's approach to structuring knowledge is thesaurus-based, not hierarchical. For example, "When clients call for access experts, they are unlikely to always use the same terms as the experts use. . . . Therefore there must be some 'translation' function performed by Teltech in connecting client needs to available expertise. This function is performed by knowledge analysts in combination with Teltech's online search and retrieval system, the 'KnowledgeScope.' [It] includes a thesaurus of over 30,000 technical terms. It is maintained by several full-time 'knowledge engineers,' who add 500 to 1,200 new concepts per month to the database and remove outdated ones as well."[20]

RETRIEVING KNOWLEDGE

In an ideal knowledge management world, everyone would be able to retrieve anything regardless of time or location. In reality, people's needs will differ, organizations' goals and culture will vary, and access approvals and access levels will be determined accordingly. Some users will want (or need) to "perform simple keyword searches across all information sources, while others will want (or need) to target specific sources. As the number of information sources increases, end users may be presented with extremely large results sets . . . with no easy way to navigate them."[21]

However, all workers will want to get what they need, or what they can, as efficiently as possible. So the initial organization of knowledge resources and the taxonomy used to enable navigation is extremely important to the usability of the knowledge base. As well, technological advances in searching capability—developing, it seems, at breakneck speed—can accomplish remarkable feats of information retrieval. Intelligent "agents" can now be instructed to retrieve particular kinds of information, in particular domains, at particular intervals. These capabilities are discussed in Chapter 5.

DISTRIBUTING KNOWLEDGE

Knowledge distribution is another way of expressing access rights to certain information. Subject matter experts will have a role in determining reliable external sources of knowledge and even in creating valuable internal knowledge—but how will that knowledge be shared?

In many organizations that have a well-functioning knowledge base, a kind of "ownership" of particular knowledge sets prevails. Usually, the head of the business unit to which a particular knowledge set pertains is the "owner" of that knowledge, at least the titular owner. He or she may delegate the granting of access to it and the management of its integrity to someone else in the unit. In large, complex organizations, there are even ladders of responsibility for updating, creating, granting access to, and pruning or archiving knowledge sets.

There are various technologies for moving or distributing knowledge in a networked organization, and the use of a partic-

115

ular technical method depends on the needs of various business units, the importance of timeliness of the information, and work management processes in place. It may be adequate for some information or knowledge to be accessed as needed by persons familiar with search techniques. In other cases, items may be delivered to the desktop by automated systems.

Real Life File: Ernst & Young Documents and Uses Its Experience

Ernst & Young has five "mega" strategic processes for its consulting business: services; new business acquisition; recruiting and development; strategic service development; and knowledge management. At a high level, these are pertinent to any large business. Ernst & Young sees knowledge management as a key enabler for the other mega processes.

"Knowledge management processes are included in what E&Y calls the 'knowledge process landscape,' which, in turn, includes sub-processes for acquiring, adding value to, storing and deploying knowledge. . . . Related processes include knowledge creation processes and end-user processes for utilizing captured knowledge (e.g., search, navigation and application). Knowledge creation processes are executed by teams that are tightly linked to specific business processes. . . .

"All of these sub-processes are explicitly designed and implemented; the acquisition sub-process is a good example. . . . A conscious effort is made to acquire as many work products as possible, and knowledge gathering is embedded in all E&Y activities. A document management system is used on every engagement to supply work products to the knowledge process. Specific people are assigned responsibility for managing the process, because without such responsibility, the process breaks down."[22]

116

Ultimately, the distribution, sharing, or movement of knowledge in the organization depends on the workplace culture and the attitude of participants in the knowledge cycle. It is the organization's responsibility to remove any cultural barriers to sharing and to put in place reliable networked systems for the movement of knowledge resources throughout the enterprise.

MAINTAINING THE KNOWLEDGE BASE

In almost every organization since the introduction of computers, there are stories of new electronic systems, installed with great promise and fanfare, that "never went anywhere," or that "died a natural death from neglect." Then, when newer ones were introduced as technology improved, someone invariably would whine, "Oh, no, not another system. Why should I learn/use this one? The others were abandoned just as I got used to them."

It does not have to be this way if care is taken to put in place a well-designed knowledge base, and useful, usable systems, as well as the supports to use them, such as cultural approval, systems support, training, and content management. Maintaining the utility, currency, reliability, searchability, and relevance of knowledge resources is probably the most important way to gain leverage from all the effort expended in establishing a knowledge management environment. Like any gardener who derives enjoyment from growing plants, knowledge stewards in an organization have to nourish, prune, fertilize, and nurture what has now been identified as a very valuable asset.

Content managers are the new stewards of the knowledge economy. They are assigned the responsibility of gathering, editing, linking, and validating knowledge in the organization. And they are made accountable for doing so in any organization with a serious commitment to knowledge management. They ensure that all information or knowledge, from both internal and external sources, is accurate, useful, and categorized so that it is easy to find. Stewardship is discussed in Chapter 5.

The K-map provides a universal index to all knowledge holdings as well as links to related knowledge assets. It needs to be kept up to date at all times. The relevance and consistency of the links must be current, and the structure must be regularly revised to keep pace with changing user and organizational needs. Adding and modifying metaknowledge plus adjusting the categorization scheme are also very important tasks.

The importance of this effort cannot be stressed enough. "Maintaining content, while often perceived as a nuisance, is crucial to success. . . . Many efforts at knowledge management have failed because content editors were not given time to perform their duties, which resulted in 'information pollution' and users abandoning the system."[23] Good intentions alone are not sufficient for accomplishing this imperative. Keeping up with content takes time and effort—the time and effort of people who already have jobs, in most cases, which is what makes them experts in various kinds of content. Knowledge management planners and enterprise managers will have to be diligent in providing the conditions that will allow this important work to get done, and they will need to select individuals who will carry out these responsibilities conscientiously in recognition of their significance for the business.

Conclusion

Unless the impetus and rationale behind knowledge management is fully understood, it is likely to be a short-lived "flash in the pan" initiative. Although everyone would like to just "get on with it," it is extremely important not to short circuit the planning phase of such an important initiative. Very few improvements succeed without a plan. The process enforces discipline and critical thinking, ensures a full understanding of the project, and provides a vehicle for communication with others.

The business plan balances the zeal of the knowledge management evangelist with real-world business issues. It makes every attempt to ensure that there are no surprises—costs and benefits are estimated, potential implementation barriers and other risks are identified, and suggestions for mitigating them discussed. Combined with the project plan, it provides a blueprint for the rollout of the initiative and continues the "selling" effort for the initiative.

The usefulness of a knowledge management environment is largely, but not solely, dependent on the care and attention taken in designing it and, to be useful to the business, it needs to serve business purposes. Therefore, the effort involved in identifying and analyzing how this will happen will pay big dividends in both the adoption and use of knowledge management practices and their benefits to the business. The K-map is the result of these efforts and is the foundation for the design of the entire knowledge management environment.

The "what" of content (use, generation, and need for information and knowledge), needs to be complemented by the "how" of capturing and moving around the content—knowledge management processes. The culture of the organization and the objectives of the knowledge initiative will influence the choice of tool or approach to be used. Since knowledge is valuable only if it is maintained and if it is used, a knowledge strategy is incomplete without the development of processes for these purposes. When the dynamics of these processes are determined, then the team can begin to consider the kind of technology infrastructure that would appropriately support the knowledge management process.

Last, but certainly not least, the composition and selection of the project team is very important. The right mix of users, technical resources, management representatives, and, possibly, external consultants can be the difference between success and failure. Belief in the initiative is as important as competence because without it the team will not have the passion needed to convince others to embrace knowledge management.

Notes

1.   J. Bair, "Knowledge Management Value Propositions," *Gartner Group Advisory Services* (24 June 1997), CD-ROM (Cambridge, MA: Gartner Group, Inc., 1998).

2.   Thomas H. Davenport, "Some Principles of Knowledge Management," *Knowledge Management Server* (1997), online, Available: http://www.bus.utexas.edu/kman/kmprin.htm.

3.   D. Brown and others, "ADM Five Year Scenario: Succeeding Amidst Chaos," *Gartner Group Advisory Services* (14 January 1994), CD-ROM (Cambridge, MA: Gartner Group Inc., 1994).

4.   Bair, "Knowledge Management Value Propositions."

5.   J. Bair, "Knowledge Management Leverages Engineering at Chrysler," *Gartner Group Advisory Services* (23 April 1997), CD-ROM (Cambridge, MA: Gartner Group Inc., 1997).

6.   Justin Hibbard, "Knowing What We Know," *Information Week* (20 October 1997), online, Available: http://www.information-week.com/653/53iukno.htm.

7.   Richard Hunter, "Knowledge Capital: Essential Active Management," in *The IT Revolution Continues: Managing Diversity in the 21st Century: Proceedings of Gartner Group Symposium/ITxpo96*, Lake Buena Vista, Florida, 7–11 October 1996 (Stamford, CT: Gartner Group, 1996).

8.   J. Bair, "Building Knowledge Maps: A Love of Labor?" *Gartner Group Advisory Services* (9 February 1998), CD-ROM (Cambridge, MA: Gartner Group Inc., 1998).

9.   Ibid.

10.   Larry E. Greiner and Robert O. Metzger, *Consulting to Management* (Englewood Cliffs, NJ: Prentice-Hall, Inc., 1983), 218-229.

11.   Ibid.

12.   Peter Vogel, "Know Your Business: Build a Knowledgebase!" *Datamation*, 42, no. 13 (July 1996), 84.

13. Anthony Patrick Carnevale, "Learning: The Critical Technology," *Training and Development* 46, no. 2 (February 1992), S1-S16.

14. C. Jackson Grayson, "Taking Inventory of Your Knowledge Management Skills," *Continuous Journey* (Winter 1996), American Productivity & Quality Center, 39.

15. Dataware Technologies, Inc., *Seven Steps to Implementing Knowledge Management in Your Organization*, Corporate Executive Briefing (Cambridge, MA: Dataware Technologies, Inc., 1998), 15.

16. V. Frick, "Changing a Century-Old Business Culture," *Gartner Group Advisory Services* (21 July 1997), CD-ROM (Cambridge, MA: Gartner Group Inc., 1997).

17. L. Edvinsson, "Intellectual Capital: A Strategic Inquiry By Paradigm Pioneers," brochure, n.d., n.p.

18. Dataware Technologies, Inc., *Seven Steps*, 14.

19. BackWeb Technologies, "Knowledge Management: An Industry Perspective," *Back Web*, Hp, 1998 [latest update], online, Available: http:// www.backweb.com/html/pwhpaper.

20. Thomas H. Davenport, "Teltech: The Business of Knowledge Management Case Study," *Knowledge Management Server* (30 March 1997), online, Available: http://www.bus.utexas.edu/kman/telcase. htm.

21. Dataware Technologies, Inc., *Seven Steps*.

22. R. Hunter, "Knowledge Management: Process and Platform," *Gartner Group Advisory Service* (19 May 1997), CD-ROM (Cambridge, MA: Gartner Group Inc., 1997).

23. Dataware Technologies, Inc., *Seven Steps*, 16.

5

Designing a Knowledge Management Technology Infrastructure

Organizations now must be able to learn, adapt, and respond to the market in a rapid and continuous cycle. . . . [They] no longer have the luxury of learning and adapting at a gradual pace. In the networked age, 'adapting organisms' must evolve rapidly and methodically. Technology delivers that capability.
—J. Bruce Harreld, Sr. V-P, Strategy
IBM Corporation

Issues

- What existing and emerging technologies support effective knowledge management?

- What are the steps for designing technological systems that capture the knowledge and expertise of employees in your organization?

- What are the essential components of a successful knowledge management architecture?

Business is evolving toward a set of activities that integrates knowledge work and the networked computing environment. Both the nature of work itself and the technological solutions applied to the work continue to change dramatically. Knowledge management needs a supportive infrastructure, and technology is just one element, albeit a critical one, for capturing, organizing, developing, sharing, and storing information.

The focus of this chapter is on the technology that supports and enables knowledge management. It provides a layperson's description of various classes of technology, the roles they can play, and the components of an architecture in which they can be applied. It focuses on the functionality and applicability of the tools rather than on technical specifications or names of products.

The remarkable increase in information available to the typical knowledge worker *and* the equally remarkable increase in the need to apply knowledge to everyday tasks have directly influenced the evolution of knowledge management. Every organization needs to connect and capitalize on its knowledge resources because of the compounding effect of environmental forces discussed in Chapter 1. Knowledge management helps to bring order to this chaos in systematic ways. And technology helps to deliver knowledge efficiently and link it effectively. It serves the need for speedy iterations of the knowledge cycle. As the knowledge management technology vendor Dataware Technologies points out, "Without new technologies designed to implement the revolutionary changes in the way knowledge workers create, communicate, and manage knowledge, a knowledge management system has little chance of improving enterprise knowledge sharing."[1]

Simply stated, there are three stages in developing a technology infrastructure that will support knowledge management:

- Determine what you want to be able to do—what functionality do you need?

- Design an architecture that will allow you to do this.

- Select the technologies that will best accomplish your objectives.

Technology is no longer something that can be used occasionally. It is an essential part of work and, often, even part of the products and services being delivered as a result of work. It is increasingly absorbed into the fabric of a knowledge worker's life. Boundaries between internal functions and external suppliers and customers are fading, and networked computing is pervasive and commonplace. The issues arising from the association of technology with work are extremely complex.

Large enterprises typically need a wide range of **functionality** in systems that serve their business purposes. Establishing technological support structures as part of implementing a knowledge strategy does not necessarily mean a complete overhaul of existing information systems. The important thing is to know what you want and for what purpose, how you plan to obtain it, in what format, and how fast it is needed. Then steps can be taken to augment or replace today's technology.

The best **architecture** will consider and support the way individuals and teams are organized and how they work. People interpret, understand, and use shared information in situation-specific and task-specific contexts, and they relate knowledge objects to other knowledge objects in different ways. As mentioned earlier, knowledge about customers is interpreted and used very differently by a sales representative and a credit manager.

Currently, no "solution-in-a-box" exists for knowledge management, despite an avalanche of promotional material to the contrary. But a "smart architecture" can take best advantage of what an organization has available and what components, available or new, can support a multiplicity of needs and enable what the firm wants to accomplish.

The two central considerations in selecting technology to support knowledge management are these: it must be easy to use, and it must be integrated into the process of actually doing work. As Gartner Group explains: "The activities supporting KM ... should be based on a dynamic and flexible infrastructure integrated within systems supporting the business and informal communication processes. If users have to go an extra step to record knowledge they will not do it."[2] Both existing and new technology applications can serve to harness knowledge.

A Technology Tour

The electronic tools used to exploit knowledge have become increasingly sophisticated and more widely used over time. Since the late 1980s, they have been further integrated into knowledge work with each significant technological development—for example, the availability and use of powerful desktop workstations, networks, and simple, inexpensive analysis software. Some features of the new have overlapped those of the old, and some new products have been built on the basis of the old, but all are important as continuing support mechanisms for knowledge management. Each development in technology further enables or facilitates effective knowledge management.

Following is a brief tour of technologies and the functions they support. From this, it becomes clear that many of them play a significant role in the knowledge management environment.

Again, this reinforces the fact that rarely does an organization need to start from scratch to develop its knowledge management infrastructure.

EARLY DAYS AND LIMITED INFORMATION

The amount of stored data and information grew dramatically as the cost of storage devices decreased and their capacity increased. Most organizations developed collections of structured, static, explicit information, such as sales data, reports, legal documents, and employee records, but there was no universal index (for the enterprise) to easily find the information or the relationships among information objects. Some early systems for storage, retrieval, and simple access made information more widely available, and relational databases, also more widely available, made information more searchable.

Information storage and retrieval programs typically provided search capabilities on large, textual databases. They served specialized market niches, for example, the medical profession, legal profession, pharmaceutical industry, and stock brokerage houses, but access to them was limited because desktops and networks were not commonplace. In some cases, **internal libraries** were supported by library automation software that integrated acquisition, cataloging, serials control, and circulation functions. However, these software packages were designed to help the librarian manage the library, not really to assist the user in accessing the valuable information contained in the holdings.

DAWN OF SHARED IDEAS

The increasing use of **e-mail** for communication and the emergence of groupware both influenced the development of electronic idea sharing by communities of common interest. Threaded electronic discussions with context cues—for example, "main topic" and "response"—immediately added value to information by making it more accessible and more meaningful.

These discussions facilitated the transfer of knowledge among participants in a process. Discussions about techniques and procedures in a particular activity often formed the basis for developing and recording best practices, as well as for identifying specific experts in processes or techniques.

Adopted initially by individual business units or project teams, groupware was generally used informally, with little technical support. The repositories that resulted from its use contained reusable information and lessons learned, but they were often poorly organized, not designed for reuse, and set up to serve a small, defined group of people. Accordingly, much of the context for the information was verbal and therefore not recorded, so an outsider trying to use the repository would find no connection between tacit and explicit knowledge. Reuse on a large scale was not feasible. However, the emergence of these early groupware tools and their collaboration capabilities, although limited, represented a major breakthrough in integrating the enablers of knowledge work into the work itself.

PULL TECHNOLOGY AND UNLIMITED INFORMATION

At the same time that groupware was emerging, there was a steady increase in the number of desktop computers and local area networks, and the use of e-mail was growing exponentially. Consequently, there was a corresponding increase in the volume of digital narrative and in the amount of textual information available electronically. The Internet came into common public use in the early 1990s. Next came the World Wide Web (which made the Internet easier to use), and the business world changed forever. The use of **pull technologies**, that is, the user "pulls" the information from the server to the desktop, signaled universal access to unlimited information using sophisticated full text retrieval tools. People's success with this new access tool was, and still is, conditional upon their inquiry skills.

The World Wide Web can be a gold mine, producing invaluable nuggets of information, but the proliferation of hyperlinks encourages aimless wandering, often producing surprising (and not always valuable) results. Steady improvements have been made to the organization of online resources into predetermined categories, allowing high-speed access to known and proven high-quality resources. And there have been remarkable advances in the search capabilities of "web crawlers" that scour the Web for results to a specific query.

Relevant to pulling information is the development of **intranets** or company-wide networks for the posting and dissemination of company information. This more than anything enabled the connected enterprise, the emergence of groupware, collaborative workgroups, and the beginnings of managing knowledge within a company. Intranets allow companies to organize their intelligence, and they provide a foundation for new knowledge systems. Companies have found that successful intranets: (1) have single desktop interface (window or browser), (2) allow merged streams of data to come together for knowledge delivery, (3) allow targeting by workgroup, by hardware, through filters, alerts, and searching.

The Web has spurred development in groupware and collaborative tools. Now, virtually every groupware maker has come out with a Web-based version. This means that a combination Web/groupware server lets Web users search company application databases, view contents, and create, edit, and delete documents, as well as have interactive forms, threaded discussions, and personal Web pages. Using a Web browser and a password, employees all over the world can access, share, and track documents.

PUSH TECHNOLOGY

Push technologies are so called because they "push" unfiltered information from the server to the desktop, providing information according to generic task requirements. The user does not have to request the information as in "pull" technology, described earlier. The challenge with this milestone, however, is to provide relevant and focused information.

"Listservs" are rudimentary examples of push technology. Persons interested in a particular topic can "subscribe" to a service that automatically provides information on specific subject areas. Subscribers regularly receive e-mail that relates to their area(s) of interest. These services are often supported by professional, academic, or scientific organizations. The range of material, however, is so broad that not all items are relevant to every subscriber, who thus receives more than he or she needs or wants. This then requires further effort to prune the items received for items of genuine relevance.

Some value-add service providers have developed push applications targeted to specific fields of interest—for example, news and stock information, or training techniques. Users can specify categories to restrict the information they receive to relevant topics. Often a push server can broadcast company news through a company network directly to employees' screens. Some systems push all information to the desktop and depend on the desktop system to discard unwanted information; more sophisticated applications customize the data stream before transmission.

INTELLIGENT PUSH TECHNOLOGY

Intelligent push technology provides relevant knowledge to the user's desktop, representing an advance in push technologies in general. The selection of information is based on learned user requirements and user context. Collaborative filters or intelligent agents are used for this purpose. The agent is a set of commands in the software that is "instructed" with a profile of an individual's interests and a territory of electronic domains to investigate. The agents build a file of each user's interests and then track each information request made by the user. The software compares one user's interests and information requests with those of another user, and proactively suggests additional information or sources to each user, based on retrievals made by other users with similar interests.

Intelligent agents can monitor the issues people research, ideas they submit to the knowledge repository, and topics covered in the documents they prepare. This information is used for a profile of that individual contained in the knowledge base.

Collaborative filtering builds on identified patterns to expand the user's knowledge. As Eric Brethenoux explains, "In addition to looking at movies or music tastes, collaborative filtering can be used to match interest profiles in Usenet news and messages . . . perform Web page filtering for specific interest topics and even derive profiles out of a user's bookmark files. . . ."[3] Intelligent agents can be used to "learn" what knowledge is created (and needed) by individual activities and processes. They also learn what knowledge is generated (and needed) by multiple interacting processes, or processes that run in parallel but which can affect the outcome of the other(s).

The use of intelligent push technology can help to leverage learning across the organization. Since experts are in short supply, this technology can greatly enhance access to expertise. It can, for example, facilitate the development and exchange of best practices information, common techniques and procedures, and project management knowledge.

In practice, this can work well for the organizational supports of knowledge management in an organization. Communities of interest or subject matter experts identify what information they consider important and relevant. **Information crawlers** or **spiders** search for the specified domains, or content categories, of information. Sometimes the user can also specify the locations in which the crawler is to look. In this way, crawlers or automated filters can refine searching to enhance the value and relevance of the content delivered. An organization introducing this technology would do well to apply it to current processes with known participants.

DAILY WORK SUPPORTS

Technology and software developments have facilitated all kinds of work activities in all kinds of businesses through work management software and supports. **Workflow systems** and document management systems have speeded up and systematized everyday activities and further enabled knowledge management practices. Workflow systems route work from one activity, role, or process to another, based on business rules. It ties activities together in a logical sequence and tracks the status of work. **Production workflow**, for example, supports processes triggered by outside events, such as by a customer or supplier, and focuses on capturing and moving a business transaction through to completion. Workflow systems improve productivity by routing work to the right person at the right time, and delivering all the information required for completing a task.

Electronic document management helps businesses put information assets to effective use. A **document** is "a data medium and the data recorded on it . . . capable of being read by [a human being] or machine," according to the International Organization for Standardization. A document can include any combination of data—text, image, voice, structure, video, organization—that can be saved online.

Document management is a process for exploiting, sharing, and distributing the information needed for the company's activities. Gartner Group estimates that professionals spend, on average, 20 to 40 percent of their time managing documents. Effectively distributing and sharing information are all key elements of effective knowledge management.

Electronic document management is a way of storing, seeking, finding, and controlling documents throughout their life cycle, on local and wide-area networks. This includes document life from information acquisition to storage, organization, retrieval, distribution, and, ultimately, destruction, for electronic or paper documents.

DECISION SUPPORT TOOLS

A number of software applications provide specialized assistance for decision making; these include case-based reasoning, simulation, data warehousing/mining, and expert systems. **Case-based reasoning (CBR)** tools provide the capabilities needed to retain, retrieve, and reuse old solutions, commonly referred to as "cases," expressed as a series of problem characteristics and solutions. When a customer or client presents a problem to the system, the symptoms are compared with the cases in the database, and a match is selected. CBR takes users through question-and-answer iterations to locate relevant experiential knowledge, to help classify the problem, and solve it. CBR allows users to benefit from captured knowledge to enrich their own expertise. If sanctioned by the organization's procedures, users may contribute new cases that have been validated in the field. CBR tools are used extensively to support help desk and other customer service environments, equipment maintenance, finance, and medical diagnosis, plus other areas with similar recurring problems.

Expert systems are computer programs that capture an expert's decision-making knowledge so it can be disseminated to others. People interact with the system much the same as if they were interacting with a human expert to get answers to their questions. The system has a knowledge base, which contains the logic of how the human expert makes a specific decision; and it has an **inference engine**, a program that uses the various facts and rules in the knowledge base to arrive at conclusions for a specific problem. The system may give a single recommendation or several recommendations arranged in order of likelihood, in the same way a human expert would. The system can also explain the logical basis for each of the recommendations, which adds credibility and educates the end-user. Expert systems were created about 1970 in the academic community; since then, tens of thousands have been created in business, industry, and government.

Simulation software lets organizations test decisions before putting them into practice. Custom-designed simulations can be expensive, but off-the-shelf applications can be used for generic skill training, such as project management. Participants can experience a project on their own PC and experiment with how they could risk failing—without being fired—and learn what not to do.

A **data warehouse** is an electronic storehouse for data from many sources and in many forms. The data are converted into a consistent, uniform format—"cleansed"—and organized so that users can extract what is relevant to their business purposes. **Data mining** tools are used to uncover implicit relationships that are difficult for human analysts to identify, to spot trends, and to extract hard-to-get data. Their uses are many and varied. Retail chains mine sales data from checkouts to discover patterns in the way people shop, make repetitive purchases, and buy associated items. Airlines use data warehouses to determine the optimum mix of fares on particular routes. Financial organizations use customer status information, from mining the data warehouse, to help cross-sell other products.

Determine Functionality Requirements

Although many potential configurations of knowledge management technology exist, there is a common set of functions that needs to be supported:

- Getting to where you need to be
- Finding what you need
- Storing what you've found
- Tracking where you've been
- Providing support for using knowledge

The first task in outlining what a **knowledge management infrastructure** needs to accommodate in your organization is to prepare a checklist of functions the system must provide and the situations in which they will be used. The latter is important because it will help in the evaluation process—some technologies and configurations will be better suited than will others. The information gathered to date can be used as a basis for this task.

Business priorities have already been identified, the K-map has helped to define the existing knowledge landscape, and proposed knowledge management processes have been designed. Now, the technology must provide the functionality needed to support these carefully considered decisions. The following section outlines some of the most typical kinds of functionality, with comments on the context in which each is important. Remember that you are considering the kinds of functionality *your* organization will need to accommodate.

GETTING TO WHERE YOU NEED TO BE

Pointers to Paper (or People) or Document Images. Most organizations have and will continue to have large quantities of paper documents, such as those received from customers or business partners, or those for which the electronic version is either unavailable or in an unusable format. One way to track them is to use the indexing schema of the records management system and identify the physical location of the documents as part of the K-map for the knowledge base. (This kind of contact navigation can also be done with people—the best source of expertise.) Alternatively, the paper can be scanned and the images stored, so that the documents can be viewed, or even manipu-

---

Real-Life File: Water Utility Provides Sales Support

A major water utility in Ontario scanned all its contracts with municipal clients into a mass storage system at the head office. The system was accessible through its wide-area network to its client service representatives across the province. In this way, through document imaging software, the sales people could have an immediate picture of the terms of the contracts when meeting with clients, while the paper contracts constituted the legal record.

---

lated, if converted to electronic format through optical character recognition (OCR). Each organization will need to determine the mix of paper and electronic documents it can or wants to accommodate, and address retention schedules in both places.

Hyperlinks—Webs of Meaning. Hyperlinking provides a way for the user to move quickly and easily between related pieces of information. The links simplify the process of understanding the relationships between the pieces, and also how one piece of information influences another. For example, if meeting minutes refer to a project schedule, a click on the hyperlink contained in the minutes allows direct access to the project schedule. In a knowledge base, context is important, so an "intelligent" hyperlink can be connected to all other relevant points in a chain or web of meaning; the user can go to any one of them or return to the starting point. Ideally, the K-map will be able to graphically display these relationships.

E-mail Hot Links. Particularly in groupware applications, hot links to the organization's e-mail system can greatly facilitate access to others and enhance the success of work groups. Any kind of electronic document can be e-mail enabled. For example, in project work, as project members record events or details about a particular project, client, or product, they can click to an e-mail hot button on the screen and type a quick e-mail to a colleague asking for more information or clarification. This function is also useful for action items, if provided for in the database or application. Filling in an action item template and hitting "save" can automatically send the template to the e-mail of the assignee because the assignee field triggers the system action of e-mailing. Also, if individuals are identified in the knowledge base as specialists or experts in the organization, others can easily contact them through an e-mail link built into the expert's profile in the expert directory.

Navigation Links—Standard Access Paths. To "pull" information from its location involves human intervention, deliberation, and effort. As the volume grows, it becomes harder to quickly locate the required information or knowledge. Standard paths of access for topics that make sense for the organization's business activities also make sense for its productivity. These provide a place to start to navigate through the store of information and also some context to the topic. A manufacturing plant, for example, could provide direct access points for maintenance issues or environmental concerns.

Internal Business Applications—Links. Knowledge must be accessible in the context of particular business activities since it is valuable only if it is relevant to your purpose. To be of practical use to the business, the knowledge base must be able to link to business applications that are already being used, such as order processing systems and decision support systems. The extent of the linking depends on what is feasible considering the nature and age of the existing application and the technology that supports it. Of course, there is greater incentive to link to applications that are critical for the success of the business.

External Sources—Live Links. Linking the organization's knowledge base to useful outside sources of valuable information and knowledge can save time and enlarge the value of a knowledge base. Such sources could include public domain databases, vendor, product, and industry research service databases, and electronic government publications. Links can also be maintained to relevant Web sites, such as those of competitors, partners, and academic organizations.

FINDING WHAT YOU NEED

Search Function. Character or string searches (keyword and Boolean) look for exact matches of strings of characters. This cannot account for meaning, or relate to a context, or find synonyms.

Knowledge workers need sophisticated search tools that are easy to use in order to effectively access the knowledge base. A simple keyword search for "ground" cannot differentiate between the verb meaning of grounding a teenager and the noun meanings of land, a rational motive for belief, coffee, or an electrical connection. Similarly, such a system cannot link "ground" to related terms such as anchor, earth, evidence, garden, or terra firma. Because these types of relationships are important to the knowledge seeker, advanced search mechanisms such as those listed below are of significant value.

- **Natural language searching:** user can enter instructions such as "find me more like ..."

- **Boolean searching:** system allows user to enter AND/OR definitions

- **Automatic root expansion:** user enters "perform"; system finds "perform," "performance," "performing," etc.

- **Thesaurus integration:** user enters "dog"; system finds "hound," "canine," etc.

- **Search by object type:** TIFF images, RTF documents, etc.

- **Search by index fields:** author, date, location, etc.

- **Concept searching:** user enters "software deals"; system finds "joint venture," "alliance," etc.

Fuzzy Searching. Users often look for knowledge using terms unanticipated by the system. Fuzzy searching allows the right documents to be located even when the query uses a similar word (cloth rather than fabric) or when the query contains misspelled words.

Query Function. A query is a specific question, as opposed to a general search. A general search provides all of the available information about a specific topic, such as how to create a business plan. A query is directed at a particular issue or concern, such as how the overhead costs are calculated for budget forecasting. More commonly now, queries can be phrased in standard English, rather than in complex query languages.

Intelligent Push Based on a Profile or Event. When push technology is combined with intelligent agent technologies, individuals can anticipate much more targeted discovery of pertinent information or knowledge. The searcher may also find relevant items that were not anticipated. The agent "knows" what to look for, does the work of searching, and results are delivered to the user.

Knowledge Mining. This is a way to "mine" knowledge, or quickly find the most relevant knowledge and gain insights as a result of implicit relationships that are difficult for human analysts to identify. This is accomplished by the system revealing significant facts, relationships, trends, patterns exceptions, and anomalies associated with the knowledge. It is also called **media mining** because the action of probing and synthesizing contents of linked repositories or a warehouse can apply to data, text, or other digital media (e.g., images, video).

STORING WHAT YOU'VE FOUND

Multidimensional Cataloging/Indexing. There are two standard ways to index information that is stored electronically: **full text indexing**, which automatically indexes every word in a document, and **structured indexing**, which creates an index "card" with prespecified attributes such as author, title, date, and keywords. Although full text indexing is thorough, any given search may retrieve far more information than is required or relevant. On the other hand, structured searching is restricted to the data that have been entered in the index fields; missing or incorrect information will cause potentially important documents to be overlooked.

There may also be a need for specific views or graphical organization of knowledge to support a business solution or application. For example, sales, marketing, manufacturing, software distribution, customer service, investor relations, and reseller communications may all use common knowledge, but in different business contexts. Accordingly, the knowledge base index allows the system to automatically arrange contents according to multiple subject areas.

With the burst of development now surrounding knowledge systems, some very sophisticated indexing software is being developed to accommodate both standard indexing types. More likely is the development of taxonomies that reflect the nature of a particular business and that support the standard access paths the business wants to accommodate. There are also new demands for cataloging multimedia holdings, and new technologies are being developed to accommodate this need. Universal database systems can now manage data in many different forms—numbers, letters, images, text, documents, spreadsheets, photographs, video-clips, sound-bites, and more.

'Unclassified' Information. The best way to maintain a knowledge base is to index and catalog all new information as it is added, but holdings are constantly changing. Pieces of knowledge evolve unevenly, so there may not be enough information to establish new categories. Also, establishing all the relevant links to other information may take time because of the complexity involved. The system needs to accommodate this kind of "limbo" content. Although it can be made available immediately, it can have markers to indicate that it is uncataloged, so users are alerted to its "orphan" status, and archivists can find it to catalog when possible and practical.

Expiration/Supersede Dates. As the content of a knowledge base will be changed and updated over time, each document, which of course has a creation date, can also be assigned an expiration date, version number, or some indicator of its currency, in accordance with the official records retention schedule. If designed with this in mind, the knowledge base can use this date to automatically remove and replace outdated items. For example, documents that explain why the world is flat can be archived and replaced with documents that describe the world as being round. A word of caution is in order, however: the value of the knowledge contained in a document (regardless of media) may exceed its legal compliance lifetime, so it is very important to assess which has the priority and, therefore, which governs retention scheduling.

Working with the records manager (sometimes in a combined role), the archivist is responsible for ensuring the identification, preservation, and use of an organization's historical record. Because the archivist's mission is to secure and help people to use authentic records, thereby ensuring the availability of evidence and the preservation of heritage—whatever the system's capabilities in this regard—the archivist plays a central role in its design and operation.

Knowledge Rules. With knowledge rules, or business rules, knowledge can be applied to business circumstances in a targeted way. For applications that use case-based reasoning, simulations, or expert applications, the knowledge base needs a place to store the rules that support them. This allows the information to be preprocessed by the system in the context of a particular knowledge requirement. For example, if a loan officer is trying to determine whether to approve a request, knowledge rules can be automatically applied to the information provided by the loan applicant and documented on the loan application form to give an initial assessment of whether the applicant is a good candidate for a loan.

Real-Life File: CIGNA Uses Rules for Knowledgeable Choices

Boston-based CIGNA (insurance and financial services) went through a reengineering exercise to become more efficient, but still found itself underwriting bad risks. It had to find ways to make more knowledgeable choices. Managers working from home had the job of building and maintaining a knowledge base, housed in the same software that every underwriter used to process applications. The custom-built software assesses risk factors such as staff training, earthquake faults, sprinkler systems, and others. "When new information comes in—expert analysis, feedback from the claims department, or insights from the underwriters themselves—the manager/knowledge-editor evaluates it and, if necessary, changes the database. Claims processors and agents have similar setups." The incremental cost was low because "they were collecting all the information anyway, but it just went in the files."[4]

Resource Directories—Subject Experts and Others. The human brain is always the best source of knowledge, but one way to tap into what is held in people's heads is to create a directory of internal and external subject experts who can act as live guides and knowledge sources. Of course, the experts have to agree to act as knowledge sources, and the list needs to be kept up to date. Other kinds of resources that could be maintained for everyone's benefit include: special training packages, accessible when people need them or have time to consult them; documentation on safety and operational procedures; and professional or industry benchmarking studies or guidelines. All of these can be designed to be hot-linked to other pertinent knowledge objects. For example, the "Project Management Lessons Learned" knowledge base could be hot-linked to "Project Management Tools" and "Computer-Based Project Management Training."

Real-Life File: Hewlett-Packard's Network of Experts

HP Laboratories, the company's research arm, began the Connex project to provide a guide to human knowledge resources within the labs. Over time, Connex covered the whole organization. It uses a Web browser as an interface to a relational database. It contains a set of expert profiles—the backgrounds and expertise of individuals who are knowledgeable about certain topics. Upon finding the right someone, the searcher can then link to the individual's home page on the intranet, if one exists.[5]

TRACKING WHERE YOU'VE BEEN

Personal Navigation Trail (Access Path). Everyone who uses the knowledge base will want to know how to navigate through it. Once you get somewhere, you want to know how you got there and how to get there again. This can be critical to building the context surrounding information and to validating information obtained from external sources. Internet browsers use bookmarks or favorites lists to approximate this function, but these provide only a direct path to a specific site, not a trail of all of the sites traveled on the way to getting to the final destination. The personal access path needs to keep track of both the journey and the destination, so that the journey can be repeated and modified as required to recreate the same collection of knowledge that was required.

Evolving Trail of Knowledge (History). Part of the value of a knowledge base is that it can keep a history of how knowledge has developed within the organization and its environment. It is important not to lose the context of how a certain conclusion was reached; otherwise, substantial rework and rethinking must take place if the conclusion is questioned in the future. The explanation of the fact that we used to think the world was flat, but we sent someone out to the "edge" of the earth and determined that indeed the world is round, is as important as the statement of the new knowledge. With more experience and information, many things that were thought to be true have been proven to be false, but without a rationale, the reversal of opinion means little.

Usage Audit Trail. Once established, a knowledge base, with all the links the organization considers relevant to the business, may languish from neglect or misuse or inefficient use unless it is monitored so that it can be modified accordingly. An audit trail is an important part of tracking what gets used, how much, and what does not get used. The audit trail should provide the frequency and duration of access, as well as the source of the access.

SUPPORT FOR USING KNOWLEDGE

Online Collaboration and Learning. The knowledge management environment needs to support collaborative and just-in-time knowledge creation and transfer. One of the best ways to do this is through an online **threaded discussion** forum in which participants can post main topics, responses, and responses to responses in their exploration of a topic. This is particularly useful in research and development functions, where new territory is being explored. Depending on the organizational structure, these forums can be developed for the organization as a whole, or for various communities of practice or interest. The same format also accommodates the posting of questions, answers, tips, and tricks—in a place where a particular user community will look first for help. It is a good way to support customer service and general inquiry activities.

Multimedia Support. Knowledge is found in many formats, and the knowledge base should be able to accommodate the ones you need. These can include, in addition to text, images, three-dimensional graphics, video, and sound. These might be accessed as they happen from online news services. They could also be used in, or generated by, real-time meetings of distant participants. An advertising or public relations company, for example, would rely heavily on multimedia resources. Organizations that are more typical can nevertheless make creative use of these capabilities for a multitude of purposes—product design, training, promotion, marketing, and capturing lessons learned, to name a few. An interesting application of knowledge management is recording oral histories of an organization by workers about to retire, including its products, services, and markets. Video and voice can also be used for capturing special knowledge from respected and expert workers. This knowledge can be used later for training, for introducing new strategies and techniques, or as part of a best practices library.

Performance Measures Support. Any organization with hopes of being successful wants to know how well it is performing on a number of fronts, and not just at annual report time. There is growing interest in monitoring performance along several dimensions in addition to the financial dimension. Measures could be developed for such things as customer and employee satisfaction, internal process productivity, market growth, and innovation or renewal and development. Thus, the functionality of any knowledge management system would need to accommodate the tracking of such performance measures in a way that integrates the measurement with daily knowledge management processes.

Real-Life File: Knowledge Links at Hewlett-Packard

At Hewlett-Packard, the Product Processes Organization (PPO) provides such services to HP product divisions as purchasing, engineering, market intelligence, change management, and environmental and safety consulting. The director of PPO put the Information Systems Group at the center of PPO, and then formed a knowledge management group within the IS group. Its initial charter in 1995 was to capture and leverage product generation-oriented knowledge for managers of the product generation process in the various HP product divisions.

They "developed a Web-based knowledge management system called Knowledge Links. Its primary content is knowledge about the product generation process; the knowledge may come from variety of perspectives, including marketing, R&D, engineering, and manufacturing. The knowledge going into Knowledge Links comes from outside the Knowledge Management group, but group members add value by identifying, editing, and formatting the knowledge, and making it easy to access and use."[6]

Design Knowledge Management Technology Architecture

The **knowledge management technology architecture** defines the functions for each part of the knowledge management environment and identifies the relationships of each to the others. It helps to turn the knowledge strategy into a reality of knowledge content, tools, connections, processes, and people.

The architecture must serve knowledge management in the following ways:

- Support the complete knowledge management life cycle and processes as described in Chapter 4 (Figure 4-8 on page 108)

- Satisfy the need to access, search, and make connections across multiple knowledge domains

- Accommodate both explicit and tacit knowledge and the role of each in the knowledge environment

As Figure 5-1 shows, the typical knowledge architecture has five distinct layers: user interface, knowledge metamodel, knowledge repository (or source repositories), knowledge access tools, and knowledge management enablers (many of which were described in the technology tour earlier in this chapter). In some frameworks, the knowledge repository is a separate physical layer; in others, this is a virtual environment represented by multiple source repositories. It is important to understand the role of each of the layers because the overall success of the knowledge infrastructure is dependent on an architecture design that capitalizes on the functionality and features provided by each of them.

USER INTERFACE

There must be a simple, easy-to-understand **metaphor** for representing the classes of information to the user because: (1) the metaphor hides the complexities of managing multiple applications from the user, and (2) it presents a uniformly logical view of the information/knowledge in the knowledge base. And, it makes the interface easy to navigate. If navigation is difficult, the knowledge base will not be used.

Every technological innovation used by a knowledge worker needs a **user interface**, a graphical, screen-based access point to

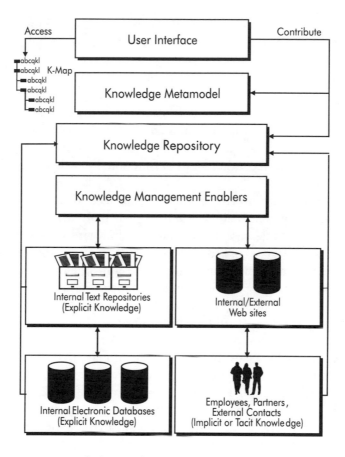

Figure 5-1—Knowledge Architecture

the holdings and functionality of the system. The interface allows the user to look around or "browse" the organization's knowledge base, which can include internal and external knowledge repositories.

The user interface ideally behaves much like an Internet browser, allowing users to access sites by specifying an address, use search criteria to find unknown locations, and to "bookmark" favorite or frequently visited sites for easy revisiting. The

147

browser is a natural fit with a search engine and, combined with collaborative and messaging software, offers a compelling solution for knowledge management.

The user interfaces should provide a range of different viewing options. For example, when the desired information has been located, the user is able to view it directly in the browser window, open it in the original application, view a summary, save it to disk, or e-mail it to someone else. As browsers become more sophisticated, other kinds of functionality will be included in this layer.

Because the knowledge workers may need to access and use a variety of business applications in their daily work, the challenge is to seamlessly integrate this capability into one easy-to-learn and easy-to-use desktop environment. This can be complex because many applications are controlled by their own interface; for example, client contact management, access to up-to-the-minute stock quotes, case-based applications, and user help may each have a unique user interface. In these cases, the knowledge system's user interface design will need to recognize and potentially incorporate the environment that dominates the user's work. User input is critical to successfully designing or selecting the user interface. As one group of designers concluded after finishing a large corporate interface for all functions for all users, "Working in a vacuum is not user-centered design, and it can be a lot of time wasted going in the wrong direction."[7]

To test functionality or usability, it is likely that user representatives will be asked to prepare scenarios using situations that are representative of what the system can be expected to support. If this stage of the technology infrastructure design is carried out conscientiously, it will save time and effort at the implementation stage of user acceptance testing.

KNOWLEDGE METAMODEL

The **knowledge metamodel** is the heart of the knowledge management environment because it houses the context that makes the knowledge valuable and meaningful. That context is "knowledge about knowledge" known to knowledge management professionals as **metaknowledge**. It comprises what we know about the knowledge asset, what its purpose is, how it is used, and what to be concerned about when it is used. Everything in the knowledge infrastructure works according to the metamodel and metaknowledge it contains.

The metamodel contains information about the types of knowledge objects—for example, a document (minutes, proposal, application); a data file (customer record, sales data); video clip; e-mail message; person with specialized expertise; or other type of "knowledge container." It describes the knowledge object, such as creation date, author, location, software used, list of persons with access, list of persons authorized to edit/change contents, related documents, and sources of information used to create contents. It will also contain definitions of terms as a particular type of knowledge object uses them. For instance, does the "date" refer to date of sale, date of creation, or date of manufacture? Without this information about attributes, it is difficult to use multiple knowledge objects for collaborative or comparative purposes.

The metamodel also contains business rules associated with the use of a particular knowledge object, such as the knowledge domain to which the knowledge object belongs; the workflow and business processes in which it is used; and other knowledge object(s) with which it is associated. It contains information about retention, disposal, and other corporate memory and records management considerations.

Early implementers may have to deal with a virtual metamodel, rather than a physical one, since each software product vendor will incorporate pieces of a metamodel in its own product(s). The whole notion of using technology to share knowledge is relatively new, so there are few standards that govern knowledge management infrastructure design and development. If several product-specific metamodels are used in a larger knowledge management infrastructure, there is a high likelihood of incompatibility. Unless a directory and pointers are designed and built, it could be difficult (or impossible) to provide universal access to the knowledge these systems contain. As a consequence, the likelihood of sharing knowledge in this environment is remote.

There is some good news, however. **Extensible markup language** (**XML**) is emerging as the metaknowledge language of choice. In essence, it defines the syntax or rules that govern the preparation of metaknowledge so that it can be interpreted, processed, and communicated by and among multiple applications, thus extending the use of the knowledge asset it describes. Completely transparent to the users, XML is used by application developers to identify or tag specific areas of documents that are different from others—for example, to isolate the name of the author, and then capture this information in the metamodel. These tags will make it easier for search engines, agents, and applications to locate specific information. XML is a subset of **standard general markup language** (**SGML**), which is the metalanguage that defines **hypertext markup language** (**HTML**), the syntax and terms used to develop well-defined Internet documents.[8]

KNOWLEDGE MAP

Also shown on the metamodel level of the architecture illustration in Figure 5-1 is the knowledge map or K-map, a visual representation of knowledge holdings. It identifies the links between existing islands of information and represents all categories of knowledge and the relationship among them.

The K-map may provide live links to an organization's knowledge repositories, regardless of type and location, as the "front end" of an integrated knowledge management product suite, or through direct connections (hot links) to various applications available from some sophisticated desktop tools. Alternatively, it could be a simple directory or diagram created by a desktop tool with information about the location of knowledge assets.

KNOWLEDGE REPOSITORY OR SOURCE REPOSITORIES

In implementations where the knowledge repository is a separate physical layer, the repository gathers all of an organization's separate knowledge objects from disparate information systems and transforms them into a structured resource. This central repository provides for contributing and retrieving knowledge through a universal access tool, such as a Web browser, while maintaining the functionality and format of the original applications. The knowledge metamodel and its K-map govern the structure and operations of the knowledge repository.

In many implementations, various kinds of source repositories form the foundation layer of knowledge management architecture. These various repositories of knowledge will be integrated in such a way that the users will still have a single point of access to the organization's knowledge assets—their own user interface.

The knowledge architecture can include fileservers, database servers, groupware servers, document management systems, and

---

Real-Life File: Meta-Help for Knowledge Repositories

Answerthink Consulting Group has taken the concept of knowledge repositories a step further. The Philadelphia IT consulting firm "uses the Knowledge Management Suite from Dataware Technologies Inc., to maintain a taxonomy, or categorization system, which organizes documents stored in different repositories. Consultants add metadata to documents they submit to the repositories, putting the contents of documents in context. For example, a successful sales proposal could have metadata explaining why the proposal won. Documents can be categorized or searched according to metadata."[9]

Web sites. It can also include mission-critical systems, such as financial reporting, human resource management, and sales automation, which represent enormous stores of legacy knowledge about products, customers, and suppliers.

KNOWLEDGE ACCESS TOOLS

The knowledge access layer and the metamodel are totally interdependent, but they need to be kept separate. This is because system management and access tools may change, and if the two layers were to be combined, maintenance could become complicated. The knowledge access layer of the architecture is a complex combination of system administration tools and **knowledge management enablers**. This layer can include:

- System administration information (security models, directory interfaces, network interfaces)
- Location information (where knowledge unit resides)
- Database type (document management, data repository)
- Access protocol for database (SQL, ftp)
- Knowledge access tools and engines (sophisticated full text search and query on knowledge object contents and on the metaknowledge)
- Distribution tools and engines (electronic publisher, connections to World Wide Web, intranets, client/server networks, CD-ROM, e-mail systems)

In organizations with a virtual knowledge repository, automated information request brokers can be used to access, with a single query, multiple repositories housed on an intranet. Sophisticated search engines can make connections between related knowledge objects, uncovering new insights or previously unknown relationships.

Select the Best Technologies (For You)

At this point in the process, an organization's planners have a good idea of the knowledge management objectives, the functionality wanted and needed, and they have prepared a high level architecture that identifies key components and relationships of the priority knowledge domains. Now there is a need to assemble the hardware and software components that will satisfy knowledge management objectives and be cost-effective for the organization. Existing systems can be realigned where appropriate to service knowledge management goals; there is no need to reinvent the wheel and incur great costs.

One organization may choose a framework that incorporates multiple products to satisfy functionality requirements. Another company may choose to develop a knowledge warehouse that links to other knowledge bases and can accommodate swift and flexible manipulation and searching of all enterprise resources. To select the best technology for its identified functional needs, an organization can benefit from answering the following questions:

1. What is required to satisfy the functional requirements identified earlier?

2. What is required to satisfy anticipated volumes—users, transactions, and storage?

3. With what systems does any new technology need to interface and integrate; what are the technology requirements to satisfy this?

4. Do existing technologies satisfy the emphasis on knowledge sharing?

5. Is there a need to add discussion databases or redesign the existing ones?

6. Does the technology have the ability to scale to large enterprise applications?

7. Will the system be able to access information sources in existing systems?

8. Does the system provide for prioritization and automatic delivery?

9. Does the technology promote timely and relevant answers?

10. Does the system promote discovery through linking the "what" and the "why"?

11. Can revisions be done easily?

12. Does the system promote feedback?

13. Does the system provide easy access?

14. Is external access to the system available regardless of the user's location?

15. Does the environment facilitate cross-business knowledge and experience sharing?

16. Is the technology infrastructure fully or partially in place?

17. Will the system replace, or add to, current information access methods?

18. Does the system take into account context and usability?

19. Can the process be integrated into employees' workflows?

20. Is system security sufficient to comply with company standards?

Most organizations already use a variety of familiar technologies, including e-mail, networks, and the Internet, and many can be included in the knowledge management infrastructure; few companies will need to build from nothing. Figure 5-2 provides some suggestions as to how these tools and applications can contribute, but it is not intended to be all-inclusive. Ultimately, however, the architecture should be designed and the components selected to serve the needs of the people who will use the knowledge system.

In addition to existing technologies, there is a wide and growing range of innovative technology products that serve knowledge management in various ways. When Monsanto designed its knowledge management architecture, it identified nine key technologies to use that were leading-edge but proven: groupware, messaging, Web browsers, document management, search and retrieval, data mining, visualization, push technology, and intelligent agents.

Current Technology	Contribution
Discussion Databases	Capture questions, responses, and on-going discussions
Workflow	Codifies internal processes; provides central repository of business processes
Electronic Document Management	Provides central repository of information; improves access to repositories of digital information
Records Management	Improves access to repositories of paper files
Library Management	Improves access to books, magazines, etc.
World Wide Web	Broadens information regarding markets, competitors, etc.
Data Mining	Lets the software answer vague questions and discover unknowns—for example, finding patterns or a correlation that had not been noticed before
Intranet	Provides an enterprise-wide publishing and information-sharing platform

Figure 5-2—Incorporation of Existing Tools

Many technology vendors focus on a specific technology or tool to be used as part of a complete knowledge management solution. Only a few offer an integrated suite as a foundation for a knowledge management environment. But their areas of specialty show impressive developments. Search tool companies are working on approaches to let users create an unstructured query against multiple types of data, information, and knowledge from sources as varied as textual databases, data warehouses and photo galleries. Database vendors are positioning a new class of database-management system, so-called **universal databases,** to play a central role in knowledge management architectures. These systems manage data in many different forms—text, numbers, photographs, video clips, or sound bites. Now e-mail, spreadsheets, and documents can all be searched in a database with the same security, backup, and recovery capabilities of relational data. Also, as search results grow more complex, the need for **intuitive visualization** increases. One product in development shows results as three-dimensional landscapes, and another product now available presents results as clustered files suspended in three-dimensional space.

A word of caution from a knowledge management industry watcher: "Knowledge is the marketer's dream word—much more appealing than data or information. It sounds sophisticated, New Age and expensive. . . . It won't be long before every database, application package, server and even peripheral vendor will be linking their products to knowledge. Prepare for the onslaught now by setting your antihype phaser to 'neutralize.'"[10]

Gartner Group sees three phases in knowledge management development over the next five to ten years. The first (and current) phase is that of **knowledge retrieval**, where the goal is retrieval relevance. In this phase, geography and reluctance to share are still barriers; information is isolated, and knowledge is still largely tacit. The second phase is one of **connectivity**, where the former barriers have been overcome, there are relationships among people and information objects, and an interlinked memory is forged through groupware, workflow, and document management media; the goal here is relationship management. The final phase is the **coordinated enterprise**, which is characterized by coordination among people, objects, and processes, with interrelated knowledge, resources, and models.[11]

When an enterprise reaches this stage of evolution, collaboration and knowledge sharing are part of the organization's culture and daily activities. The technological infrastructure fully supports the entire knowledge management process and life cycle. There is universal access throughout the enterprise to all relevant knowledge, usually through the type of browser-based interface described earlier. In this way, the knowledge management system serves multiple users and multiple uses.

This is an environment in which **anytime, anywhere collaboration** is an integral part of sharing and managing knowledge. This demands that the meaning of any content is well represented and well communicated—and even done in new ways, but new ways that preserve the integrity of the meaning.

Figure 5-3 shows a suite of technologies that supports anytime, anywhere collaboration. The mix will depend on what the organization needs.[12] For a global organization wanting to capitalize on a broad base of widely dispersed skills, the technologies in the top right-hand quadrant provide maximum support.

In the future, we will need new tools to represent, structure, and transfer knowledge to others, including graphics, music, interactive Web sites, videos, virtual meetings, and avatars. An **avatar**, for example, is a digital presence that represents an indi-

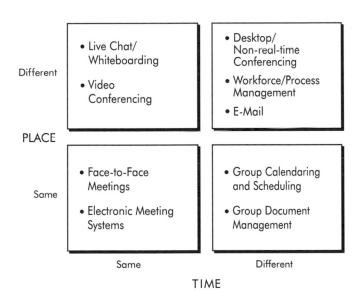

Figure 5-3—Framework for Collaborative Technologies

vidual user to others in a digital environment. The new tools must be capable of encouraging knowledge workers to look in new places—looking harder and better in the same place is not enough. The knowledge system will capitalize on these new knowledge sources; it will seek them out and add them to its already rich stores. As well, these new tools must support organizational learning. The organization should be smarter because of its relationship with the individual and vice versa.[13]

It is expected that the knowledge workspace will need to be highly visual, and that corporate stories will need to be represented by models of meaning that can be shared across thousands of miles and cultures, and among thousands, and even millions, of people. Depiction mechanisms will be needed that are simple to apply and easy to understand, and that preserve the richness of the knowledge they represent. Sophisticated modeling and synthesis tools will also become part of the decision-making process, which even now requires business leaders to anticipate the future. These, too, will gradually be incorporated into the knowledge architecture.

As new technologies are introduced to the knowledge environment, many new questions will arise. For example, most **enterprise resource planning** (**ERP**) software packages create their own version of metaknowledge, as do most desktop tools. This can result in a duplication of metaknowledge if each particular system has its own "metadescription" of attributes that are common to all of them. Moreover, none of the knowledge contained in any one of them can be accessed by any other system including the legacy systems a company may use. It will not be surprising therefore if the creation of multiple sets of metaknowledge will be called into question. Also, as the mix of technologies becomes more complex, it will be important to establish which **application programming interface(s)** (**API**) will dominate the technology environment.

Ultimately, knowledge management practitioners can look forward to a knowledge repository or knowledge base that is able to take advantage of existing metaknowledge to seamlessly access all of its knowledge assets and that will not jeopardize the ability of designers to enrich the metamodel with additional contextual information. Figure 5-4 shows a picture of how this future might look.

Conclusion

Unfortunately, there is no total "out-of-the-box" knowledge management solution, so finding systems and software with the functionality appropriate for knowledge management is a major challenge for those who are undertaking a knowledge management initiative. Over time, this is expected to change as vendors offer more integrated tools. But, today it is necessary to draw from available and emerging technologies in order to assemble an appropriate infrastructure. It is important for the system to allow knowledge to be captured in many forms, and to use the knowledge to dynamically link various corporate entities, thus

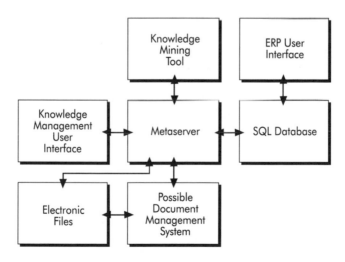

Figure 5-4—Potential Integrated Knowledge Management Environment

providing the foundation for the creation of new knowledge. At the same time, the knowledge environment as a whole must unify the silos or islands of information stored in different systems across an organization.

There is the risk that knowledge management tools and architectures will fail to integrate the wide variety of information, data, knowledge, and systems that exist today (and that continue to be introduced), making it impossible for enterprises to reconcile the different formats for later reuse. Since there are few standards associated with the knowledge management environment, it is important to focus on those that do exist in order to maximize versatility and longevity and reduce the risk of obsolescence. Claims that knowledge management and document management are one and the same or that groupware will fulfill all knowledge management requirements are false.

If the knowledge management system is used extensively, and it encompasses a wide variety of data types, the impact on local and wide-area networks can be significant, particularly if the environment incorporates real-time collaboration, voice, and video. Also, the appropriate security measures must be in place to ensure that the knowledge asset is available whenever and wherever needed, but that access is limited to those who need it and have permission to use it, when they need it.

Notes

1. Dataware Technologies, Inc., *Knowledge Management*, Corporate Executive Briefing (Cambridge, MA: Dataware Technologies, Inc., 1997), 1.

2. J. Bair, J. Fenn, R. Hunter, and D. Bosik, "Foundations for Enterprise Knowledge Management," *Gartner Group Advisory Services* (7 April 1997), CD-ROM (Cambridge, MA: Gartner Group Inc., 1998), 13.

3. E. Brethenoux, "User-Targeted vs. User-Centered Techniques," *Gartner Group Advisory Services* (30 July 1997), CD-ROM (Cambridge, MA: Gartner Group Inc., 1997).

4. Thomas A. Stewart, "Getting Real About Brainpower," *Fortune*, 27 November 1995, 202.

5. Thomas H. Davenport, "Knowledge Management at Hewlett-Packard, Early 1996," *Knowledge Management Server* (30 March 1997), online, Available: http://www.bus.utexas.edu/kman/hpcase.htm.

6. Thomas H. Davenport, "Some Principles of Knowledge Management," *Knowledge Management Server* (1997), online, Available: http://www.bus.utexas.edu/kman/kmprin.htm.

7. Susan Hopper et al., "Real World Design in the Corporate Environment: Designing an Interface for the Technically Challenged," in *CHI 96: Electronic Proceedings, Association for Computing Machinery, Special Interest Group on Computer-Human Interaction*, 16-18 April 1996 (ACM, 1996), online, Available: http://www.acm.org/sigchi/chi96/proceedings/desvbrief/Hopper/Hwh_txt.html.

8. R. Knox, "Why is Metadata Important?" *Gartner Group Advisory Services* (13 May 1998), CD-ROM (Cambridge, MA: Gartner Group Inc., 1998).

9. Justin Hibbard, "Knowing What We Know," *Information Week* (20 October 1997), online, Available: http://www.information-week.com/653/53iukno.htm.

10. Thomas H. Davenport, "The Knowledge Biz," *Intellectual Capitalism* (15 November 1997), online, Available: http://www.cio.com/archive/enterprise/111597_intellectual_content.html.

11. J. Bair, "Knowledge Management Scenario," in *The Future of IT: Proceedings of Gartner Group Symposium/ITxpo97*, Lake Buena Vista, Florida, 6-10 October 1997 (Stamford, CT: Gartner Group, 1997).

12. David Coleman, "Collaboration, Knowledge Management and the Rise of Intranet Communities" (New Orleans: The Office Systems Research Association, 27 February 1998, transcription).

13. Edward W. Rogers, "Designing the 'Tools' Needed for Crafting Knowledge at Cornell," *Cornell Chronicle* (1996), online, Cornell University, Available: http://www.news.cornell.edu/Chronicles/2.29.96/commentary.html.

6

Implementing the Knowledge Strategy: Making It Work

The illiterate of the 21st century will not be those who cannot read and write, but those who cannot learn, unlearn, and relearn.
—ALVIN TOFFLER

Issues

- What cultural, organizational, and methodological changes will organizations need to make in order to maximize leverage on their investments in knowledge management?

- How can an organization encourage attitudes of sharing and of contributing to team success rather than hoarding and individual achievement?

- What roles and responsibilities are fundamental to the success of a knowledge management initiative?

The implementation process aims to put in place the three key elements of the knowledge management system: people, process and technology. These are all needed in appropriate measure for the knowledge strategy to become successfully integrated into the life of an organization. This is the last stage of making the knowledge management system operational, and it needs to be approached in a balanced way—all the parts have to work, and they all have to work together.

The primary objective of the knowledge strategy is to encourage people to develop and share knowledge in the best way possible with the result that it has a noticeable and visible impact on the business. Spending great amounts of money on computers, networks, and software does not guarantee that knowledge will be created or transferred. The challenge of the implementation phase is to orchestrate the elements of change so that a culture develops in the organization to complement the technology that is put in place in this phase. This is a climate in which the power dynamics are at least somewhat changed and where widespread knowledge sharing is encouraged and rewarded. Such a climate is needed for knowledge management to flourish, and it depends on relationships built on continuing trust.

Ideally, there is a parallel evolution in an enterprise of technological enablers and cultural enablers of knowledge management. This evolution of supports builds on the cultural and technological changes that have taken place in the workplace over the last decade. Many of them were impelled by automated systems, and recently jolted to further change with the World Wide Web. Knowledge management does include new technology with new capabilities, but it is built on existing systems. Knowledge management also requires cultural change, and an intensification of what people have already adapted to with the advent of e-mail, groupware, and search and retrieval capabilities.

The **implementation phase** of the knowledge management project is highlighted by the installation of technical systems, but it is also a time when cultural conditions must be considered a priority. Like any project, the knowledge management initiative needs a good implementation team for continuity, and a clear plan for methodical progress.

Testing and installation of technical systems is perhaps the most straightforward part of the implementation phase. The systems may be advanced, and the live links, special functions, and connectivity may be complex, but skilled technical people and communicators can do the job well. Other elements of the transition may be more difficult and potentially contentious. For example, it may be difficult to encourage people to contribute to the knowledge base, or equally difficult to encourage people to trust and use the contents. These difficulties may be the result of lack of information, poor communication, reluctance to change, or one of many other human issues. Figure 6-1 outlines some of the challenges one might encounter during the implementation process.

Making knowledge management work requires the right cultural conditions to be present. These include leadership that demonstrates commitment to the initiative and sanctions structural supports for it; organization structures that facilitate shar-

Implementation Guidelines	Implementation Challenges
• Guide activities by clearly defined business need; link human performance to corporate vision	• Maintaining the highest value, e.e., discouraging dilution of repository content
• Start small and test thoroughly	• Belief that knowledge management is an all-or-nothing initiative
• Focus on speed, specificity, and relevance	• Information overload caused by lack of focus
• Leverage existing knowledge, experience, and capacities	• Specialists who fear knowledge sharing will reduce their value
• Recognize contributors through reward and recognition; encourage and nurture teamwork	• Culture that favors knowledge ownership instead of knowledge sharing
• Build on what you know and what you learn	• Employees and their knowledge constantly moving in and out of the organization
• Monitor, revise, and leverage best practices	• Need for constant renewal—may not be the "best" anymore
• Work across silos; knowledge benefits everyone in the organization	• Subject matter expertise needed to be an effective content filter
• Discover innovative ways to empower people; set up structures that encourage trust and sharing	• "Command and control" style of management
• Create an environment that sustains and nourishes ingenuity	• Tight focus on structured process with little or no room for innovation

Figure 6-1—Implementation Guidelines and Challenges

ing, collaboration, teamwork, and creativity; and recognition and reward systems that actively promote knowledge sharing and contributions to, and use of, the organization's knowledge resources.

Finally, to make knowledge management work, there needs to be an acknowledgement of certain special roles within the collective responsibility of all employees. A variety of these are evolving as knowledge management programs take shape in a wide range of organizations. All the special roles for knowledge management somehow involve a notion of **stewardship of intellectual resources.** Everyone has a particular role to play according to his or her strengths and inclinations.

Select a Team and Make a Plan

An **implementation team** should be put in place at an early point in the initiative to move the implementation process along and make sure that it proceeds smoothly. The team can include an executive sponsor, the team leader, subject matter experts, business unit heads, architects, and technical experts. It must include, however, representation from a cross-section of the user community. Without them, the initiative can easily fail very early. They can best represent their own interests and provide feedback on such things as functional characteristics of the infrastructure or the kinds of activities or approaches that would be most well received by their colleagues.

The project manager should have a successful track record managing similar high-profile projects with high cultural challenge or projects that are cross-functional. Finally, it is important to maintain some continuity in the team's composition, difficult as this may be with busy people.

Any sensible implementation will be measured and progressive. It will proceed in a series of steps, since everything cannot be done at once anyway. More than that, however, the steps will unfold as part of a strategic implementation plan, designed to satisfy the objectives set for the knowledge management strategy. Thus, this practical phase of putting elements in place should begin with pilot projects that deliver sustainable, repeatable, and measurable results. Advice to knowledge management implementers: *Start small and let momentum and demand drive growth, or risk having the initiative collapse under its own weight.* For all these reasons, it is recommended that the steps be outlined in a plan, so the team can proceed clearly.

A community of practice or interest is an ideal place to begin implementation because the members already share a common interest and engage in similar work practices—so there is an obvious benefit from sharing knowledge. As Michael Zack, associate professor, Management Science Group at Northeastern University College of Business, points out, when communicators have a common work purpose the focus of the communication is more likely to be explicit, factual knowledge. This does not require heavy interaction and can be supported by relatively lean technologies, such as e-mail, computer conferencing, and shared repositories. Conversely, sharing tacit knowledge across different knowledge communities involves highly expressive interaction and requires technology that is more robust and sophisticated to support it.[1]

It is appropriate, and easiest, to focus on capturing explicit knowledge first, with the objective of making it widely available. Electronic publishing is possibly the least complex knowledge-sharing application. It represents one-way distribution of explicit knowledge, which is then referenced and applied in day-to-day activities. The subject matter is often of interest to a wide variety of workers (not necessarily in the same community of interest) and rarely requires interaction between users—for example, a policy and procedures manual. Although this is a practical and easy way to start, the effort should not stop here, or even drift along in a comfortable way at this level. It may be convenient for workers to find explicit information as a result of this early stage of the initiative, but the real benefits of knowledge management accrue at later stages of implementation.

The implementation plan subscribes to similar principles as the project plan (see Chapter 3). It should have clearly defined deliverables, milestones, accountabilities, and timeframes. The complexity of the implementation plan will depend on the level to which new technology is being implemented. A balanced approach is needed for managing the technology installation and managing the cultural changes that knowledge management and new technology together will demand.

In all ways, the implementation plan must reflect a balanced approach to every aspect of the implementation: people, processes, and technology. This is important because it is the implementation process that converts strategy into actions; educates the organization on changing roles and responsibilities; initiates the execution of new procedures and processes; and facilitates the adoption and integration of new technology.

Figure 6-2 provides a summary of the major activities that might be included in the technical system implementation plan, as part of a knowledge management initiative.[2]

Technical System Implementation

The main objectives of the technical implementation in this phase are to:

- Finalize any elements required for implementation
- Confirm that the objectives have been achieved
- Train the appropriate personnel
- Obtain final approval from all participants
- Ensure that the new system is successfully put into production

The major deliverables of the implementation phase are:

Objectives	Description
• Implement an operational system. • Provide support for users/ operating personnel.	• Conduct acceptance tests. • Train users. • Install production environment. • Put system into production.

Activities	Goals
1. Conduct user acceptance tests.	1. Have users validate the acceptability of the system.
2. Conduct technical acceptance tests.	2. Ensure that the system meets technical quality and operability criteria.
3. Review the implementation, conversion, and contingency plans.	3. Revise the plans based on the acceptance test results.
4. Conduct user training.	4. Give users the knowledge they need to use the system effectively.
5. Conduct operations staff training.	5. Provide operating staff with the knowledge they need to operate and maintain the system.
6. Ensure organizational readiness.	6. Ensure that organizational changes are in place.
7. Install the production environment.	7. Ensure that the requisite technical production environment is in place.
8. Convert existing knowledge to new system as needed.	8. Develop a foundation knowledge base.
9. Prepare system maintenance strategy.	9. Implement maintenance processes that support continuous repopulation of the knowledge repository.
10. Implement the new system.	10. Put the system into production and make necessary adjustments.

Figure 6-2—Summary of Major Technical Implementation Activities

- **Organization.** Established organizational environment; trained users; trained operating staff; maintenance plan; contingency plan

- **Processing and Information.** Test results; system documentation; converted data and loaded databases; implemented system

- **Technology.** Operational production environment

As indicated, a number of key activities need to be undertaken to satisfy these deliverables.

CONDUCT ACCEPTANCE TESTS

No new technological infrastructure will be used well, or even used at all, if users find it onerous to operate or do not like the way it works. Before a system is implemented, therefore, it needs to be tested for its acceptability to users. Users can verify whether it will satisfy their needs and expectations. In some cases, this activity is a confirmation of usability or functionality tests that were conducted at the earlier stage of designing the technology infrastructure. As a way of providing some structure to the testing process, users are requested, at this point as well, to prepare testing scenarios, using situations that are representative of what the system can be expected to support. Also at this point, the new system's workability in relation to existing systems can be checked.

In much the same way, technical acceptance testing allows information technology (IT) staff to validate the quality of the technical aspects of the system, such as performance reliability and recovery. To do so, IT staff generally prepare test scripts that represent certain working scenarios such as those tested for user acceptance. The system's performance will be measured against these scripts.

REVIEW AND APPROVE IMPLEMENTATION PLANS

All plans should be reviewed against the results of the acceptance tests to ensure that implementation continues to proceed smoothly. Delay may occur while adjustments are made, or the order of implementing certain elements may be changed. Some alternatives may have to be considered in anticipation of some implementation challenges. The important thing is to know what changes need to be made, know what the risks are, and mitigate the impacts.

When the bumps in the road are known, and plans have been adjusted accordingly, approval to proceed is needed from management. All adjusted budgetary, timing, and organizational issues should be identified in the plan submitted for approval. This represents the final "sign off" prior to putting the system into production.

CONDUCT TRAINING

There should not be much need for training in a formal sense. With each new iteration, applications have become more "intuitive," that is, programs that reasonably competent people can learn to use on their own. Much online help and performance support may already have been built into the knowledge base system, making it easier for users to get help in operating the system, and also in finding information they need to do their work. Performance support technology enables employees to immediately access databases, learning resources, and productivity-enhancing software tools. Gloria Gery, the doyenne of the performance support movement, calls it "the reapplication of all resources now spent on training, documentation, help desks, and peer support."[3] Other parts of the framework for real-time learning include interactive multimedia, groupware, networks, and telelearning technology.

Study after study has shown that people learn most productively by doing. What they need to know, therefore, should be accessible at the point and the moment of need—that is, *online.*

Also, any "training" on the new system would be most productively constructed around "doing" a number of situations the users need to do or would likely encounter in a normal workday, and for which they could effectively use the new system. How-to-do scenarios and stories would help learning. This is the world of real-time learning—when you need it.

So, systems training, if any, should be brief. More appropriate, perhaps, in a knowledge environment, are sessions on how various functions in the new system contribute to enhancing the access and use of knowledge in the organization, and its importance to the firm and the individuals in it. People need to know that what they know is valuable and how and with whom to share knowledge. Coaching and support are the methods of choice here. Such face-to-face sessions are not really training, but rather, more accurately, relationship building or strategic skill development sessions. Network interactivity may be too impersonal for certain development or motivational efforts.

> **ImplemenTip: Be empathetic to employees' sensitivities by asking,**
> - **How comfortable are the users with the system?**
> - **What do users expect from new systems?**
> - **What do users know (now) and need to know to handle new information/ processes?**

SYSTEM INSTALLATION AND MAINTENANCE STRATEGY

A fully operational production environment means the system is ready for use. All hardware and software are in place, and are functioning faultlessly; upgrades, if any, have been completed; backup procedures and recovery mechanisms are established and working; and data conversion has been done.

A successful knowledge management environment needs the continuing support of a well-functioning technological infrastructure to facilitate the real-time acquisition, exchange, and generation of knowledge. At the very least, the system should not be allowed to fail; the people, of course, need constant attention. For this reason, a **system maintenance strategy** is essential, and should:

- Outline the roles and responsibilities of the maintenance team

- Define procedures for processing system modification requests (some organizations use a system user resource group to help set priorities for requests)

- Identify functions that would be interesting to consider for later development

- Define management metrics for systems performance and use (with users and IT group)

Cultural Transition

Early in the evolution of the knowledge management "movement," it was recognized that lack of attention to the cultural aspects of a knowledge management initiative would doom it to failure. People, processes, and technology were like a three-legged stool supporting learning organizations and robust businesses. Processes had to be in place to encourage people to move knowledge around, and people needed to be motivated to do so. Technology was ever there, the clever servant waiting for instructions.

Maria Andresino, a marketing consultant, remarked in the mid-1990s that successful performance-support solutions come when there are both management structures and employee attitudes to support change and encourage performance. "When you put this great technology in place but you haven't spent any time dealing with the people, dealing with their attitudes and beliefs, or putting the structures in place that will support this—that's when [it] fails."[4] Cultural transitions that enable knowledge management are similar: they need to happen in processes to handle knowledge (create, transmit, generate), and in people themselves.

ORGANIZATIONAL ENABLERS

An organization cannot actually manage knowledge in the sense that other activities can be managed; knowledge creation/capture/transfer is not amenable, as an activity, to general management tasks such as issue analysis and resource deployment. But the company can provide workers with a knowledge-friendly environment. How exactly is that done? Not just with a prominently displayed plaque listing company values. Not with a reward system based on functional cost centers competing with each other for the best gross/net numbers. It is done with organizational structures and processes that enable and encourage sharing; it is done with coaching, mentoring, and putting resources into knowledge-managing roles. And it is very much a matter of people realizing and appreciating that the new knowledge management environment is actually making them more successful at what they do, and a matter of management rewarding those achievements and people's participation in the knowledge cycle.

In today's dynamic business environment, successful organizations are highly adaptive—they learn and act on what they learn rapidly and efficiently. This cannot be done if key issues have to be channeled to a single point for decision, and then the decision filtered through another hierarchy of authority. One way to resolve this sluggishness in decision making is to provide employees with access to the knowledge needed for making appropriate decisions on behalf of the organization. That accessibility involves various kinds of organizational instruments in the same way that financial transactions flow through certain institutional instruments and technologies.

A typically hierarchical "command and control" organizational culture is unlikely to have a workforce that can capitalize on its capabilities and act responsibly and autonomously. A "feudal" information and social environment is an unlikely and unwelcome home for a knowledge management initiative. Successful implementations need to focus on things like sharing, trust, nurturing, mentoring, and coaching—not on controlling. An initiative of such major and far-reaching proportions needs champions and good captains to steer it through rough waters.

A knowledge-friendly environment will have the following organizational attributes:

- **Policies** that encourage employees to use and contribute to the knowledge management system, according to their own learning styles
- **Procedures** that allow capable, responsible, autonomous individuals to use their knowledge
- **Processes** that enhance communication, collaboration, and creativity, allowing people to develop their own communities of interest
- **Management style** that allows employees to be comfortable with questioning what is done as well as the way things are done
- **Business processes** that incorporate and encourage the knowledge management process

ImplemenTip: Consider a special orientation program for developing innovation as a competency. Include topics such as: idea generation techniques; creative problem solving; overcoming obstacles; maximizing results; choosing and managing productive teams.

Some of the cultural needs are obvious, others less so. Regardless, it is important that organizations equip themselves to play in the knowledge market where people can get what they need, and can give others what they have.

Leadership. Leaders need to do two main things to ensure that knowledge management gets off to a good start and continues without faltering:

- They must put in place the organizational enablers that allow all members of an organization to be successful users and benefactors of knowledge management.

- They must demonstrate by example that sharing information and knowledge is valued by the organization and is without penalty (for example, loss of status).

Leaders cannot afford to be complacent about either of these obligations. If processes and reward structures and other resources are not available, people will not use knowledge effectively, or even at all. If management demonstrates a lack of commitment to the initiative—by not putting enough resources toward it, by not rewarding participation, by letting other short-term priorities override its interests—then people will quickly see through the superficiality. In addition to their vision of a more dynamic, innovative, and profitable organization, leaders need to have a great deal of energy and patience to keep the momentum of the initiative going; otherwise, their good efforts may be overcome, like many other great projects, by organizational inertia.

> **ImplemenTip: Make sure there are senior sponsors for the knowledge management initiative—sponsors who are able to secure support for it, make things happen, and continue to guide it over considerable time before handing the role on to a successor.**

Interdependence. A knowledge environment must support the use of knowledge. Knowledge can be considered to be knowledge precisely because it is actionable. People who can solve problems, take responsibility, and collaborate with other people are the ones who can use knowledge intelligently, in a targeted way, for the benefit of themselves and the business. An individual needs to have the right knowledge in order to be in a position to take responsibility for decisions and actions. Best practices (described in Chapter 1) are collections of lessons learned and proven solutions to known problems—therefore, they are reliable sources of knowledge.

Using knowledge is the exercise of power, certain kinds of power, different levels of power, but an activity of power nevertheless. The gridlock of failed knowledge exchange encountered by some organizations occurs when employees are not empowered to access knowledge as they need it and contribute or transfer it as they deem appropriate, and when management's need for control blocks avenues or stifles inclinations for knowledge transfer.

People have a need to hold on to their own know-how. They fear they will no longer be valued by the company after they

---

Real-Life File: Xerox a Leader in Leveraging Best Practices

"Perhaps the leading example of the success of this Process [leveraging internal best practices] is Rank Xerox, the European arm of Xerox Corporation. By relentlessly identifying and replicating internal best practices, the company has saved more than $1.5 billion over the past five years. It has experienced year-over-year, double-digit improvements in productivity by leveraging knowledge that already existed within its European operations. The program has been expanded to become a worldwide initiative for Xerox, and Rank Xerox has now begun identifying and replicating internal best practices on the revenue side of its business, anticipating similar dramatic gains. . . .

"Internal best practices are a practical means to begin capitalizing on the vast store of knowledge, skill, and experience of a large organization. It has proven to be the starting point for many companies' knowledge-management efforts, because it directly addresses the issue of paramount importance to line managers—results."[5]

178

have "given up" their know-how. They still have it, of course; they have simply relinquished exclusive use of it. They need reassurance that they are important for what they know, and particularly valued because they have shared this knowledge with the organization. They need to know that lighting another candle does not diminish an existing candle.

Managers also like to hold on to knowledge as a lever of influence and a measure of status. This has traditionally been the case, and young managers have taken their cues from those representing the past. This is no longer relevant. Managers who are leaders are encouraged and energized by the innovative energies of their employees, not threatened by them. They love the ideas that bubble up from the idea pool of such a workforce, as well as the fact that ideas are being generated regularly. If it can do so, the management team needs to refresh its perception with the notion that knowledge generation is the source of their business success and longevity.

A new covenant between employer and employee is needed to reassure both managers and workers that knowledge management activities in that organization are beneficial to both groups. This is true also for functional groups that have often distrusted other such groups, currying favor and support for their own interests to the exclusion of those of others. Everybody can help everybody else because all are subject to the same demands and deadlines. Knowledge management allows everyone to learn and to act faster and better. As Lewis Perelman, technology consultant and head of the Kanbrain Institute observes, "Time is precious. You have to act. The idea that you should prepare first and then act is vanishing. We are moving toward a work environment of real-time learning."[6] Creating and sustaining reciprocal trust in an organization is accomplished in small steps. As the value of sharing is made explicit and demonstrated, people can learn to trust each other, be more comfortable about sharing what they know, and see this as a way of working in businesses that prosper.

179

ImplemenTip: The organization has to demonstrate that it values sharing knowledge in the organization and will not tolerate resistance or reprisals. It can also set up channels or structures that encourage workers to put diverse views on the table or online, and to discuss and debate issues.

Reward and Recognition. Ideally, an organization's knowledge management system is so closely integrated with normal business functions and practices that using it effectively is no more effort for people than is doing their normal work. Most organizations fall short of this ideal, however, because their employees need to do more and do it faster. To record a summary of best practices used in a successful engagement in the knowledge base, for example, is extra work for an employee, however minimal. There need to be various kinds of incentives for employees to do this, at least at first.

To keep itself renewed for the future, an organization needs to recognize who has the knowledge that will make it successful in the long term, and to keep these people around. In today's business world, recognition includes not only money but also choice of work location or working hours, and corporate recognition of good ideas from today's knowledge worker. The last is becoming the most compelling for them: *explicit recognition of good ideas from which the company can benefit, and recognition of individual contributions to a team, a solution, a new product.* Effective knowledge management creates a smart workplace that will attract, reward, and retain the best workers.

Drucker has long espoused the theory that one cannot manage knowledge workers, one can only make them productive.[7] He contends that although knowledge workers are paid for their efforts, they are not "employees" per se; they are volunteers. Since they own the means of production—knowledge—they can move as quickly and as often as they wish. They can be attracted to stay if they: know what is expected of them; know their responsibilities and help set goals; provide valued input;

and can rise to become leaders. He suggests that because knowledge workers expect to be challenged, they be placed in positions that capitalize on their strengths, positions where they can be productive and successful.

> **ImplemenTip: Make demands on workers and give them responsibility. Make sure they keep learning. Develop and stretch goals. Let them shine and become better than they were yesterday.**

To confirm its support for the value of knowledge, the organization needs to make it easy for workers to see the advantages of stocking and using the knowledge base, and the disadvantages of not doing so. As Tom Davenport says, "If my knowledge is a valuable resource, why should I share it? If my job is to create knowledge, why should I put my job at risk by using yours instead of mine?"[8] Successful reward systems encourage lasting change, and knowledge management needs long-term sustainability to be successful.

There are several ways to do this: messages, performance reviews, rewards, metrics, and targets. Knowledge management fosters a culture of collaborative work in which both individual and team contributions are important. People need to know why they should share, work collaboratively, and use the knowledge base. Desirable behaviors need to be clearly articulated, communicated, and understood. Messages from management first of all make this clear to everyone, and second, reinforce the importance of collaborative activity for the organization.

It is becoming more common in organizations that have an established knowledge management operation to build into periodic performance reviews an assessment of the worker's contributions to and use of the knowledge base, both in terms of quantity and quality. There is in these organizations "a shift from measuring and rewarding the direct contributions of individuals to measuring and rewarding the individual's contribution to the performance of the team as a whole."[9] Firms are beginning to evaluate and reward employees for knowledge sharing and use.

Quantitative metrics can be used to track specific contributions to the knowledge base, along with an estimate of their value, based on the number of times the knowledge is used by others. "Lotus Development, . . . a division of IBM, devotes 25% of the total performance evaluation of its customer support workers to knowledge sharing. Buckman Laboratories recognizes its 100 top knowledge sharers with an annual conference at a resort."[10]

Real-Life File: Price Waterhouse Makes Sharing Personal

"Members of the consulting organization have an assessment of their contribution to and use of the knowledge base built into their performance reviews. Part of the assessment involves the use of quantitative metrics. For example, specific contributions are tracked and an indication of their value is captured by monitoring the number of requests for the information. Although revenue generation has certainly not been forgotten as a criterion, advancement in the firm now also depends on demonstrating knowledge contributions to the 'team' as a whole. In addition, alternate career paths are now available to contributors who may not excel at revenue generation or choose not to pursue partnership."[11]

Targets can be useful for encouraging participation in the organization's knowledge cycle. Nick Bontis, assistant professor of strategic management at the Michael G. DeGroote School of Business, McMaster University, suggests that as a requirement for evaluation purposes, each employee must aim to learn something that the organization currently does not know.[12] Also, an organization could require employees to target what their knowledge acquisition will be in the next period. It could be to learn a new skill, understand a new process, improve the design of a computerized report, or extensively study a competitor, channel, or product.[13] It could be that a team of employees decides what the targets are and then decides who should receive compensation for the best contribution, such as most relevant information or most used information.

ROLES AND RESPONSIBILITIES

If one can make knowledge workers more productive (rather than merely "managing" them), then it follows that various roles can encourage productivity by measures similar to those for any sports team. These are clearly defined roles for "players," as well as specially assigned resource personnel with clear responsibilities for facilitating players' success, like coaches, managers, trainers, and promoters. There is a place for knowledge owners, stewards, guardians, coaches, and players in the knowledge-intensive organization, but there is no place for information or knowledge hoarders, hiders, or blockers.

Most observers agree that new organizational roles are needed to support the knowledge management process. In the mid-1990s, Thomas Stewart, award-winning member of the Board of Editors of *Fortune* magazine and author of *Intellectual Capital: The New Wealth of Organizations*, saw a role emerging of **knowledge integrator**. "People who specialize in organizing a company's information, knowledge integrators, are part librarian, part entrepreneur, part social director who are also charged with persuading people to use the system and identifying topics that need to be represented and researched."[14] It's a big job, and there are roles for many kinds of integrators.

At present, however, there are few role models to emulate, and there is a great deal of uncertainty about the precise nature of the responsibilities. This situation is subject to all the same tensions and uncertainties of any ill-defined structure: people are uncertain and uneasy about what to do; other people try to carve out their own role; still others try to impose their views on the group. This can lead to difficulties, especially in the context of political unrest that often accompanies the breakdown of the "knowledge is power" culture.

Knowledge is different from information because it needs the insight and comprehension of human beings, who assimilate and process information to produce knowledge. Knowledge management needs the same insight and comprehension to work, so it can be considered mainly a cultural undertaking.

Because it must be pervasive in an organization's culture, it can be said that, ultimately, knowledge management is really everybody's job. "The most successful organizations will be those in which knowledge management is part of everyone's job," observe Davenport and Prusak in *Working Knowledge*. "Knowledge management will not succeed . . . if it is solely the responsibility of a staff group, no matter how large or small. Ultimately, managers and workers who do other things for a living (designing and engineering, manufacturing, selling, marketing, providing service to the customers) must do the bulk of the day-to-day KM activities."[15] Managers, in their day-to day roles, are also responsible for driving the processes required. Accountability for performance—good, bad, or knowledge enabling—rests with operating managers. They make sure that everyone is focused on the goals of the knowledge management process and understand its importance to the company's performance and its success.

Knowledge management cannot be left to everyone in general to make it work, however. Special responsibilities need to be undertaken to keep the knowledge management processes working and their substance relevant and useful; these are quality-control, custodial, and coordinating roles. These need to be identified, together with the accompanying accountability for their execution, throughout all phases of the knowledge management life cycle. If this is not done, knowledge management will not get done. No one will be responsible for anything, but everybody will expect somebody to do it.

The knowledge culture is characterized by the natural flow of knowledge and is therefore not amenable to prescription or edict. In any value-laden commercial interaction, there are various necessary roles—promoters, makers, brokers, traders, sellers, buyers, owners, evaluators, and regulators. In the knowledge marketplace, the same applies. People will fulfill roles most suitable to their place in the market, or their skills, or their motivations. Roles will emerge and need to be filled according to the organization's business needs, its structure, and its model for workability.

The next few sections discuss some suggested knowledge-related positions and responsibilities. Each can be customized to the needs of a particular organization. There could be different titles for essentially the same role, or there could be variations on a role with the same title. More will likely evolve as experience is gained with knowledge management implementations, and will vary according to different needs and corporate cultures.

Chief Knowledge Officer. With the knowledge age, the business community is looking for leadership that can extract value from vast storehouses of information now available to everyone as a result of galloping technological innovations. This role is commonly called chief knowledge officer (CKO). The CKO has a big job; he or she "articulates and champions the knowledge management vision, proactively leads the enterprise to implement and sustain knowledge management, and is the ultimate role model for knowledge users, creators and sharers."[16] The cardinal skill set of this individual includes business acumen, enterprise, human leadership, cross-functional experience, an ability to synthesize disparate information into a workable vision, and the people skills to forge coalitions among the company's many information communities.

Sometimes this role is called chief learning officer (CLO). Anthony Rucci, chief administrative officer of Sears, is responsible for Sears becoming a learning organization, but he is not called the CKO or the CLO. "I don't like that title," he says of CLO, "because it suggests the opposite of what we want, that learning will emanate out of one executive's office. The learning function is about giving people the information they need to have an enlightened opinion about how to do their job better."[17]

The CKO can come from any part of the organization that champions knowledge and promotes the organization's strategic interests: management (executive or operational), strategic planning, research and development, human resources, office of best practices, corporate learning centers, or, as is often the case because of familiarity with technology, information systems. Based on the results of Gartner Group research,[18] Figure 6-3 outlines a typical CKO position.

Chief Information Officer. By this time, most organizations have a chief information officer (CIO) who is the caretaker of an organization's business information and the systems in place to support its processing. If a knowledge management initiative is undertaken, this person is likely to lead the knowledge architecture team and help to make sense of scattered, heterogeneous technology systems. Under the CIO's direction, the information technology manager is usually the one who "implements and oversees the information technology that supports the knowledge architecture."[19] The precise nature of this responsibility will differ in each organization.

The CIO is responsible for implementing the technology infrastructure recommendations of the knowledge management project team. That includes such things as access control levels, business results reporting, user preferences, and system production levels.

Knowledge Broker. In the knowledge marketplace, there is ample opportunity for individuals to act as matchmakers or brokers for a transaction involving knowledge. Librarians evolved into "information brokers" in the late 1980s and have long considered themselves to be playing such a role. A **knowledge broker** can be considered a single-transaction kind of role, rather than one that is part of a longer term relationship, although that certainly may develop. According to Gartner Group, "The knowledge broker is a deal maker who links buy-

CKO Roles and Responsibilities

The chief knowledge officer (CKO) is the primary advocate for implementing knowledge management as an organizational discipline and is instrumental in supporting senior management in its efforts to build and sustain a knowledge-based enterprise. The CKO assumes the following responsibilities:

- Leads the development of an enterprise-wide knowledge strategy, ensuring that it:
  - reflects and supports the organization's business goals and objectives
  - capitalizes on existing data and information
- Develops the timetable for knowledge strategy implementation and rollout across the organization, ensuring that:
  - knowledge management is integrated into everyday processes and job activities
  - processes are designed to encourage participation in and contribution to the knowledge management program
- Secures funding for the implementation of the knowledge management strategy
- Guides the implementation of the knowledge strategy, ensuring that:
  - all aspects of the knowledge life cycle are addressed
  - the benefits of sharing knowledge are clear to everyone
  - operating processes reflect the need for participation
  - appropriate security, use, and maintenance policies are in place
- Directs the design, development, and implementation of a supporting technological infrastructure
- Monitors knowledge management trends, networking with other CKOs, tools vendors, and consultants, recommending changes to the knowledge management strategy as appropriate
- Enhances the organization's external image by assuming a leadership role in the knowledge management community at large

Figure 6-3—CKO Roles and Responsibilities

ers and sellers (who may play those roles literally, as in a transaction for money, or figuratively, as in an internal service-oriented transaction) by ascertaining buyer needs, locating the suppliers, facilitating the transfer of knowledge from supplier to buyer, and collecting a fee for the service. The broker may add little value to the knowledge 'product'; the broker's main way of adding value is by making a more efficient market for buyers and sellers.[20]

Real-Life File: Teltech's Business Booms by Brokering Knowledge

"Teltech was founded on the assumption that people are effective guides to information and knowledge. Expert, database, and vendor searches are all mediated through the Teltech knowledge analyst. While clients are entitled to search through Teltech's expert database themselves, most do not choose to do so. . . . Most clients who call Teltech have not perfectly articulated their information need. It is only through the dialogue with the knowledge analyst that the connection between the true information need and the available sources really emerges. . . . Teltech's people aid its clients in defining what information is desired, clarifying concepts and terms, interpreting search results, and knowing when and where to seek further information. Such tasks are unlikely to be the province of machines in our lifetime."[21]

Knowledge Content Specialists. **Knowledge content specialists** are guardians of the quality of the content of the knowledge base. Because each is very familiar with a particular knowledge domain or subject area, these people act as commentators who rate the value of offerings to the knowledge base. This quality control is based on agreed-upon criteria in a given domain. They also ensure the utility of contributions by eliminating any that fall short of users' needs and standards. This role can be played by subject matter experts, leaders of communities of interest, or managers in particular knowledge domains. For a complex knowledge base, many such specialists will be required to maintain content integrity. As everyone knows, if the content is of poor quality, irrelevant, or outdated, there will be no audience, no contributions, and no success.

Real-Life File: Industry Giants Need Clear Roles and Content Watchdogs

Chrysler developed an *Engineering Book of Knowledge* on Lotus Notes to reuse automotive design engineering knowledge across its major divisions. (See Chapter 4.) The process of knowledge development, review, and reuse was made user-friendly by establishing "technology clubs" for content areas such as electrical, interior, chassis, and scientific labs. Participants in the clubs had distinct roles and responsibilities.

In a pyramid of responsibilities, there is Reader at the lowest level; then in ascending order, Book Author; Book Owner; Technology Club Coordinator, and Executive Level for Technology Club. (These responsibility levels generally correspond to access levels on Notes.) The user-friendly book metaphor for organizing knowledge also helped to structure roles.[22]

Knowledge Stewards. In a knowledge-intensive business that has a knowledge-friendly environment in which knowledge resources are systematically and effectively used, exploited, leveraged, and acted upon for business benefit, the notion of stewardship of resources is a natural one. In an environment that encourages collaboration, learning, and creativity, not much can be compelled or dictated. However, the participants in this knowledge cycle can be motivated to take care of the resources on which they draw and to which they contribute. If the culture supports and rewards knowledge sharing, members will recognize the win-win proposition of cultivating healthy intellectual resources.

Organizations are calling this role **knowledge steward** or knowledge integrator, in recognition of the need for maintaining the integrity and richness of the knowledge holdings. Stewards have a more constant role than other players do, rather like the role of curators. They are responsible for reviewing and culling the knowledge base on an ongoing basis, for ensuring that the knowledge is current and accurate, and for maintaining the overall organization of the knowledge base—in conjunction with fellow stewards.

Real-Life File: Consulting Giants Need K-Stewards

"Andersen Consulting understood that in order to make its knowledge repository useful and keep it fresh, it would have to be more than a dumping ground of documents. Instead of looking like somebody's attic, it needed to look like a library—complete with librarians. Andersen spelled out specific job requirements for knowledge professionals. These employees are subject matter experts who cull through documents to ensure quality, relevance and currency. They make sure that documents are appropriately categorized and summarized. They make particularly worthwhile 'gems' easy to find, and eliminate redundant or obsolete content. In this way, Andersen ensures that the company's most relevant and current knowledge is not only captured, but reused. Andersen has dubbed this role knowledge integrator, which is also referred to as a knowledge steward in some knowledge management literature."[23]

Librarians. "Librarians are in a position to observe trends [in knowledge being sought] and are actual seekers of knowledge; they are well positioned to facilitate human connections between individuals pursuing similar interests separately.[24] **Librarians** are like matchmakers: they have no particular attachment to the transactions they facilitate except their pride in making the match well. In the business of connecting people with information, librarians are in a pivotal position in this age of information overload, digital resources, and networked intelligence.

Responsibilities are changing for librarians, as their roles expand towards a digital universe of connected meaning, especially in knowledge management environments, and as better and more interesting ways appear to perform their roles. The term "cybrarian" has been used since the late 1980s, and is increasingly being used to reflect the changing role of the traditional librarian in a digitized, networked information environment. Librarians can easily take advantage of their information-organizing skills to become the stewards of intranet- and Internet-based knowledge. They are the "door" to externally based knowledge, and they bring valuable resources into the organization or to the attention of its members.

This changing role concerns librarians themselves, as they strive to meet the challenges of their profession. The Special Libraries Association responded recently with a Special Committee on Competencies for Special Librarians. In the Association's outline of professional competencies, the special librarian:

- Has expert knowledge of the content of information resources, including the ability to critically evaluate and filter them

- Has specialized subject knowledge appropriate to the business of the organization or client

- Develops and manages convenient, accessible, and cost-effective information services that are aligned with the strategic directions of the organization

- Provides excellent instruction and support for library and information service users

- Assesses information needs and designs, and markets value-added information services and products to meet identified needs

- Uses appropriate information technology to acquire, organize, and disseminate information

- Uses appropriate business and management approaches to communicate the importance of information services to senior management

- Develops specialized information products for use inside or outside the organization or by individual clients

- Evaluates the outcomes of information use and conducts research related to the solution of information management problems

- Continually improves information services in response to changing needs[25]

The key differentiators of librarians from other kinds of "brokering" roles are the librarians' special contribution of value to the corporate client. This includes the points highlighted above: critical evaluation and value-added services. Another aspect of the librarian role is that librarians who tend to work on the information users' behalf over an extended period of time develop a relationship with them. Librarians, according to one observer, were the first "push technology."

Records Manager. According to William Saffady, professor of information management at Long Island University and respected authority on records management,

> Records and recordkeeping systems are valuable knowledge resources. Recorded information, whether in human-readable or electronic form, is an important embodiment of an organization's knowledge and intellectual capital. It is the principal manifestation of explicit knowledge, which is externalized in documents and data repositories. An organization's records document its strategies, intellectual property, products and services, business processes, customer knowledge, and competitive intelligence.... The explicit knowledge they contain remains available after employees depart.[26]

192

Records managers are in a unique position to make valuable contributions to their organization's knowledge management initiatives and the stewardship of its knowledge assets. They are poised at the edge of a new order, a new valuation of resources, a new mode of technological utility. They can help others make the transition without losing the supports needed for stability in both the historical and emerging contexts of corporate value. The Association of Records Managers and Administrators (ARMA) reflects the records managers' interest in this area in its mission statement:

> The mission of ARMA International is to provide education, research, and networking opportunities to information professionals, to enable them to use their skills and experience to leverage the value of records, information, and knowledge as corporate assets and as contributors to organizational success.

As the custodians of all that an organization values about itself, its way of doing business, its strengths, and its performance, records managers keep safe what is needed for minimizing risk and meeting outside legal and regulatory requirements. The question of what constitutes a record today is a fascinating challenge. According to Gartner Group, "In the most general terms, a record is any information-bearing media generated or received by an organization. This includes documents, spreadsheets, images, Web pages and e-mail. Records management involves the systematic organization and managed storage of these diverse information sources through the end of their life cycles. While many organizations have records management, most have barely addressed the issue of managing diverse record types."[27] It is an interesting challenge for records managers in a knowledge management world. Some interesting niches exist if records managers choose to occupy them. Following are some ways records managers can enlarge their role to play an important facilitating part in the emergence and development of knowledge management environments in businesses everywhere.

Contribute Foundation Information for Knowledge Management. There is a fundamental connection between a knowledge inventory, required to identify knowledge resources in order to determine their characteristics and value, and the holdings of records management, which inventories explicit knowledge resources for different reasons. Since explicit knowledge is documented as recorded information (in the records), both records and knowledge management activities encompass databases, paper files, library materials, microform collections, and other electronic and nonelectronic sources. These records can form a starting point for developing a knowledge inventory or knowledge base. Records management can be "a way to exploit the corporate knowledge contained in a records management repository," and it "should be incorporated into KM strategic planning as an interface to applications that support KM."[28] In the course of the development of a knowledge base, records managers can help to remedy gaps in explicit knowledge by improved documentation practices and better retrieval or distribution methods. Information organization skills map extremely well to the knowledge steward role.

Expand Guidance on Legal Implications. The records manager has traditionally been a kind of risk manager, with record holdings reducing risk for the corporation. The knowledge base (or repository, or warehouse) may contain duplicates of official records. It may also contain discussion databases, frequently asked questions and answers, and insights that provide competitive advantage (competitive intelligence) that appear nowhere else. In the event of litigation, where do these fall in the records management program? Records managers may now be called on to find answers to proprietary issues regarding questions of intellectual property. This will be interesting since there are few answers yet.

Co-evolve Corporate Policies on Knowledge Assets. The records manager and knowledge managers or stewards need to define corporate polices that reflect the changing views of the use and value of the knowledge assets. This is a transition-facilitating role that maps the value of information to the value of knowledge. Some murky issues must be addressed by the records manager:

- Is the context in which a decision was made considered part of the record? What about the circumstantial variations in repetitive implementations?
- If something in the knowledge base has infinite value in the knowledge context, how does this affect retention of the official record? Which is the dominant retention period: the records management date or the knowledge management date?

Facilitate Shift from Paper to Electronic Records. Records managers can find an important role in managing and facilitating the shift from paper to electronic records. They can help to translate the value of legacy systems into the new digital age. Records managers can also take advantage of this shift by orienting their skills more to the electronic management of information and knowledge.

Alert Company to Value from Intellectual Property. Astute knowledge managers, from whatever part of the organization, will be interested in extracting maximum value from intellectual property, since knowledge is embodied in patents, trademarks, copyrights, proprietary technologies, and trade secrets. Astute records managers can similarly be alert for opportunities to gain value from selling or licensing these assets. For example, older patents or proprietary technologies may be overlooked or forgotten, despite continuing value. Also, they can identify reuse opportunities for new knowledge products or services.

Track Records from Other Systems. When the knowledge management initiative is in the process of developing a knowledge inventory, the records manager can assist the effort by pointing out useful relationships between various entities of explicit knowledge. If there is a good records management program, particularly if it is supported by current records management software, there will be little need to replace or rebuild explicit knowledge maps.

In all these ways, records managers can facilitate the development of knowledge management in an organization. If they are observant of the dynamics around them as companies move to knowledge-based business processes and objectives, they can find ways to contribute to the challenges of an ever more complex work environment. As Saffady advises, prepare yourself; get involved (in knowledge management activities in your workplace); learn about enabling technologies; and do your job, because "if a records management program is intelligently conceived and systematically implemented, knowledge management initiatives will benefit."[29] Knowledge stewardship is becoming a core competency of leading-edge organizations, and the knowledge steward a vital player in its strategic considerations.

Conclusion

There are two main tasks to accomplish in the final, implementation phase of establishing a knowledge management environment: put the technological support systems into production; and ensure that the organization has adopted the practices of a working knowledge environment. The first task is relatively straightforward—system testing, installation, and maintenance. The other is the more challenging, but essential for the whole initiative. Knowledge management cannot work without the cultural attributes described here, nor, it seems, can businesses be successful without them.

In today's business environment it is important to be predictive as well as responsive. Leading-edge organizations promote information sharing, openness and trust, cooperation and collaboration, continual search for knowledge and truth, risk-taking, experimentation, and a respect for others' knowledge and expertise. All this is done for the sake of good business in a demanding business environment. Breakthrough ideas and those that can be leveraged for commercial benefit depend on creative thinking, which is nourished by a knowledge management environment. The strongest contributors to this process are an organization's most valuable assets. The challenge is encouraging them to participate.

There are many ways to encourage participation, not the least of which is a reward and recognition program that reflects the objectives established for knowledge management. Identifying special roles for knowledge capture, quality assurance, and maintenance is becoming a necessary part of making a knowledge environment a workable reality. Unless participation in knowledge cultivation, and all that it entails, is undertaken throughout the enterprise, this garden of great promise can languish in neglect.

The organization that encourages knowledge development and avails itself of the benefits of knowledge and experience can be considered a learning organization. The constant renewal of knowledge and the discourse that occurs naturally throughout the organization both contribute to the development of a learning space where employees and the organization can learn what they want, when they want, according to their own style. Organizations that encourage employees to work in teams will benefit from the development of knowledge through the natural team learning process.

Notes

1. Michael H. Zack, "Interactive and Communication Mode: Choice in Ongoing Management Groups," *Information Systems Research* 4, no. 3 (1993): 207-239.

2. LGS Group Inc., *Inspiration for Systems Development* (Montreal: LGS Group Inc., 1991).

3. Britton Manasco, "Enterprise-wide Learning: Corporate Knowledge Networks and the New Learning Imperative," *Knowledge Inc.* (1995), online, Available: http://www.webcom.com/quantera/ps95.html.

4. Ibid.

5. Richard Baumbusch, "Internal Best Practices: Turning Knowledge into Results," *Strategy & Leadership* (July/August 1997), 44.

6. Manasco, "Enterprise-wide Learning."

7. Peter F. Drucker, *Keynote Session*. (San Diego: 1998 International Knowledge Management Summit, June 1998, transcription).

8. Thomas H. Davenport, "Some Principles of Knowledge Management," *Knowledge Management Server* (1997), online, Available: http://www.bus.utexas.edu/kman/kmprin.htm.

9. V. Frick, "Obstacles to Knowledge Management," *Gartner Group Advisory Services* (23 January 1998), CD-ROM (Cambridge, MA: Gartner Group Inc., 1998).

10. Davenport, "Some Principles of Knowledge Management."

11. V. Frick, "Changing a Century-Old Business Culture," *Gartner Group Advisory Services* (21 July 1997), CD-ROM (Cambridge, MA: Gartner Group Inc., 1997).

12. Nick Bontis, "There's a Price on Your Head: Managing Intellectual Capital Strategically," *Business Quarterly* 60, no. 4 (Summer 1996), 40-47.

13. Ibid.

14. Thomas A. Stewart, "Mapping Corporate Brainpower," *Fortune*, 30 October 1995, 221.

15. Thomas Davenport and Larry Prusak, *Working Knowledge* (Boston: Harvard Business School Press, 1998).

16. K. Harris, "Chief Knowledge Officer: Managing Intellectual Assets," *Gartner Group Advisory Services* (20 March 1997), CD-ROM (Cambridge, MA: Gartner Group Inc., 1997).

17. Stratford Sherman, "Bringing Sears into the New World," *Fortune* (13 October 1997), online, Available: http://www.pathfinder.com/fortune.1997.971013/fro.html.

18. K. Harris, "Chief Knowledge Officer."

19. Ibid.

20. Richard Hunter, "Knowledge Management Case Studies," in *The Future of IT: Proceedings of Gartner Group Symposium/ITxpo97*,

Lake Buena Vista, Florida, 6-11 October 1997 (Stamford, CT: Gartner Group, 1997), 6.

21.   Thomas H. Davenport, "Teltech: The Business of Knowledge Management Case Study," *Knowledge Management Server* (30 March 1997), online, Available: http://www.bus.utexas.edu.kman/telcase.htm.

22.   J. Bair, "Knowledge Management Leverages Engineering at Chrysler," *Gartner Group Advisory Services* (23 April 1997), CD-ROM (Cambridge, MA: Gartner Group Inc., 1997).

23.   Lotus Institute, "Real World Insights," *Lotus, IBM and Knowledge Management Index*, White Paper, nd, online, Available: http://www.lotus.com/news/topstories.nsf.

24.   Hunter, "Knowledge Management Case Studies."

25.   Special Committee on Competencies for Special Librarians, "Competencies for Special Librarians of the 21st Century," *Special Libraries Association* (October 1996), online, Available: http://www.sla.org/professional/comp.html.

26.   William Saffady, *Knowledge Management: A Manager's Briefing* (Prairie Village, KS: ARMA International, 1998) 13.

27.   M. Gilbert and D. McCoy, "Records Management: Taking the Next Steps," *Gartner Group Advisory Services* (23 August 1998), CD-ROM (Cambridge, MA: Gartner Group Inc., 1998).

28.   Gilbert and McCoy, "Records Management."

29.   Saffady, *Knowledge Management*, 15.

7

The Next Few Years

*In this networked world . . . the future is
no longer a matter of destiny but of choice.*
—Derek DeKerkhove

Issues

- Why is it critical to invest in knowledge management today?

- What types of business change can be anticipated over the next few years?

- Can the cost of knowledge management really be justified?

While there is something magical involved in predicting what might occur before a major time-related event—a new year, a new century, a new decade—knowledge is expected to continue to be the most valuable asset an organization has long after the millennium excitement dies down. Therefore, this chapter is not limited to events that will occur in the next couple of years, but rather to those that are expected to happen during the next decade or so.

This concluding chapter recaps the key concepts presented earlier in the book and uses them as the basis for a vision of knowledge management over the next five to ten years. One of the most important aspects of knowledge management is ensuring that it is self-sustaining. Part of this is ensuring that the knowledge base is organic, allowing growth and change as the organization learns more about its capacity to generate knowledge and as its appreciation for the value of its knowledge assets increases. The underlying message is that successful knowledge management is the key to prosperity in a world where knowledge work is the largest component of the workforce and where people who can manipulate information and create new knowledge from it have the brightest future of all.

The approach of a new century is invigorating; it stimulates the desire for a new start, for renewal, and transformation. It encourages all of us to consider what the future might hold because that is the environment in which we expect to live and work. This contemplation of the future is fraught with uncertainty and simultaneously engenders an atmosphere of excitement, anticipation, fear, and anxiety.

Marilyn Norris, editor of *Strategy & Leadership* reminds us to be "optimistic about the possibilities of the future, sensing the natural pull within every living organism—from individual to organization—toward growth and development rather than disintegration and decay."[1] It is this positive attitude, coupled with a resurgence of appreciation for the value of knowledge, innovation, and human intellect, that will lead to individual, organizational, and possibly global prosperity.

Much change is to be expected as we proceed, and while the principle espoused in earlier chapters is that managing knowledge will help us to anticipate upcoming events, in reality, none should be so bold as to think that we can accurately predict the future. Nor should we fool ourselves into thinking that as new ways emerge, the old ways will immediately become irrelevant. Radically new ways of doing business will emerge as we are still struggling to perfect the current way of operation.

Challenges will occur as we face new organizational structures, new mandates, new demands, and new ideas. It is vital that we maintain a fresh—but pragmatic—approach to moving forward and be willing to accept that the past may not represent the ideal state for the future. Some of the issues, concerns, and potential impacts are discussed in this chapter.

The Changes

There is no doubt that we are participants in a period of significant change, one that has encouraged the search for new paradigms. We are grappling with changes over which we have no control: economies rise and fall, corporations succeed and fail, and stars ascend and just as quickly descend. Knowledge is a factor in all of these changes; perhaps knowing more would have helped, but certainly those who made the connections between discrete pieces of knowledge were better prepared to deal with the change.

ORGANIZATION

Charles Handy, renowned business thinker, author, and teacher, suggests that we would be wise to consider that the "organizations of the next century are going to be very different from the ones which we knew in this one . . . and . . . much of the past analysis and writing on the subject will be . . . wrong or irrelevant."[2] If we accept that this is true, then the challenge ahead of us is significant. There are no absolute role models and no blueprints for the organization of the future.

Organizations have already started to change. They are no longer the premises-based, physical entities we have known for many years. They are increasingly becoming virtual, intangible, interconnected workspaces and are unconstrained by time and place.

The result of these developments has been profound. Work and workers continue to evolve in these knowledge-based "nonstructures" and people, technology, and process co-exist in a sometimes-happy union. Financial institutions trade currency and commodities 24 hours a day through a linked chain of trading floors. Retailers sell goods to people around the world, again on a 24-hour basis, with little regard for local currency or taxation laws. The dominance of English as the language of business becomes increasingly apparent as the Internet assumes a more significant role. Technology has become a ubiquitous tool, part of almost everything we do.

The relationship between employer and employee is also changing. The flexibility afforded by technology will encourage an increase in telecommuting. It is no longer necessary for everyone to work from the same physical location, or at the same time. The disillusionment that follows downsizing will have a profound effect on traditional loyalties—no more jobs for life, no more employees for life. It is expected that the number of freelancers or contract employees will increase dramatically, moving from organization to organization as the need arises. As a result of these phenomena, there will be major changes in communication patterns, decision-making processes, and in how teams work together. Talking computers, voice-activated systems, intelligent agents, and other advances in technology will facilitate many of these activities.

As we try to deal with the external forces that are driving change, we will be trying to deal with many internal forces: retention of top performers; merging of work and pleasure; and cultural complexities, to name but a few. We can expect new organizational issues and ideas to surface as we try to deal with all of these and it will be difficult to maintain our equilibrium. If we assume that knowledge is a key asset and its management is a core process or competency, the success of the knowledge management initiative will have a profound effect on any success we can expect in managing these forces.

Sustainable Learning Communities. Knowledge-based organizations recognize the need for continuous learning, and knowledge workers readily accept the necessity for lifelong learning. Employees have an inherent desire and capacity to learn, and it is the organization's responsibility to provide an environment that encourages growth through the continuous generation and exchange of knowledge. This is very similar to the proposals suggested by Stephanie Pace Marshall in her paper, "Creating Sustainable Learning Communities for the Twenty-First Century," in which she describes why the school system of today is inappropriate for the needs of tomorrow.[3]

In this environment, learning is connected to real issues and involves the learners in the research and analysis needed to produce a solution. Knowledge is freely generated, used, and shared. The communities of learning are dynamic, adaptive, and are allowed to grow and change to accommodate differing needs.

Sustaining this type of learning environment so that it continues to generate knowledge depends on the organization's willingness to recognize the value of the process and its products. A sense of community will encourage the participants to continue their learning experience long after the training session is over. The knowledge-based organization will recognize the need to support this continuity as one of the links in the learning organization's chain of self-sustenance.

New Employment Contract. Peter Drucker's view that employees are really volunteers and that new ways of managing them are required was noted earlier. As we continue on the journey through the cultural transformation that is under way, this view becomes more and more critical.

The members of this "volunteer" community are primarily knowledge workers doing knowledge work in a knowledge-based organization. As such, they represent the principal assets of an organization and, if they leave, the organization's real value leaves with them. In an ironic way, therefore, the employees are the "owners" of the organization whether or not they have shares.

This leads directly to the need for a new covenant between employer and employee—a new employment contract. The workers will have different rights than today, and managers will likely play a different role. In a "member-owned" organization, the manager must lead by effective persuasion, as a coach or mentor, not by command or directive. The job of the manager will certainly be more difficult, but in many ways more legitimate.[4]

Self-Organizing Work Units. The unbounded nature of the organization will naturally lead to self-organizing virtual work units that are linked through technology. In such cases, a sense of community is developed through competency and common interest, rather than through title or function. When there is a shared sense of meaning and purpose, as well as a shared or common identity to provide cohesion and synergy, there is an increase in collective intelligence. This in turn helps to sustain the learning communities so important to success in the knowledge economy.

The relationship between these work units and knowledge is twofold. First of all, they are dependent on communication, information, and knowledge for survival. Only with these can the work unit undertake to support the decision-making process in a better, faster way. Second, since there is a common bond and shared intelligence, these work units are by nature collaborative and interactive. Consequently, they generate a significant amount of new knowledge through their communal development and testing of hypotheses.

BUSINESS ENVIRONMENT

The knowledge economy is still in its infancy and the opportunities it offers remain largely unexplored. This is expected to change dramatically as countries of varying industrial sophistication join the knowledge society. The ability to share and exchange knowledge based on a worldwide communications network reaches into every corner of the world. As the knowledge economy takes hold, the business environment becomes more expansive: the field becomes wider, the number of players increases, and the opportunity to score a goal increases dramatically.

Never before have we been able to do business around the clock, around the world. Never before have individual countries had so little control over their own economic well-being. Never before has the cost of entry into new markets been so low. These forces (plus many more "never befores") combine to cause a business environment that will be volatile, lacking equilibrium, and potentially unstable. This kind of environment demands **organizational adaptability**, if the organization's objective is long-term profitability and sustainable success. These objectives will be impossible to achieve without constantly refreshed knowledge and continuous innovation.

TECHNOLOGY

Collaborative technologies play a key role in capturing questions, responses, and ongoing discussions. Knowledge sharing comes from debate and interaction, and technology that supports online communities of interest (chat rooms, forums, multicasting) can make a valuable contribution to encouraging collaboration. Other technologies help move information around and make it accessible and reliable: workflow assists in codifying internal processes and document management technology improves access to vast repositories of digital information. Technology can also help to provide access to people and the tacit knowledge they hold. Systems that help to identify the best resource, human or otherwise, to solve a particular problem are part of the overall knowledge management environment.

One thing is certain when discussing technology: bigger, better, faster is always around the corner. Earlier technologies (for example, information retrieval, groupware, and GUIs) are being used as the foundation for the development of new technologies to support knowledge retrieval. But, from a knowledge management perspective, some key technological developments are on the horizon that will contribute to the development of a fully linked, dialogue-based, interactive enterprise as described in Chapter 5. Gartner Group portrays these advancements as the three legs of the knowledge management stool: semantic tools, collaborative extensions, and visualization interfaces.[5]

First, it is reasonable to expect that there will be increased use of neural networks to detect similar patterns in indexes or content and to identify documents that have similar meaning. This should result in much improved relevance performance. Second, better support for collaboration will result in much improved access to tacit knowledge and also in better ways to identify experts. Profiling and profile comparisons will group users of the knowledge base by common interest and make comparative assessments of expertise.

Third, technology will become increasingly visual. This will result in much improved user interfaces and in easy-to-interpret representations of content. Both of these should contribute to increased use of the knowledge base as well as an increased appreciation for the usefulness and value of its contents.

But, perhaps the most important technology issue is the tremendous advancement we need and expect in order to better support the knowledge economy. First and foremost, technology must continue to become increasingly intuitive, powerful, and mobile. No one has the time nor the inclination to sit for hours learning how to use a software tool; if technology is to be truly ubiquitous it must have sufficient intelligence to learn how each individual does his or her work, and what that person's preferences are. New technology needs to be powerful to support the use of visual representations, modeling and simulation tools, and for running multiple real-time collaboration sessions. Mobility needs technology that is small, wireless, portable, and usable wherever and whenever. Access to the knowledge repository must be available to everyone regardless of the time and location.

The Challenges

The challenges of implementing and sustaining the knowledge strategy are many, and have been covered extensively throughout this book. However, as our journey together comes to a close, it is worthwhile to recap what some of these challenges might be.

MOVING FROM CONCEPT TO REALITY

It is important to remember that organizations with a knowledge-oriented culture—those who reward idea generation, encourage new product ideas, and learn from experiences—will move quickly to incorporate knowledge management tools and techniques into their core processes. It is likely that these organizations profit from knowledge and depend on work that is "brain intensive." In this type of organization, once the knowledge strategy implementation has matured, intellectual assets will be considered as important as physical and financial assets for valuation purposes.

In other types of organizations, moving the knowledge strategy from concept to reality could be more difficult. Even though we understand what knowledge is, how it is developed, and the contribution it makes to our lives, it is difficult to articulate what it represents as a "hard" or tangible thing. Its benefits can be expressed in terms of "soft" attributes such as its contribution to tracking competitors; developing strategic plans; revealing insights about your industry; or tapping into employees' knowledge about the market, products, and competitors.

The urgency of moving the knowledge strategy to reality can be expressed only in terms of how it contributes to achievement of the organization's strategic goals and objectives and the competitive necessity of knowledge reuse. It is imperative that this be understood if knowledge management is to become a key business process and a core competency.

SUSTAINING KNOWLEDGE VALUE

The key to sustained appreciation for the knowledge strategy is continued knowledge creation. Without it, knowledge management has little lasting value. It is important to update the knowledge strategy as the business environment changes and to identify new content areas and new communities of interest that complement the changes.

Regularly monitoring the progress of the knowledge system is important for two reasons: to assess how the processes are working and to see how knowledge sharing and collaboration are developing. From a technology perspective, introducing new and increasingly sophisticated knowledge management tools as well as expanding the integration with existing (legacy) systems are important steps.

But perhaps the most important contributors to sustainability are identifying and making known the support that the knowledge strategy gives to mission and vision, and making certain that the knowledge in the repository is current, accurate, and relevant.

JUSTIFYING THE EXPENDITURE

Knowledge management itself is relatively low risk, since the extent of the risk is limited to the investment in knowledge management facilities and processes. However, it is not necessarily low cost. The costs of building and maintaining a knowledge management infrastructure can be much higher than the benefits of cost reduction.

Knowledge management is about revenue generation, not cost reduction. It is more easily justified in terms of its impact on time-to-market and quality (or value) and other leverage opportunities than it is on productivity. It is worth repeating the quotation by Thomas Stewart that appeared at the beginning of this book:

> *The benefits of preserving and organizing intellectual capital have not been quantified yet, but the sense is that millions of dollars can be saved and better work can be done as a result.*[6]

One may well think twice about the expense of implementing knowledge management, but unless consideration is given to the consequences (and cost) of not managing knowledge, then any conclusions are invalid. The cost of not responding to customers, or of answering their questions incorrectly, can be enormous. Decisions and actions based on inaccurate, out-of-date, or irrelevant information put the organization's future at risk. It is unwise to dismiss knowledge management as a passing fad without carefully thinking about the consequences and of the missed opportunities.

VALUING THE RESULTING ASSET

There has been much discussion regarding the use of innovative accounting techniques to value intangible assets, but the conclusion is always the same—it is difficult to translate corporate knowledge into corporate assets or bottom-line results. However, since we agree that knowledge is the organization's principle asset, then there must be ways to place a value on it.

All knowledge-based objects owned by the organization that will produce or contribute to a future stream of revenue (or other benefit) for the organization represent knowledge assets. Many of the knowledge assets are intangible—they have no physical form and no obvious financial value—and they are often difficult to identify. Knowledge management in itself is not the issue; the real issue is its contribution to the processes that contribute to the organization's bottom line. The value of knowledge management lies in our ability to think strategically, in a nonlinear and holistic way.

So, some models for measuring intangibles in business are emerging, developed by thinkers and businesspeople who are committed advocates of a new age. All use some model to categorize intellectual capital. Most use some variations in detail and terminology on the key categories of human, structural, and customer capital. The companies that use them have found success with them; these are primarily large multinationals that also have a knowledge management program. These models have all been implemented, tested, accepted by practitioners and commentators, and translated into actions in various corporate settings, but are not yet in wide use. The most significant of these intellectual capital measurement schemes are the following:[7]

- The Skandia Navigator was developed and is used by Skandia AFS, a Swedish financial services company. It tracks the organization's financial and intangible capital, and balances accounting ratios for follow-up and control with indicators for renewal and development. The Intangible Assets Monitor (developed by Karl Eric Sveiby) uses three categories of knowledge assets: competence, external structure (customer, suppliers), and internal structure (processes, systems, management, databases). Indicators in these categories are further classified according to whether they support stability, efficiency, or growth and renewal.

- Brothers Johan and Goren Roos developed the Intellectual Capital Index (IC Index) after extensive research. It addresses the strategic impact of changes in intellectual capital, identification

212

of the most important intellectual capital categories, and cross-comparisons over different business units and companies.

- The Inclusive Valuation Methodology (IVM) was developed by Prof. Philip M'Pherson of City University (U.K.). Like the Intellectual Capital Index, it has hierarchies of weighted indicators in combination and uses relative, but not absolute values.

Conclusion

What we have described in this book are the design and implementation of a knowledge management environment that supports collaboration and consensus in how conclusions are reached, solutions are identified, and problems are resolved. The process is made more difficult because the rules *and* the game continue to change. This book provides a foundation for the design and implementation of a knowledge management environment that will support your business through this period of radical change.

Managing knowledge in organizations will lead to a variety of new problems and issues. The serious pursuit of knowledge in organizations will be challenged, and its introduction will not be without resistance. We will continue to ask, "How can we place a value on knowledge management when it is still being defined?"

It will be necessary to continue to capitalize on current markets, operate in existing structures, and manage using today's reward and recognition systems, while beginning to exploit new markets, investigate new organizational models, and develop new reward and recognition systems. Moving too quickly is risky, but so is moving too slowly. The ability to capitalize on knowledge and experience will assist organizations to manage this shift and allow them to simultaneously focus on multiple vectors, some of which have been discussed in this chapter. The objective now is to tap the potential of the continuing revolution in information technology to support this knowledge imperative.

Notes

1. Marilyn W. Norris, "Editor's Page," *Strategy & Leadership* 26, no. 1 (January/February 1998).

2. Charles Handy, "Unimagined Futures," in *The Organization of the Future*, ed. Frances Hesselbein, Marshall Goldsmith and Richard Beckhard (San Francisco: Jossey-Bass, 1997), 377-384.

3. Stephanie Pace Marshall, "Creating Sustainable Learning Communities for the Twenty-First Century," in *The Organization of the Future*, ed. Frances Hesselbein, Marshall Goldsmith and Richard Beckhard (San Francisco: Jossey-Bass, 1997), 177-189.

4. Handy, "Unimagined Futures."

5. J. Bair, "Adoption Time Frame for Knowledge Retrieval Technologies," *Gartner Group Advisory Services* (12 January 1998), CD-ROM (Cambridge, MA: Gartner Group, Inc., 1998).

6. Thomas A. Stewart, "Mapping Corporate Brainpower," *Fortune*, 30 October 1995, 209-221.

7. Margaret Tanaszi and Jan Duffy, "Measuring Knowledge Assets in the Knowledge Economy," Draft Management Accounting Guideline (Hamilton, Ontario: The Society of Management Accountants, April 1999).

Appendix

Value Proposition for Senior Management	**Value Proposition for Middle Management**	**Value Proposition for Nonmanagement Employees**
Aggressive management of our knowledge capital will reduce the time ABC Company takes to develop new products by six months, without significant increases in overtime or massive restructuring. Capture and reuse of lessons learned support the redundancy needed to ensure accelerated product introduction, thus supporting our goal of sustained market leadership. The investment is estimated to be less than $600,000.	Aggressive management of our knowledge capital will reduce the time ABC Company takes to develop new products by six months, without significant increases in overtime or massive restructuring. Capture and reuse of lessons learned support the redundancy needed to ensure accelerated product introduction, thus supporting our goal of sustained market leadership. Strong employee commitment and an increased sense of identity with our vision and with the organization will reduce turnover and minimize dependence on contract staff.	Aggressive management of our knowledge capital will reduce the time ABC Company takes to develop new products by six months, without significant increases in overtime or massive restructuring. Employees will have increased involvement in the decision-making process and more opportunity for collaboration. Most importantly, employees will be rewarded for innovative reuse of existing knowledge and previous experiences. Capture and reuse of lessons learned support the redundancy needed to ensure accelerated product introduction, thus supporting our goal of sustained market leadership.

Figure 3-4—Sample Knowledge Management Value Propositions

Suggested Elements of the Communications Plan

- **Position statement.** The position statement consists of one or two succinct sentences that describe the business drivers providing the impetus for the knowledge management initiative. The vision forms the focal point of this section. This statement is the foundation of the entire communications plan.

- **Background description.** The background description acts as an introduction and explains why knowledge management is important and what it will accomplish. This section covers all of the "who, what, when, and why" addressed by the plan. The core of this section is the knowledge management value proposition. The context provided by this section ensures that the reader will be able to understand the rationale behind the communications plan.

- **Analysis of the initiative in the context of the organization.** This section identifies stakeholders, influencers, opinion leaders, and other groups affected by the impending introduction of knowledge management. It also provides insight into potential difficulties, concerns, and pitfalls.

- **Target audiences.** The plan identifies who the target audiences are for the communications plan. For all audiences, the communications plan addresses their unique characteristics, their relative importance, how best to reach them, and how best to persuade them. The messages contained in the knowledge management value proposition developed for each group are incorporated into this section to reflect these differences.

- **Objectives and goals of the plan.** The objectives and goals clearly articulate what the communications plan is going to achieve, that is, the objectives of the plan are to communicate the purpose, outcomes, and scope of the knowledge management initiative. The goal is a statement of the tangible results expected from the communications (for example, the degree of penetration of the message or the measurable level of buy-in to the change).

- **Communications strategy.** The strategy describes how the message will be communicated. Since knowledge management is a collaborative endeavor, one that demands trust and commitment, the communications strategy should reflect the same values. The choice of communications vehicle will depend on the audience, the potential level of resistance or lack of understanding, and

(continued)

Figure 3-6—Elements of a Communications Plan

how well the knowledge management advocate has laid the groundwork. Group discussion is a powerful tool that allows for interaction, exchange of ideas, and, most important, clarification of any gray areas. Each group, or even individual, may have different motivators and concerns, but in all instances, the best way to obtain support is to ask for input and provide information on a regular basis.

- **Schedule.** The schedule documents the timing and critical path of the communications roll-out and ensures that everyone receives the required messages before implementation actually begins.

Knowledge Management Readiness Assessment
TECHNOLOGY AND SYSTEMS ENVIRONMENT
**Rate your organization's readiness on a
scale of 1 (strongly disagree) to 7 (strongly agree)**

Conditions Responses	
1. Do most employees have a workstation with sufficient power to handle a full suite of collaborative desktop tools?	
2. Is the major portion of the organization networked (local and wide area)?	
3. Do the majority of users use the same type and version of software?	
4. Do all users have access to the Internet/WWW ?	
5. Do you know current uses and current users?	
6. Is an intranet installed and used?	
7. Do you know the intranet's usage volume and patterns?	
8. Is groupware installed and used?	
9. Is electronic document management technology installed and used?	
10. Is a functioning records management system installed and used?	
11. Is library management software installed and used?	
12. Does the organization have teleconferencing capability?	
13. Are the organization's major systems interconnected?	
14. What is the availability of intranet/Internet connectivity?	
15. Are there standards in place for information technology (IT) acquisition, operation, and maintenance?	
16. Is the current system adaptable to interfacing with new technologies?	

(continued)

Figure 3-7—Technology Readiness Assessment Checklist

Conditions Responses	
17. Does IT have a policy/procedure for introducing new infrastructure, e.g., a migration policy?	
18. Are there levels of access (security) in place on current systems?	
19. Is an inventory of hardware/software in use, and does it include locations?	
20. Are resources available for IT training/performance support?	

Knowledge Management Readiness Assessment
BUSINESS ENVIRONMENT
**Rate your organization's readiness on a
scale of 1 (strongly disagree) to 7 (strongly agree)**

Conditions Responses	
1. Does the organization routinely repeat mistakes?	
2. Does work often get duplicated?	
3. Are customer relations generally strained?	
4. Is the organization unable to keep up with market leaders?	
5. Is the organization dependent on key individuals for various mission-critical functions?	
6. Are good ideas hoarded by business units and not shared with other parts of the company?	
7. Is the organization slow to launch new products/services?	
8. Are employees suffering from information overload?	
9. Is there a constant requirement to do more with less?	
10. Are there limited opportunities, channels, and mechanisms to share knowledge?	
11. Does the company consider doing/acquiring market research a "nice to have" expense that it cannot afford?	
12. Does the company lack or have limited/poor business intelligence knowledge?	
13. Does each department lack a system to evaluate and track the successes and failures of its projects?	
14. Does the company consistently miss recognizing/tracking deficiencies and learning from them?	
15. Does the company respond only haphazardly (without a system in place) to customer complaints, suggestions, and requests?	

(continued)

Figure 3-8—Business Readiness Assessment Checklist

Conditions Responses	
16. Is there often no follow-up to customer contacts?	
17. Is there no accountability for who is going to do what about customer contacts?	
18. Does the organization establish priorities based on the latest crisis?	
19. Is the rest of the organization "in the dark" about management's business directions, however short term?	
20. Are shareholder interests only rarely considered?	

Knowledge Management Readiness Assessment
ORGANIZATIONAL ENVIRONMENT
Rate your organization's readiness on a scale of 1 (strongly disagree) to 7 (strongly agree)

Conditions Responses	
1. Does the company have "enterprise thinkers" (people with broad vision) supporting the knowledge management initiative?	
2. Are roles and responsibilities well defined?	
3. Are employees empowered to make decisions?	
4. Are employee decisions supported by information/knowledge and company policy?	
5. Is the company able to take advantage of the information/knowledge it owns?	
6. Are people in the company encouraged to be innovative?	
7. Is risk rewarded?	
8. Are employees rewarded on the basis of both individual and shared performance?	
9. Is the employee turnover rate relatively low, or at least stable?	
10. Does the organization chart reflect the actual power structure?	
11. Does the organizational structure enable appropriate and workable two-way communication channels?	
12. Does the organization communicate policies, procedures, and standards relatively effectively and in a timely fashion?	
13. Is management open to communication, suggestions, and concerns from employees?	

(continued)

Figure 3-9—Organizational Readiness Assessment Checklist

Conditions **Responses**	
14. Is there a workable method for maintaining continuity between corporate memory (no context), culture and values, and day-to-day knowledge demands?	
15. Is there a relatively constructive and methodical way to bring new employees up to speed quickly?	
16. Does the organization have a commitment to training, performance improvement, performance support, and human development, with budgeted resources for this purpose?	
17. Are business units or locations discouraged by policy and reward systems from operating as independent entities?	
18. Does the organization have procedures to mitigate stress from conditions of rapid growth or change?	
19. If new management processes and structures have been implemented, have these been introduced in accordance with change management principles?	
20. Is the organization a lively, interesting, fun place to work?	

One-Time Costs
(usually incurred once only,
often at the outset of the initiative)

- **Internal meetings or reporting.** It is difficult to assign a precise cost to staff participation in these important and time-consuming activities which could affect other critical activities.
- **External consultants.** Often used to support knowledge management initiatives, the extent and type of involvement will vary by enterprise. Consulting assistance can range from occasional expert facilitation and guidance to full-time on-site support from a team of people. The cost is dictated by time and expertise used.
- **Software acquisition and installation.** Specialized knowledge management tools are now starting to emerge. Typically, these offer sophisticated search and retrieval functions, hyperlinks to assist in organizing and synthesizing knowledge, and knowledge mapping tools. Standard office tools, such as document management software, groupware, and intranets may also be required.
- **Hardware and infrastructure upgrades.** Effective knowledge

Ongoing Costs
(incurred on an ongoing basis
as part of the knowledge
management function)

- **Conferences.** During the discovery phase of the project, early participants might benefit from attending knowledge management-related conferences and seminars. Continued participation in such events is advisable for developing awareness of best practices.
- **System administration.** The knowledge management environment, once in place, will need ongoing care and support. The system administrator is responsible for monitoring system usage, maintaining high running rate, ensuring connectivity, adding and removing users, and adjusting their access rights as required.
- **Categorization.** Rapid and easy access to the contents of the knowledge base is critical to success. Developing a schema for knowledge categorization, and categorizing new contributions to the knowledge base are key processes and involve ongoing time and effort on the part of knowledge stewards and subject matter experts.
- **Populating and maintaining knowledge.** The knowledge base

(continued)

Figure 4-1—One-time and Ongoing Costs

One-Time Costs

management needs good system response time and an effective communications network. This might mean installing a new server, putting more memory in desktop hardware, or even implementing a new electronic mail system. With the pace of change in hardware and software, this activity may creep onto the "ongoing" side of the ledger.

Ongoing Costs

needs to contain the kinds of information and knowledge that people need and use. It can include policies, procedures, client data, reports, meeting minutes, work engagement details, and product specifications. The knowledge content needs to be continually edited, packaged, and pruned, and will require significant effort on the part of subject matter experts, "new" records custodians and special librarians, and appropriate business unit workers. Information archiving and deletion and maintaining the knowledge map can be part of this responsibility.

- **Training and education.** Staff needs training in the use of new systems as well as in the creation, sharing, and use of knowledge. There will be an ongoing activity of teaching people to integrate knowledge management activities and system use into their day-to-day work.

Questionnaire on Information Used, Generated, and Needed

As you know, there is a concerted effort under way to assess and evaluate the knowledge management requirements for a highly successful customer service operation. Since it is important to determine what information is currently being used in this connection, would you please complete the following questionnaire and return it within five days? **All prompt responses will be rewarded with a video discount coupon.**

---

* Identify which of the following internal information repositories you use regularly in connection with your customer-service-related activities, and rank them [7 is high (good) and 1 is low (poor)]:

	Type of Information	Usefulness	Ease of Access	Frequency of Use
Documents Stored on the LAN Servers				
Documents Stored on Your Own Hard Drive				
Archives				
Electronic Discussion Databases				
Paper Records				
Financial Systems				
Customer Databases				
Data Warehouses or Data Marts				
Policy and Procedure Manuals				

(continued)

Figure 4-5—Sample Questionnaire on Information Used, Generated, and Needed

- Identify which of the following external information repositories you use regularly in connection with your customer-service-related activities, rank them [7 is high (good) and 1 is very low (poor)]:

	Type of Information	Usefulness	Ease of Access	Frequency of Use
World Wide Web				
Electronic News Feeds				
Magazines				
External Databases, e.g., Credit Records, Market Research Data				

- Are there information sources that would be useful to you but are unavailable? What would they allow you to do that you can't do today?

- Are there specific people in the organization that you go to for job-related information? If so, who are they and what types of questions do you ask them? What do you do if they are not available?

- Are there specific people in the organization who come to you for job-related information? If so, who are they and what types of questions do they ask you? What do they do if you're not available?

- What technologies do you use on a regular basis and for what are they used?

- Do you ever discover that several of you are working on very similar projects or trying to answer the same questions? What do you do in this situation?

- Do you have enough customer information available to you to satisfy the need for a high level of customer service? If not, what is missing? What would this allow you to do that you can't do today?

- What are the most frequently stated customer frustrations? What would help you to resolve them more easily or quickly?

Interview or Workshop Guideline

1. What is the most important thing for people to know about your job in order to understand what you do?

2. In your response to the Information Questionnaire, you indicated that you use certain types and sources of information on a regular basis. Please explain what makes this particular information valuable. What do you do with this information and what do you need to know in order to use it properly?

3. How does this information relate to activities depicted in the business process diagram? Do you need to use it in conjunction with other information?

4. What kinds of knowledge do you need from experts? How do you access this knowledge and how do you ensure that it is correct and current?

5. How complex is this knowledge? Does its complexity affect its utility? How important is the timeliness of this (kind of) knowledge?

6. Do you or others in the organization use unique critical- or creative-thinking processes that convert into value for the organization? Do you apply unique configurations and applications of assumptions, patterns, logic, and processes or other scientific techniques? What are they, who knows about them, and where are they recorded?

7. What specific activities of your work require insights gained from experience, e.g., forecasts, trends, lessons learned?

8. Can the knowledge you need/value be captured, transferred, and validated? Can it be made explicit?

9. What do you know that might be useful to others? How could this be categorized so that people who need it can easily find it?

10. What benefits could accrue from capturing and using knowledge that is currently not captured or that is currently not applied?

11. What new knowledge do you generate, how do you share these lessons learned, and with whom? How are they retained for future use?

12. How well do you (as an individual and as an organization) learn from past mistakes and take advantage of your successes? If you don't, why don't you? If you do learn, how do you do so?

(continued)

Figure 4-6—Interview or Workshop Guideline

13. Do you (or does your organization) have trade secrets, special recipes, and other things you can do that other organizations can't do? If so, how and where are they captured and stored for future use?

14. Are there sources of knowledge and experience that would be useful to you but are unavailable? How do you compensate for this lack?

15. What is *your* signature skill? For what particular area of expertise are you known and respected? How did you gain this level of credibility?

16. Do your competitors have someone with a role similar to yours? Do those individuals have the same levels of expertise and experience as you? Do they have access to the same information sources? If not, what other sources to they use?

17. How do other people in the organization take advantage of what *you* know?

18. What technologies do you use to support the management, sharing, or development of knowledge?

19. What additional opportunities do you see to use information technology to enhance learning and knowledge management?

20. What does it take to be successful in your organization? What aspects of the work are most emphasized, recognized, rewarded? How are mistakes/failures treated?

Sample Inventory

	Physical Location and/or Source	Subject Matter, i.e., Knowledge Domain	Owner/Party Responsible for Updating	Format and/or Media	Age and/or Years of Data	Used By, Used For, and Frequency of Use
Internal Information						
Electronic Documents						
E-mail Messages						
Electronic Discussion Databases						
Paper Records						
Financial Data						
Customer Information						
Data Warehouses or Data Marts						
Policies						
Procedures						
Competitive Intelligence						
Copyrights						

(continued)

Figure 4-7—Sample Inventory Data Gathering Form

	Physical Location and/or Source	Subject Matter, i.e., Knowledge Domain	Owner/Party Responsible for Updating	Format and/or Media	Age and/or Years of Data	Used By, Used For, and Frequency of Use
Special Formulae or Recipes						
Skills Inventory						
Patents and Trademarks						
External Information						
World Wide Web						
News Feeds						
Credit Records						
Market Research Data						
Regulations/ Legislation						

Glossary

anytime, anywhere collaboration the ability for a group of people to work together, regardless of time or geography

application programming interfaces (API) the mechanism that provides for one software application to exchange information with another software application

audit trail the monitoring of a knowledge base; tracks what is used and what is not used, how much, by whom, and when

automatic root expansion an advanced search mechanism that produces variations of a key word, such as "perform," "performance," and "performing"

avatar a digital presence that represents an individual user to others in a digital environment

benefits in the case of knowledge, these are the advantages that accrue as a result of identifying, capturing, and applying knowledge to provide business advantage to the organization

best practices business processes, or major subsets of business processes, that represent the most effective way of achieving specific objectives

Boolean search an advanced search mechanism that allows a user to enter AND/OR definitions

business case builds on the value proposition and high value definition that have already been developed; grounds these principles in practical business realities

business environment an organization's operational culture; reflects how an organization manages its learning processes

business process diagram a graphical representation of the tasks and activities involved in completing an organization's work

case-based reasoning (CBR) tools that provide the capabilities to retain, retrieve, and reuse old solutions, commonly referred to as "cases," expressed as a series of problem characteristics and solutions

cataloging creates an index "card" with pre-specified attributes such as author, title, date, and keywords

collaboration a process of shared creation or development of shared understanding that requires involvement of more than one person; the foundation of teamwork

collaborative filtering separation of irrelevant from relevant knowledge prior to it being "pushed" to the user's desktop; the selection of information is based on "learned" user requirements

communications plan action steps required to communicate anticipated changes resulting from any new initiative

communities of interest people who have joined together to use and develop their skills and resources and to work together on issues of common interest; they share ideas and experiences to identify new opportunities in their field or to solve problems confronting them as a community

communities of practice a group of people who have a common interest or shared responsibility for a particular subject area or field of work and are held together by a common goal and purpose that is supported by a desire to share knowledge

concept search an advanced search mechanism through which users enter a keyword but receive similar topics; for example, entering "software deals" might produce "joint venture" or "alliance"

connectivity formation of an enterprise-wide electronic memory through the use of groupware, workflow, and document management technologies

content managers the new stewards of the knowledge economy; assigned the responsibility of gathering, editing, linking, and validating knowledge in an organization

context the circumstances at the time of the event, e.g., who was involved, why the decision was made, what events triggered the process, etc.

coordinated enterprise the coordination of people, objectives, and processes with interrelated knowledge, resources, and models

corporate memory constitutes a historical record of an organization's significant events and decisions

costs include all anticipated monetary outlays, risks (both technical and nontechnical), organizational and cultural implications, and potential impacts on other key initiatives that are planned or are already under way

cultural transition changes to business processes and employee behaviors to support the management of knowledge (create, transmit, generate)

cybrarian an individual with the skills of a librarian who can also develop a knowledge map; often a lead member of the knowledge mapping team

data the lowest level of known facts

data mining used to uncover implicit relationships that are difficult for human analysts to identify, to spot trends, and to extract hard-to-get data

data warehouse an electronic storehouse for data from many sources and in many forms

document a data medium and the data recorded on it . . . capable of being read by [a human being] or machine

document management a process for exploiting, sharing, and distributing the information needed for the company's activities

electronic document management a way of storing, seeking, finding, and controlling documents throughout their life cycle using networked technology

e-mail messaging technology and the messages it transmits

enabling conditions an environment that is conducive to success

enterprise resource planning (ERP) application software designed to provide enterprise-wide support for corporate processes, e.g., human resources management, financial management, etc.

expert systems computer programs that capture an expert's decision-making knowledge so it can be disseminated to others

explicit knowledge knowledge that is documented and public; structured, fixed-content, externalized, and conscious

extensible markup language (XML) defines the syntax or rules that govern the preparation of metaknowledge language so that it can be interpreted, processed,

238

and communicated by and among multiple applications, thus extending the use of the knowledge asset it describes

full text indexing automatically indexes every word in a document

functionality the functions or tasks the system performs, either on its own without human intervention, or in conjunction with the user

fuzzy search a search mechanism that allows the right documents to be located even when the query uses a similar word ("cloth" rather than "fabric") or when the query contains misspelled words

groupware technology that supports collaboration and cooperation and allows users to work together on a specific project or to coordinate group activities

high value knowledge definition a confirmation of what the organization expects to accomplish through its implementation of knowledge management processes—what value it will add

hot link allows the user to send an e-mail message directly from any application without exiting that application

hyperlink provides a way for the user to move quickly and easily between related pieces of information; simplifies the process of understanding the relationships between the pieces and also how one piece influences another

hypertext markup language (HTML) the syntax and terms used to develop well-defined Internet documents

implementation phase the stage of a project that includes installation of technology, modification of processes, reallocation of responsibilities, etc.

implementation team group of individuals that is carefully selected to support the implementation of the knowledge strategy

inference engine a program that uses the various facts and rules in the knowledge base to arrive at conclusions for a specific problem

information the result of data which are organized, analyzed, and interpreted

information and knowledge holdings information that is relevant to the business of an organization; includes both tacit and explicit information and knowledge

information and storage retrieval programs computer software that supports searching large, textual databases

information crawlers or spiders technology that can search for specified domains, or content categories, of information; crawlers or automated filters can refine searching to enhance the value and relevance of the content delivered

innovation development and application of new and creative ideas

intelligent agent a pre-programmed software routine that learns the habits and preferences of a user and adjusts its performance accordingly

intelligent push technology provides relevant knowledge to a user's desktop; represents an advance in push technologies

internal libraries a library that is owned and operated by an organization for use by its employees

interpretive context perspective; the lens through which a situation is viewed

intranets the use of Internet technology to provide enterprise-wide access to internal information and knowledge; often restricted to employees

intuitive visualization visual representation of search results that simplify the user's analytical process

knowledge information that has been validated

knowledge "construction" the process of developing new knowledge through testing, validating, and building on the results of prior knowledge generation efforts

knowledge access tools sophisticated full text search and query on knowledge object contents and on the metaknowledge

knowledge architecture defines the functions for each part of the knowledge management environment and identifies the relationships of each to the others

knowledge base the accumulation of knowledge in an organization; often refers to the physical store of knowledge

knowledge broker a deal maker who links buyers and sellers by ascertaining buyer needs, locating the suppliers, facilitating the transfer of knowledge from supplier to buyer, and collecting a fee for the service

knowledge content specialists guardians of the relevance of the knowledge base; may also refine and filter knowledge content to satisfy specific knowledge user requirements

knowledge domains key knowledge topics for an organization, categories that represent the major stakeholders, business drivers, and other major influences

knowledge economy an economic environment where intellect has become the kind of capital most in demand

knowledge integrator an employee responsible for reviewing and culling the knowledge base on an ongoing basis, for ensuring that the knowledge is current and accurate, and for maintaining the overall organization of the knowledge base

knowledge management a process that drives innovation by capitalizing on organizational intellect and experience

knowledge management enablers distribution tools and engines, e.g., electronic publishers, connections to World Wide Web, intranets, client/server networks, CD-ROMs, e-mail systems

knowledge management infrastructure people, processes, and automated systems that support an organization's knowledge management initiative

knowledge management processes the ways that an organization handles knowledge at various stages of its life in an organization; acquisition, organization, retrieval, distribution, and maintenance

knowledge management technology architecture technology framework or foundation on which the knowledge management system is developed

knowledge management value proposition articulation of the real value of knowledge management to the organization; important for helping the prospective users to understand the knowledge management initiative and the contribution it will make

knowledge management vision a positioning statement that provides a view of where the knowledge management initiative will lead, what direction it is expected to take, and how it will help the organization to achieve its goals

knowledge management vision statement statement of direction providing a definition of what and how knowledge management will contribute

knowledge map (K-map) a navigation tool that provides a visual representation of the overall knowledge management environment; it points to knowledge sources and locations and provides a graphical view of their relationships

knowledge metamodel houses the context that makes knowledge valuable and meaningful

knowledge mining the way to quickly find the most relevant knowledge and gain insights as a result of implicit relationships that are difficult for human analysts to identify; accomplished by a system revealing significant facts, relationships, trends, patterns expressions, and anomalies associated with knowledge

knowledge repository part of the knowledge management technology architecture that stores the knowledge base; may include multiple source repositories

knowledge retrieval access and retrieval of relevant knowledge

knowledge rules rules that allow knowledge to be applied to business circumstances in a targeted way

knowledge sharing one of the core attributes of the knowledge management life cycle, it is supported by all of the knowledge management processes: acquisition, organization, retrieval, distribution, and maintenance

knowledge steward an employee responsible for reviewing and culling the knowledge base on an ongoing basis, for ensuring that the knowledge is current and accurate, and for maintaining the overall organization of the knowledge base

knowledge strategy a description of how an organization plans to use its knowledge to support its corporate objectives; an outline of the program for implementing the processes that form the knowledge management life cycle: acquire, organize, retrieve, distribute, and maintain

knowledge work work that involves independent thinking and creative problem solving

knowledge workers a term first coined in 1959 by Peter Drucker; people who are, in essence, intellectual craftspeople whose products are decisions, ideas, and actions

knowledge-intensive organization an organization that capitalizes on creating, harvesting, assimilating, and applying knowledge to gain economic leverage, producing a smarter and more competitive organization

librarians professional information brokers; librarians are in the business of connecting people with information

library management collection development and acquisitions: deciding what materials to obtain for the user community, finding out how to get hold of the chosen materials, and buying them; cataloging and classification: arranging the collection in such a way that users can find items within it, using search tools such as indexes and catalogs; circulation: lending items to users, reserving items for users, and getting the items back again and reshelving them; reference work: discussing users' information needs with them and advising users how best to use the library's resources to find the information they need; preservation, conservation, and archiving: ensuring that materials remain available to users in perpetuity (e.g., images, video)

"listserv" an electronic subscription service that provides periodic, regular updates on a specific topic to subscribers, using e-mail as the distribution mechanism

live link provides the user with uninterrupted access to relevant Web sites

managing capturing, using, generating, sharing, exploiting, storing, accessing, transferring, and gaining leverage from "know-how"

media mining also called "knowledge mining"; the action of probing and synthesizing contents of linked repositories or a warehouse; applies to data, text, or other digital media

metaknowledge "knowledge about knowledge" known to knowledge management professionals

metaphor legend or key that increases the user's ability to understand how the system works

multimedia more than textual or narrative documents, includes video, voice, etc.

natural language search an advanced search mechanism through which a user can enter instructions such as "find me more like . . ."

navigation link a standard path of access for topics that make sense for an organization's business activities

navigation trail bookmarks or other electronic identifiers provide users with immediate access to favorite or frequently used knowledge locations

new knowledge the result of proving that personal theories are valid through direct experience or deduction

organizational adaptability the willingness and ability to predict and respond to the changing business environment

organizational enablers organizational structures and processes that enable and encourage knowledge sharing

organizational environment the internal cultural environment; how an organization is managed and its employees motivated

performance achievement of objectives, growth, and increased customer satisfaction

performance measures indicators of how well the organization (or the system) is meeting its objectives

production workflow supports processes triggered by outside events, such as by a customer or supplier, and focuses on capturing and moving a business transaction through to completion

productivity output by employees

productivity paradox the lack of tangible returns on investment in information technology

project deliverable any predetermined entity to be delivered as a result of a project

project planning document definition of a project's scope, objectives, and terms of reference; a summary of all activities required for the design and implementation phase

pull technology technology that allows the user to "pull" or electronically retrieve information from a server to a desktop

push technology technology so called because it "pushes" unfiltered information from the server to the desktop, providing information according to generic task requirements

quantitative metrics used to track specific contributions to the knowledge base, along with an estimate of their value, based on the number of times the knowledge is used by others

query a specific question, as opposed to a general search; directed at a particular issue or concern, such as how the overhead costs are calculated for budget forecasting

readiness assessment a process of identifying areas needing attention or having potential problems and risks

records management organization and management of all records including off-site and on-site records throughout the entire document life cycle

records managers professionals who are charged with managing records, information, and knowledge as valuable corporate assets

resource directories a directory of internal and external subject experts who can act as guides and knowledge sources

simulation software lets organizations test decisions before putting them into practice

smart reuse reuse of practices, processes, or techniques based on a good understanding of the circumstances surrounding their successful application

source repository a component of the knowledge repository

standard general markup language (SGML) the metalanguage that defines hypertext markup language (HTML)

stewardship of intellectual resources ensuring that knowledge is current and accurate; assuming responsibility for the quality of the knowledge base

structured indexing creates an index "card" with pre-specified attributes such as author, title, date, and keywords

subject matter experts (SMEs) representatives of users of the knowledge base; subject matter experts have the responsibility of providing input into which links are most appropriate, which sources are most valuable, and what should be included in a knowledge base

system maintenance strategy outlines the roles and responsibilities of the maintenance team; defines procedures for processing system modification requests; identifies functions for later development; defines management metrics for systems performance and use

tacit knowledge personal, undocumented knowledge; context-sensitive, dynamically created and derived, internalized, and experience-based; often resides in the human mind, behavior, and perception

targets employee goals and objectives

teamwork shared effort to achieve a group goal

technology environment combination of technologies that are available or planned in an organization; includes hardware, software, applications, networks, etc.

threaded discussion an online forum in which participants can post main topics, responses, and responses to responses in their exploration of a topic; particularly useful in research and development functions where new territory is being explored

unclassified information accumulation of information/knowledge that has not yet been cataloged or indexed

universal database a new class of database-management system that manages data in many different forms – text, numbers, photographs, video clips, or sound bites

unlimited information unrestricted access to infinite volumes and types of information through electronic access to technologies such as the Internet

user interface a graphical, screen-based access point to the holdings and functionality of a system; allows the user to look around or "browse" the organization's knowledge base

workflow systems route work from one activity, role, or process to another, based on business rules

References

Amidon, Debra. *Collaborative Innovation and the Knowledge Economy.* Hamilton, Ontario: The Society of Management Accountants of Canada, 1998.

_____. "Evolving Communities of Knowledge Practice." *International Journal of Technology Management* 16, nos. 1/2/3 (1998).

Andrus, Christopher. "Knowledge Management: Components and Methodology." Lotusphere98, Lake Buena Vista, Florida (February, 1998).

Austin, T. "Information Sharing Chaos: Much Change." *Gartner Group Advisory Services* (3 July 1997). CD-ROM. Cambridge, MA: Gartner Group Inc., 1997.

BackWeb Technologies. "Knowledge Management: An Industry Perspective." *Back Web*, Hp, 1998 [latest update]. Online. Available: http://www.backweb. com/html/pwhpaper.

Bair, J. "Adoption Time Frame for Knowledge Retrieval Technologies." *Gartner Group Advisory Services* (12 January 1998). CD-ROM. Cambridge, MA: Gartner Group, Inc., 1998.

_____. "Building Knowledge Maps: A Love of Labor?" *Gartner Group Advisory Services* (9 February 1998). CD-ROM. Cambridge, MA: Gartner Group Inc., 1998.

_____. "Knowledge Management Is About Cooperation and Context." *Gartner Group Advisory Services* (14 May 1998). CD-ROM. Cambridge, MA: Gartner Group Inc., 1998.

_____. "Knowledge Management Leverages Engineering at Chrysler." *Gartner Group Advisory Services* (23 April 1997). CD-ROM. Cambridge, MA: Gartner Group Inc., 1997.

_____. "Knowledge Management Scenario." In *The Future of IT: Proceedings of Gartner Group Symposium/ITxpo97 Held in Lake Buena Vista, Florida, 6-10 October 1997.* Stamford, CT: Gartner Group, 1997.

_____. "Knowledge Management Value Propositions." *Gartner Group Advisory Services* (24 June 1997). CD-ROM. Cambridge, MA: Gartner Group, Inc., 1998.

Bair, J., J. Fenn, R. Hunter, and D. Bosik. "Foundations for Enterprise Knowledge Management." *Gartner Group Advisory Services* (7 April 1997). CD-ROM. Cambridge, MA: Gartner Group Inc., 1997.

Baumbusch, Richard. "Internal Best Practices: Turning Knowledge into Results." *Strategy & Leadership* (July/August 1997).

Bontis, Nick. "There's a Price on Your Head: Managing Intellectual Capital Strategically." *Business Quarterly* 60, no. 4 (Summer 1996).

Brethenoux, E. "User-Targeted vs. User-Centered Techniques." *Gartner Group Advisory Services* (30 July 1997). CD-ROM. Cambridge, MA: Gartner Group Inc., 1997.

Brown, D., and others. "ADM Five Year Scenario: Succeeding Amidst Chaos." *Gartner Group Advisory Services* (14 January 1994). CD-ROM. Cambridge, MA: Gartner Group Inc., 1994.

Buckman, Robert H. "Collaborative Knowledge: The Worldwide Implications." *International Knowledge Management Summit Held in Austin, Texas, 11 March 1997.* Transcription.

Byrd, Richard E. *The Creatrix Inventory.* San Diego: Pfeiffer & Company, 1986.

Carnevale, Anthony Patrick. "Learning: The Critical Technology." *Training and Development* 46, no. 2 (February 1992).

Coleman, David. "Collaboration, Knowledge Management and the Rise of Intranet Communities." New Orleans: The Office Systems Research Association (27 February 1998). Transcription.

Dataware Technologies, Inc. *Seven Steps to Implementing Knowledge Management in Your Organization.* Corporate Executive Briefing. Cambridge, MA: Dataware Technologies, Inc., 1998.

Davenport, Thomas H. "The Knowledge Biz." *Intellectual Capitalism* (15 November 1997). Online. Available: http://www.cio.com/archive/enterprise/111597_intellectual_content.html.

_____. "Knowledge Management at Hewlett-Packard, Early 1996." *Knowledge Management Server* (30 March 1997). Online. Available: http://www.bus.utexas.edu/kman/hpcase.htm.

_____. "Some Principles of Knowledge Management." *Knowledge Management Server* (1997). Online. Available: http://www.bus.utexas.edu/kman/kmprin.htm.

_____. "Teltech: The Business of Knowledge Management Case Study." *Knowledge Management Server* (30 March 1997). Online. Available: http://www.bus.utexas.edu/kman/telcase.htm.

Davenport, Thomas, and Larry Prusak. *Working Knowledge.* Boston: Harvard Business School Press, 1998.

Drucker, Peter F. "Introduction: Toward the New Organization." *The Organization of the Future.* Edited by Frances Hesselbein, Marshall Goldsmith and Richard Beckhard. San Francisco: Jossey-Bass, 1997.

_____. *Managing in a Time of Great Change.* New York: Truman Talley Books/Dutton, 1995.

_____. *Post-Capitalist Society.* New York: HarperCollins Publishers, 1993.

_____. *Keynote Session.* In *1998 International Knowledge Management Summit, Held in San Diego, June 1998.* Transcription.

Duques, Ric, and Paul Gaske. "The 'Big' Organization of the Future." *The Organization of the Future.* Edited by Frances Hesselbein, Marshall Goldsmith and Richard Beckhard. San Francisco: Jossey-Bass, 1997.

Edvinsson, L. "Intellectual Capital: A Strategic Inquiry By Paradigm Pioneers." Brochure, n.d., n.p.

Frick, V. "Best Practices and Knowledge Management." *Gartner Group Advisory Services* (22 January 1998). CD-ROM. Cambridge, MA: Gartner Group Inc., 1998.

_____. "BPR TOPView." *Gartner Group Advisory Services* (24 September 1997). CD-ROM. Cambridge, MA: Gartner Group Inc., 1997.

_____. "Changing a Century-Old Business Culture." *Gartner Group Advisory Services,* (21 July 1997). CD-ROM. Cambridge, MA: Gartner Group Inc., 1997.

_____. "Obstacles to Knowledge Management." *Gartner Group Advisory Services* (23 January 1998). CD-ROM. Cambridge, MA: Gartner Group Inc., 1998.

Gilbert, M., and D. McCoy. "Records Management: Taking the Next Steps." *Gartner Group Advisory Services* (23 August 1998). CD-ROM. Cambridge, MA: Gartner Group Inc., 1998.

Grayson, C. Jackson. "Taking Inventory of Your Knowledge Management Skills." *Continuous Journey* (Winter 1996). American Productivity & Quality Center. Online. Available: http://www.apqc.org/b2/b2stories/story1.htm.

Greiner, Larry E., and Robert O. Metzger. *Consulting to Management.* Englewood Cliffs, NJ: Prentice-Hall, Inc., 1983.

Grove, Andrew. *Only the Paranoid Survive.* New York: Doubleday Currency, 1996.

Hamel, Gary, and C. K. Prahalad. *Competing for the Future.* Boston: Harvard Business School Press, 1994.

Hammer, Michael. "The Soul of the New Organization." *The Organization of the Future.* Edited by Frances Hesselbein, Marshall Goldsmith and Richard Beckhard. San Francisco: Jossey-Bass, 1997.

Handy, Charles. "Unimagined Futures." *The Organization of the Future.* Edited by Frances Hesselbein, Marshall Goldsmith and Richard Beckhard. San Francisco: Jossey-Bass, 1997.

Harris, K. "Chief Knowledge Officer: Managing Intellectual Assets." *Gartner Group Advisory Services* (20 March 1997). CD-ROM. Cambridge, MA: Gartner Group Inc., 1997.

Hibbard, Justin. "Knowing What We Know." *Information Week* (20 October 1997). Online. Available: http://www.informationweek.com/653/53iukno.htm.

Hill, Linda. "Faultlines a Manager Must Walk on the Way to the 21st Century." *Harvard Business School Publishing* (June 1996). Online. No longer available: http://www.hbsp.harvard.edu/groups/newsletters/update.html.

Hopper, Susan, et al. "Real World Design in the Corporate Environment: Designing an Interface for the Technically Challenged." In *CHI 96: Electronic Proceedings, Association for Computing Machinery, Special Interest Group on Computer-Human Interaction, 16-18 April 1996* (ACM, 1996). Online. Available: http://www.acm.org/sigchi/chi96/proceedings/desvbrief/Hopper/Hwh_txt.html.

Hunter, R. "Knowledge Management: Process and Platform." *Gartner Group Advisory Services* (19 May 1997). CD-ROM. Cambridge, MA: Gartner Group Inc., 1997.

_____. "The Whys and Hows of Knowledge Management." *Gartner Group Advisory Services* (4 February 1998). CD-ROM. Cambridge, MA: Gartner Group Inc., 1998.

_____. "Knowledge Capital: Essential Active Management." In *The IT Revolution Continues: Managing Diversity in the 21st Century, Proceedings of Gartner Group Symposium/ITxpo96, Held in Lake Buena Vista, Florida, 7-11 October 1996.* Stamford, CT: Gartner Group, 1996.

_____. "Knowledge Management Case Studies." In *The Future of IT: Proceedings of Gartner Group Symposium/ITxpo97 Held in Lake Buena Vista, Florida, 6-11 October, 1997.* Stamford, CT: Gartner Group, 1997.

Ikujiro, Nonaka, and Hirotaka Takeuchi. *The Knowledge Creating Company.* New York: Oxford University Press, 1995.

Institute for the Future (The). Recent Reports. "Institute for the Future." Online. No longer available: http://www.iftf.org/Whats_New.html.

Kanter, Rosabeth Moss. *When Giants Learn to Dance.* New York: Touchstone, 1989.

Kleiner, Art, and George Roth. "How to Make Experience Your Company's Best Teacher," *Harvard Business Review* (September-October 1997).

"Knowledge Management." American Productivity & Quality Center (1998). Online. Available: http://www.apqc.org/pordserv/courses.htm.

Knox, R. "Why is Metadata Important?" *Gartner Group Advisory Services* (13 May 1998). CD-ROM. Cambridge, MA: Gartner Group Inc., 1998.

Koulopoulos, Thomas M. "Leverage Knowledge Management to Create Corporate Instinct." *The Delphi Group* (1998). Online. Available: http://www. delphigroup.com/km/KMandInstinct.html.

Leonard-Barton, Dorothy. *Wellsprings of Knowledge: Building and Sustaining the Sources of Innovation.* Boston: Harvard Business School Press, 1995.

LGS Group Inc. *Inspiration for Systems Development.* Montreal: LGS Group Inc., 1991.

Lotus Institute. *Lotus, IBM and Knowledge Management Index.* White Paper (1997). *Lotus*, Hp, 1998. Online. Available: http://www/lotus.com/news/ topstories.nsf.

_____. "Real World Insights." *Lotus, IBM and Knowledge Management Index.* White Paper, nd. Online. Available: http://www.lotus.com/news/ topstories.nsf.

_____. "The Lotus/IBM Knowledge Management Framework: Structuring the Problem." *Lotus*, Hp, 1998. Online. Available: http://www.lotus.com/news/ topstories.nsf.

Malhotra, Yogesh. "Knowledge Management for the New World of Business." *Business Researcher's Interests* (1998). Online. Available: http://www.brint. com/km/whatis.htm.

Manasco, Britton. "Enterprise-wide Learning: Corporate Knowledge Networks and the New Learning Imperative." *Knowledge Inc.* (1995). Online. Available: http://www.webcom.com/quantera/ps95.html.

Marshall, Stephanie Pace. "Creating Sustainable Learning Communities for the Twenty-First Century." *The Organization of the Future.* Edited by Frances Hesselbein, Marshall Goldsmith and Richard Beckhard. San Francisco: Jossey-Bass, 1997.

McClure, Charles R. "Network Literacy in an Electronic Society: An Educational Disconnect?" *The Aspen Institute* (1993). Online. Available: http://www. aspeninst.org/dir/polpro/CSP/IIS/93-94/McClure.html.

Norris, Marilyn W. "Editor's Page." *Strategy & Leadership* 26, no. 1 (January/February 1998).

Rogers, Edward W. "Designing the 'Tools' Needed for Crafting Knowledge at Cornell." *Cornell Chronicle* (1996). Online. Cornell University, Available: http://www.news.cornell.edu/Chronicles/2.29.96/commentary.html.

_____. "Knowledge Construction." *Mayjjer Corporation* (1995). Online. Available: http://www.mayjjer.com/knowledge.html.

Saenz, Pedro. "The Knowledge Economy." *Vita* (n.d.). Online. Available: www.vita.org/technet/kaarch/0013.html.

Saffady, William. *Knowledge Management: A Manager's Briefing.* Prairie Village, KS: ARMA International, 1998.

Saia, Rick. "Thirsting for Knowledge" *Computerworld* (10 May 1997).

Schein, Edgar. *Organizational Culture and Leadership.* San Francisco: Jossey-Bass, 1990.

Senge, Peter M. *The Fifth Discipline: The Art and Practice of the Learning Organization.* New York: Doubleday, 1990.

Sethi, Deepak. "The Seven R's of Self-Esteem." *The Organization of the Future.* Edited by Frances Hesselbein, Marshall Goldsmith and Richard Beckhard. San Francisco: Jossey-Bass, 1997.

Sherman, Stratford. "Bringing Sears into the New World." *Fortune* (13 October 1997). Online. Available: http://www.pathfinder.com/fortune.1997.971013/fro.html.

Skyrme, David. *Measuring the Value of Knowledge.* London: Business Intelligence Limited, 1998.

Smith, Anthony F., and Tim Kelly. "Human Capital in the Digital Economy." *The Organization of the Future.* Edited by Frances Hesselbein, Marshall Goldsmith and Richard Beckhard. San Francisco: Jossey-Bass, 1997.

Special Committee on Competencies for Special Librarians. "Competencies for Special Librarians of the 21st Century." *Special Libraries Association* (October 1996). Online. Available: http://www.sla.org/professional/comp.html.

Stewart, Thomas A. "Getting Real About Brainpower." *Fortune* (27 November 1995).

Stewart, Thomas A. "Mapping Corporate Brainpower." *Fortune* (30 October 1995).

Tanaszi, Margaret, and Jan Duffy. "Measuring Knowledge Assets in the Knowledge Economy." Draft Management Accounting Guideline. Hamilton, Ontario: The Society of Management Accountants, April, 1999.

University of Kentucky. "Kentucky Initiative for Knowledge Management." Online. No longer available: http://uky.edu/man/dsis/KIKM.htm (24 July 1997).

Vogel, Peter. "Know Your Business: Build a Knowledgebase!" *Datamation* 42, no.13 (July 1996).

Wheatly, Margaret J. *Leadership and the New Science: Learning about Organizations from an Orderly Universe.* San Francisco: Berrett-Koehler, 1992.

Wolrath, Björn. "Power of Innovation." Supplement to *Intellectual Capital.* Copenhagen: Skandia Corporation, 1996.

Zack, Michael H. "Interactive and Communication Mode: Choice in Ongoing Management Groups." *Information Systems Research* 4, no. 3 (1993).

Zuboff, Shoshana. *In the Age of the Smart Machine: The Future of Work and Power.* Britton Manasco "Enterprise-Wide Learning: Corporate Knowledge Networks and the New Learning Imperative." *Knowledge Inc.* (1995). Online. Available: http://webcom.com/quantera/enterprise.html.

Index

A

Access path, 142–143
American Productivity & Quality Center, xvii, 37, 67
Amidon, Debra, xi-xii, 14, 21, 44
Andersen Consulting, 190
Andresino, Maria, 174
Andrus, Christopher, 70
Answerthink Consulting Group, 151
Anytime, anywhere collaboration, 157
Application programming interface (API), 158
Architecture, 125–126
ARMA International (Association of Records Managers and Administrators), 193
Arthur Andersen's Business Consulting Practice, 70
Aurelius, Marcus, 1
Austin, T., 40
Automatic root expansion, 138

B

Baumbusch, Richard, 64
Benefits
    of knowledge management, 84–87
    linked to corporate goals, 84
    types, in knowledge management, 85–87
Best practices, 3, 11–12, 54, 178
Bontis, Nick, 182
Boolean searching, 138
Botkin, Jim, 33
Brethenoux, Eric, 131
Buckman Laboratories International, Inc., 38, 39, 81, 182
Buckman, Robert, 37–38, 41, 81
Business analysts, as part of team, 91

Business case, 69
    defined, 80
    developing, 81–83
    See also Costs; Benefits; Opportunities, prioritizing
Business environment
    assessing readiness in, 75
    checklist, 222–223
Business process diagrams, 105
Business processes, review of, 102–108
Byrd, Richard E., 64

C

Carnevale, Anthony Patrick, 50, 108
Case-based reasoning (CBR), 132–133
Champion Road Machinery, 107
Change, 44
    business environment and, 207
    organizations and, 204–207
    speed and complexity of, 20–21
    technology and, 207–209
Chief information officer (CIO), 186
Chief knowledge officer (CKO), 185–186, 187
Chief learning officer (CLO), 185–186
Chrysler, 83, 189
CIGNA, 141
City University, 213
Collaboration, 40, 53
    interpretive context and, 41
Collaborative filters, 130–131
Collaborative technologies framework (illustration), 157
Command and control organizational culture, 175-176
Communication, 96
    knowledge management value proposition and, 73
Communications plan, 73, 95

(illustration), 218–219
Communities of interest, 3, 14–15, 52, 168
Communities of practice, 3, 14, 52, 168
Competing for the Future, 35
Competition, 21–22
Computerworld, 64
Concept searching, 138
Conduct acceptance tests, 171
Conduct training, 172-173
Connex project, 142
Content managers, 117
Context, 7
    defined, 4
    interpretive, 41
Cooperation, 53
Coordinated enterprise, 156
Core competency, 44
Corporate memory, 3, 12–14
Costs
    of knowledge management, 83–84
    one-time and ongoing (illustration),
        226–227
"Creating Sustainable Learning
    Communities for the Twenty-First
    Century," 205
Cultural transition, in knowledge manage-
    ment implementation plan, 174-196
    See also Organizational enablers; Roles
        and responsibilities
Customers, relationship building, 22–23
Cybrarians, 99, 191

D

Daily work supports, 131–132
Data, defined, 4
Data mining, 134
Data warehouse, 134
Databases, universal, 155–156
Dataware Technologies, 110, 125, 151
Dataware Technologies Knowledge Suite
    II, 101
Davenport, Tom, xix, 181, 184
Davis, Stan, 33
Decision support tools, 132–134
DeKerkhove, Derek, 201
Delayering, 47
Document, 132
Document management, 132
Dow Chemical, 88
Drucker, Peter, xv, 6, 35–36, 180, 206
Duques, Ric, 45

E

E-mail, 127
E-mail hot links, 136
Edvinsson, Leif, 112
Electronic document management, 132
Employee empowerment, 47
Employment contract, new, 206
Enabling conditions, 63
Enterprise resource planning (ERP), 158
ENTOVATION International, 14
Ernst & Young, 81, 116
Evolving trail of knowledge, 143
Experience, defined, 3
Expert systems, 133
Expiration/supersede dates, 140–141
Explicit knowledge, 7–8
Extensible markup language (XML), 150
External forces affecting organizations, 17
    change, 20–21
    competition, 21–22
    customer relationship building, 22–23
    globalization, 18–19
    renewal, need for, 19–20

F

Fifth Discipline (The), 35

First Data Corporation, 45
Fortune, 183
Full text indexing, 139
Functionality requirements, in knowledge
   management technology infrastructure
   automatic root expansion, 138
   Boolean searching, 138
   concept searching, 138
   e-mail hot links, 136
   evolving trail of knowledge, 143
   expiration/supersede dates, 140–141
   external sources, 137
   full text indexing, 139
   fuzzy searching, 138
   hyperlinks, 136
   index fields search, 138
   intelligent push technology, 138–139
   internal business applications, 137
   knowledge mining, 139
   knowledge rules, 141
   live links, 137
   media mining, 139
   multidimensional cataloging/indexing,
      139–140
   multimedia support, 144
   natural language searching, 138
   navigation links, 136–137
   object type search, 138
   online collaboration and learning,
      143–144
   performance measures support,
      144–145
   personal navigation trail (access path),
      142–143
   pointers, 135–136
   query function, 138
   resource directories, 142
   search function, 137–138
   structured indexing, 139
   thesaurus integration, 138
   unclassified information, 140
   usage audit trail, 143
Fuzzy searching, 138

G

Gartner Group, xvii, 24, 82, 83, 90, 126,
   132, 156, 186, 193
Gaske, Paul, 45
General Electric, 51
Gery, Gloria, 172
Globalization, 18–19
Grayson, C. Jackson, Jr., 37, 110
Groupware, 127
Grove, Andrew, xiv

H

Hamel, Gary, 21, 35
Hammer, Michael, xix, 15–16
Handy, Charles, 204
Harreld, J. Bruce, Sr., 123
Harvard Business School, 9, 10, 42, 63
Hewlett-Packard, 142, 145
High-level classification scheme (illustra-
   tion), 102
High value definition (strategic), 62, 68–71
Hill, Linda, 42
Hunter, Richard, 24, 37, 90
Hyperlinks, 136
Hypertext markup language (HTML), 150

I

IBM, 43, 123, 182
Ikujiro, Nonaka, 45
Implementation process, 164
   defined, 165

Inclusive Valuation Methodology, 213
Index fields search, 138
Indexing, 139
Inference engine, 133
Information, defined, 4
Information and knowledge holdings, 106
Information crawlers (spiders), 131
Information/knowledge inventory, 106–8
Information storage and retrieval programs, 127
Information systems specialists
  as part of team, 91
Innovation, 46-48
  defined, 44–45
  Institute of the Future, xviii
Intangible Assets Monitor, 212
Intellectual Capital Index (IC Index), 212–213
Intellectual Capital: The New Wealth of Organizations, 183
Intelligent agents, 130–131
Intelligent push technology, 130–131
  profile or event and, 138–139
Internal business applications, 137
Internal forces affecting organizations, 23
  complexity, 25–26
  geographic dispersion, 28
  information, increase in, 27–28
  resources, shortage of, 26–27
  technology, 24–25
International Organization for
  Standardization, 132
Internet, 128–129
Interpretive context, 41
Interview, 100–101
  (illustration), 230–231
Intranets, 129
Intuitive visualization, 156
Inventory (illustration), 232–233

J

Junnarkar, Bipin, 39

K

Kanbrain Institute, 179
Kanter, Rosabeth Moss, 16, 51, 63
Keilty, Goldsmith & Company, 26, 45
Kelly, Tim, 26, 51
Know-how, 2
Knowledge
  acquiring and capturing, 109–112
  best practices and, 11–12
  communities of interest and, 14–15
  corporate memory and, 12–14
  defined, 3–5
  different from information, 184
  distributing, 115–117
  explicit, 7–8
  importance of, 5–7
  kinds of, 7–10
  life cycle of, 108–109
  linkages to learning, 34
  necessity for managing, 48
  new, 8–9, 53
  new, defined, 5
  nurturing workplace, 9
  organizing and storing, 112–114
  perspective and, 39–40
  renewal of, 7
  retrieving, 114–115
  sources of, 10–15
  sustaining value of, 210
  tacit, 7–8
  valuing resulting asset, 211–213
Knowledge access tools, 152
Knowledge architecture (illustration), 147
Knowledge base, 104

Knowledge broker, 186, 188
Knowledge "construction", 9
Knowledge content specialists, 188–189
Knowledge domains, 70
Knowledge economy, 6, 15–28, 17, 35
Knowledge integrator, 183, 190
Knowledge-intensive organization, 35, 36, 53
Knowledge management, 2, 15–28
  benefits of, 84-87
  costs of, 81, 83-34
  defined, 13
  justifying expense of, 211
  learning and, 53–55
  self-sustaining, 202
Knowledge management champions, 72, 90–91
Knowledge management enablers, 152
Knowledge management environment integrated (illustration), 159
Knowledge management implementation phase
  cultural transition, 174-196
  guidelines and challenges, 166
  plan for, 167–169
  team selecting, 167–169
  technical system implementation
  See Technical system implementation
  See also External forces; Internal forces
Knowledge management infrastructure, 134
Knowledge management initiative
  assessing readiness for, 63, 73–77
  communication, importance of, 73
  communications plan and, 72
  (illustration), 61
  getting commitment for, 62, 71–72
  knowledge management value proposition and, 62, 67–71
  setting direction for, 60, 62, 63–67
  strategic high value definition and, 62, 68–71
Knowledge management innovator, 63–64
Knowledge management life cycle, 108-118
Knowledge management process (illustration), 18
Knowledge management processes, defined, 108
Knowledge management project, initiation of, 79-80
  benefits, 84–87
  business case development, 81–83
  costs, 83–84
  knowledge assets, existing
    business processes reviewed, 102–108
    knowledge map, 96–99
    mapping tools and techniques, 99–102
  knowledge management processes, defining, 108
    acquiring and capturing knowledge, 109–112
    distributing knowledge, 115–117
    maintaining a knowledge base, 117–118
    organizing and storing knowledge, 112–114
    retrieving knowledge, 114–115
  opportunities, prioritizing, 87–90
  project plan development, 92–96
  project team identification, 90–91
Knowledge management assessment questionnaire, 220-225
Knowledge management technology architecture, 145
  anytime, anywhere collaboration, 157

application programming interface
(API), 158
coordinated enterprise, 156
enterprise resource planning (ERP), 158
extensible markup language (XML),
150
hypertext markup language (HTML),
150
(illustration), 147
incorporation of existing tools (illustration), 155
intuitive visualization, 156
knowledge access tools, 152
knowledge management enablers, 152
knowledge map (K-map), 150
knowledge metamodel, 148–150
knowledge repository, 151–152
knowledge retrieval, 156
metaphor, 146–148
selecting technology, 152–159
source repositories, 151–152
standard general markup language
(SGML), 150
universal databases, 155–156
user interface, 146–148
Knowledge management technology infrastructure
See Functionality requirements;
Knowledge management technology
architecture
Knowledge management value proposition, 62, 67–71
(illustration), 217
Knowledge management vision, 63, 64
scope of, 65–66
situational statement, 65
strategic statement, 66
Knowledge management vision statement,
60, 62

Knowledge map (K-map), 96–99, 118, 150
Knowledge metamodel, 148–150
Knowledge mining, 139
Knowledge repository, 151–152
Knowledge retrieval, 156
Knowledge rules, 141
Knowledge stewards, 189–190
Knowledge strategy, challenges, 209–213
Knowledge strategy connections, 42–50
(illustration), 44
innovation and, 44–47
objective of, 164
performance and, 48–50
productivity and, 47–48
Knowledge work, 6
learning and, 35–42
Knowledge workers, 22, 34, 35, 53
defined, 6
skills needed by, 54
as volunteers, 180, 206

L

Leadership, 176–177
Learning
importance of, in organizations, 50–55
individual and organizational, 51–53
knowledge management and, 53–55
knowledge work and, 35–42
value of, in organizations, 52
Learning communities, sustainable,
205–206
Learning environment
collaboration, 40–41
how achieved, 36–42
sharing knowledge, 36–40
teamwork, 41–42
Learning organization
defined, 35

Leonard-Barton, Dorothy, 9, 39–40, 50
Lessons learned, 54–55, 75
Librarians, 190–192
    as part of team, 91
Listservs, 130
Live links, 137
Long Island University, 192
Lotus, 43
Lotus Development, 182
Lotus Notes, 189
Lotusphere98, 70

M

Managing, 2
Mapping tools and techniques, 102
    interview, 100–101
    questionnaire, 99–100
Marshall, Stephanie Pace, 205
McClure, Charles, 54
McKinsey & Co., 81
McMaster University, 182
Media mining, 139
Metaknowledge, 113, 149–150
Metamodel, knowledge, 148-150
Metaphor, 146–148
Monsanto, 39, 46, 47, 154
Monsanto Life Sciences, 46
Monster Under the Bed (The), 33
M'Pherson, Philip, 213
Multidimensional cataloging/indexing,
    139–140
Multimedia support, 144

N

National Geographic Television, 26
Natural language search, 138

Navigation links, 136–137
New knowledge, 5
Norris, Marilyn, 203
Northeastern University College of
    Business, 168

O

Object type search, 138
O'Dell, Carla, 67
Online collaboration and learning, 143–144
Opportunities, prioritizing in knowledge
    management project, 87–90
Organization
    knowledge-intensive, 35
    learning, 35
Organization of the Future (The), 15–16
Organizational adaptability, 207
Organizational enablers, in knowledge
    management implementation phase
    interdependence, 177–180
    leadership, 176–177
    quantitative metrics, 182
    reward and recognition, 180–183
    targets, 182-183
Organizational environment
    assessing readiness in, 75–77
        (illustration), 224–225
Organizational environment readiness as-
    sessment checklist
        (illustration), 224–225
Organizational learning, 51–53
    speed of (illustrated), 27
Organizational structure
    command and control, 175–176
    feudal information and social environ-
        ment, 176
    knowledge-friendly environment, 176

Organizations
    changes in future, 204–207
    external forces affecting, 17–23
    importance of learning in, 50–55
    internal forces affecting, 23–28
    responsibility to workers, 36
    See also External forces affecting organizations; Internal forces affecting organizations

P

Perelman, Lewis, 179
Performance, 48–50
Performance measures support, 144–145
Personal navigation trail (access path), 142–143
Perspective, knowledge and, 39–40
Petrash, Gordon, 88
Pointers, 135–136
Prahalad, C.K., 21, 35
Price Waterhouse, 111–112, 182
Prioritization assessment model, 89
Process re-engineering, 47–48
Product quality, 49
Production workflow, 132
Productivity, 47–48
Productivity paradox, 47
Project deliverables, 94
Project plan development, 92–96
Project planning document, 92–96
Project team, identification of, 90–91
Prusak, Larry, 184
Pull technology, 128–129
Push technology, 129–130

Q

Quantitative metrics, 182

Query function, 138
Questionnaire, on information used, generated, and needed, 99–100
    (illustration), 228–229

R

Readiness
    assessing for knowledge management initiative, 63, 73–77
Readiness assessment (illustrations)
    business environment, 222–223
    organizational environment, 224–225
    technology environment, 220–221
Records managers, 192
    as part of team, 91
    role in businesses, 193–196
Renewal, in organizations, 19–20
Renewal of knowledge, 7
Resource directories, 142
Rogers, Ed, 8–9
Roles and responsibilities, in knowledge management implementation phase
    chief information officer (CIO), 186
    chief knowledge officer (CKO), 185–186, 187
    chief learning officer (CLO), 185–186
    knowledge broker, 186, 188
    knowledge content specialists, 188–189
    knowledge stewards, 189–190
    librarians, 190–192
    records managers, 192–196
Roos, Johan and Goren, 212–213
Rucci, Anthony, 185

S

Saenz, Pedro, 16–17

Saffady, William, 192, 196
Saia, Rick, 64
Saveri, Andrea, xviii
Search function, 137–138
Searching, 137–138
Sears, 185
Self-organizing work units, 206–207
Senge, Peter, 35
Service delivery, 49
Service reliability, 49–50
Sharing, reluctance in, 46
Sharing knowledge, 36–40
Simulation software, 133
Skandia AFS, 212
Skandia Corporation, 10, 112
Skandia Navigator, 212
Smart architecture, 126
Smart reuse, 43
SmartPatent Workbench, 88
Smith, Anthony, 26, 51
Source repositories, 151–152
Special Committee on Competencies for
    Special Librarians, 191–192
Special Libraries Association, 191
Standard general markup language
    (SGML), 150
Stewart, Thomas, 183, 211
Strategy & Leadership, 203
Structured indexing, 139
Subject matter experts (SMEs), 97, 99
    as part of team, 91
Sustainable learning communities, 205–206
Sveiby, Karl Eric, 212
Swift, Jonathan, 59
Syracuse University, 54

T

Tacit knowledge, 7–8

Targets, 182-183
Team leader, 91
Teamwork, 41–42
Technical system implementation, in
    knowledge management implementa-
    tion phase
    activities (illustration), 170
    conduct acceptance tests, 171
    conduct training, 172–173
    objectives, 169, 171
    review implementation plans, 172
    system installation, 173–174
    system maintenance strategy, 173–174
Technology, 24–25
    future, in organizations, 207–209
    linkages with human capital and, 17
    selecting, 152–159
Technology environment
    assessing readiness in, 74–75
    (illustration), 220–221
Technology infrastructure, 125
    daily work supports, 131–132
    decision support tools, 132–134
    history, 127–128
    information storage and retrieval pro-
        grams, 127
    intelligent push technology, 130–131
    pull technology, 128–129
    push technology, 129–130
    unlimited information, 128–129
Technology readiness assessment checklist
    (illustration), 220–221
Teltech, 114, 188
Thesaurus integration, 138
Toffler, Alvin, 163
Tools
    incorporation of existing (illustration),
    155

U

Unclassified information, 140
Universal databases, 155–156
Unlimited information, 128–129
U.S. West Communications, 64
Usage audit trail, 143
User interface, 146–148

V

Value-add service providers, 130
Vogel, Peter, 107

W

Web crawlers, 129

Wheatley, Margaret J., 45
When Giants Learn to Dance, 16
Whitehead, Alfred North, 79
Work units, self-organizing, 206–207
Workflow systems, 131–132
Working Knowledge, 184
World Wide Web, 128–129, 165

X

Xerox, 178

Z

Zack, Michael, 168
Zuboff, Shoshana, 50–51

About the Author

Jan Duffy is vice president, specialty practices, with LGS Group Inc., one of Canada's leading management and information technology consulting firms. Jan is a senior business improvement professional with a special interest in designing total systems—people, processes, and technology—to support knowledge work and knowledge workers. Managing and exploiting business information and knowledge and designing supportive business processes and technology systems as well as complementary organizational environments are within her sphere of experience and focus.

Prior to joining LGS, Jan was the president of Duffy Consulting Group Inc., an independent management consulting firm and a partner with an international professional services firm. A frequently published author and respected speaker, she has chaired and participated in many conferences, symposia, and seminars and has guest lectured at North and South American universities.

About the Association

ARMA International is the leading professional organization for persons in the expanding field of records and information management.

As of May 1999, ARMA has about 10,000 members in the United States, Canada, and 37 other countries around the world.

Within the United States, Canada, New Zealand, Japan, Jamaica, and Singapore, ARMA has nearly 150 local chapters that provide networking and leadership opportunities through monthly meetings and special seminars.

ARMA's mission is to provide education, research, and networking opportunities to information professionals, to enable them to use their skills and experience to leverage the value of records, information, and knowledge as corporate assets and as contributors to organizational success.

The ARMA International headquarters office is located in Prairie Village, Kansas, in the Kansas City metropolitan area. Office hours are 8:30 a.m. to 5 p.m., Central Time, Monday through Friday.

ARMA International
4200 Somerset Dr., Ste. 215
Prairie Village, KS 66208
913/341-3808
U.S./Canada WATS: 800/422-2762
FAX: 913/341-3742
E-mail: hq@arma.org
http://www.arma.org